GREAT
COMPANIONS

BOOKS BY MAX EASTMAN

Enjoyment of Poetry
Child of the Amazons and Other Poems
Journalism versus Art
Understanding Germany
Colors of Life, Poems
The Sense of Humor
Since Lenin Died
Leon Trotsky, The Portrait of a Youth
Marx and Lenin, The Science of Revolution
Venture, A Novel
Kinds of Love, Collected Poems
The Literary Mind, Its Place in an Age of Science
Artists in Uniform
Art and the Life of Action
Enjoyment of Laughter
Stalin's Russia and the Crisis in Socialism
Marxism: Is It Science?
Heroes I Have Known
Enjoyment of Living, An Autobiography
Lot's Wife, A Dramatic Poem
Poems of Five Decades
Reflections on the Failure of Socialism
The Road to Abundance (with Jacob Rosin)

TRANSLATIONS

Gabriel, by Alexander Pushkin
The Real Situation in Russia, by Leon Trotsky
The History of the Russian Revolution, by Leon Trotsky
The Revolution Betrayed, by Leon Trotsky

EDITED

Capital and Other Writings, by Karl Marx
Anthology for the Enjoyment of Poetry
Czar to Lenin, A Moving-Picture History of the Russian Revolution

Max Eastman
GREAT COMPANIONS

CRITICAL MEMOIRS
OF
SOME FAMOUS FRIENDS

Farrar, Straus and Cudahy
NEW YORK

ACKNOWLEDGMENTS

Two of the twelve memoirs in this book appeared in somewhat different form in the *Reader's Digest*. Parts of three others appeared in my book, *Heroes I Have Known,* published by Simon & Schuster in 1942. Other parts appeared in the *Freeman, The American Mercury, Étude,* and the *National Review*. The portrait of my mother is republished "by request" from my earlier book and from the *Reader's Digest*.

Contents

E. W. Scripps

Albert Einstein

Ernest Hemingway

Edna Millay

Berenice Abbott

George Santayana

Pablo Casals

Leon Trotsky
and one of his daughters

Sigmund Freud

Bertrand Russell

*Charles Chaplin and the author
at Chaplin's studio in 1919*

John Dewey

Rev. Annis Ford Eastman

GREAT
COMPANIONS

Explanatory

Companion is a word with a warm current flowing through it, usually in two directions. It means that two people walk hand-in-hand a good long distance, or more etymologically—and less exhaustingly—they "break bread together." I think I have broken bread, or at least a symbolic tea-biscuit or two, with all but one of the famous people portrayed in this book. With some of them I have been close friends. But that is not what I mean by Great Companions. I found the phrase in Walt Whitman's *Song of the Open Road:*

Allons! After the great companions, and belong to them!
They too are on the road—they are the swift and majestic
men—they are the greatest women. . . .

It does not necessarily imply a two-way relation, but is
just a way of describing contemporaries whom one has
known and greatly admired. I like to admire people. In
boyhood I was an intemperate hero-worshipper. You had
only to inform me that somebody was "great," whether a
poet or a football player, and I would stick his portrait up
on the walls of my bedroom—not I fear, for purposes of
emulation, but mere passive adulation. I can still see a
small white plaster bust of Mozart that stood on my bureau.
He was a "great composer," though I could not at that time
have distinguished his music from a tune on the hurdy-
gurdy. Nature designed me, it seemed, for an adept of the
Leader cult, but I got interested after a while in seeing
what I could do with my own humble self. I still cherish
my heroes, but I have learned to look upon them with a
critical eye, and draw their portraits without too much awe.

It is significant that by the time he reaches the end of
his stanza, Walt Whitman has included among his Great
Companions everybody who is vividly alive. That, to be
sure, is far from everybody. But the implication seems to
be that heroes are not so different from everyday people,
or what is potential in everyday people, and for one with
a "vice of admiration," as my propensity has been called,
that I suppose is worth remembering. I could have written
a book like this about a number of my friends who never
achieved anything more than a life keenly lived, and who
will leave no name in history. But a certain mundane glory

would be lacking to which I am sensitive, and a forgetfulness of my own mundane ambitions. "To belong to them" —or better, take part in them—is a fair description of the effort I have made in these reminiscent portraits. It is not quite such hard work as trying to amount to something in your own person.

Old Man Scripps

A SUCCESS STORY WITHOUT A MORAL

E. W. Scripps was nearing sixty when I met him—a multimillionaire and the owner of a chain of thirty newspapers with a circulation running into millions. I was editing the *Masses,* a revolutionary magazine selling 10,000 copies and losing $12,000 a year. It was Lincoln Steffens who caused our coming together. Steff was a sort of cherishing godfather to all revolutionary enterprises, and he said to me one day, returning from the west: "Old man Scripps might give you some money for your magazine—he reads it every month." The money end of this seemed highly improbable to me, but the news that I had such a reader was exciting. I was curious to look into his eyes.

E. W. had bought, in middle age, a two-thousand-acre ranch upland from the sea near La Jolla, California, built a sixty-room ranch house, and retired there to think his thoughts, boss his family, and let his newspaper empire— except for an occasional peremptory order over the long distance telephone—expand and blossom of its own sweet will. Coming to the end of a lecture tour at San Diego, I trekked out in an old Model-T Ford car to call on him. We enjoyed each other so much that I stayed a week, and then subsequently I spent other weeks in that hospitable ranch house.

They were weeks devoted almost entirely to abstract thought—mingled, to be sure, with gusts of laughter and clouds of tobacco smoke. We never gossiped; we never took a walk; we never took a drink; we never went driving. He put at my disposal a "real car" and allowed me to tear its guts out teaching myself to operate a grown-up gearshift, but aside from that our friendship consisted of sitting together in his study smoking an endless chain of mild, made-to-order Key West cigars, and talking about ideas from three to six hours at a stretch.

He was tall, lanky, blotchy-faced, copper-headed, had a cast in one eye and a deadly quiet look in the other—a natural for the role of pirate if properly made up. He used to carry a gun in the old days in Cleveland when his penny *Press* opened an era in American journalism by publishing uncomfortable facts recklessly, cheaply, briefly, and from the workingman's point of view. He told me that one day in the antechamber of a courtroom, a mob incited by his enemies backed him into a corner with arguments that came close to physical violence. Suddenly somebody yelled, "He's going to shoot!" which may or may not have been true, but he was alone in about ten seconds.

"I looked in a mirror afterward," he told me, "and wondered whether it was the gun or my looks that caused the evacuation."

It was mainly, I surmise, his looks. He pulled that gun more than once, but he never had to shoot. He was a mental and moral athlete, but physically soft, with slim weak hands like a woman's—a frightening combination, especially when a gun is in the hands.

He sits very clear in my imagination, slanting back from his desk in a swivel chair, squinting quizzically through the smoke, laying down the law as though he knew everything on all subjects, and yet as strongly intimating— whether with the intellectual mirth in his eyes, the deprecating gestures, the occasional wistful question—that, like the rest of us, he probably knew little or nothing at all. Every once in a while he would get up and walk over into an alcove and come back with a manuscript. It would be a "Disquisition" by himself on the subject we were discussing. He would read it to me with an expression of delighted surprise at the wisdom he found in it—a surprise which I fully shared. Scripps had a mind like Montaigne's—fertile, discursive, full of extremely rational doubts and speculations about everything under the sun. And though he lacked the gift of great language, his Disquisitions had the same qualities of personal candor, intellectual daring, and ultimate unanswerable doubt that Montaigne's Essays have. But instead of publishing them, he locked them up in an old black steel box to lie there until his grandchildren were grown up.*

Montaigne may seem far afield, but there is certainly no American, least of all among those who attain wealth and power, with whom to compare this rich-minded yet angular character. He was as different from Hearst as his utilitarian ranch-house was from the gaudy show of St. Simeon. He was different from all the journalistic big shots in his intense intellectuality and reckless individualism—qualities that made some people call him a crank, though no crank was ever so canny and astute.

He was an avowed atheist; he never went to church or the theater or a political rally or a ball game. He felt that "whatever is, is wrong." He had so low an opinion of mankind, including himself, that he cared nothing for their respect and little for their affection. Fame he regarded as a bauble; he never made an effort even to retain his self-respect. At least so he said, and to prove it he boasted that for twenty-five years he "consumed enough whiskey to keep three or four men drunk all the time," stopping only when his health faltered. He was a restless traveler, an omnivorous reader, a lover of poetry—much of which he found in the Bible in spite of what he called "the imbecility of Sunday Schools and so-called Sunday School teachers." He knew all the maxims in *Poor Richard's Almanack* and didn't agree with any of them. He made it a point to sleep all he could, and never got up until he felt like it. He never

---

* Selections from these Disquisitions were published in 1951 in a book called *Damned Old Crank,* and I learned from the editor's introduction that I was one of the two or three "respected cronies" to whom he ever showed them.

kept books, and regarded the usual set of books kept by businessmen as "an unbearable nuisance." And yet he was one of the most successful businessmen in the history of our country. Starting as a farm boy coming to Detroit with eighty dollars sewn into the lining of his vest, he died at sea in a palatial private yacht, leaving an estate of over fifty million dollars.

Nothing like Scripps could have come to pass outside of America, and yet nothing is more un-American—more unlike the national success story—than the way he piled up a fortune without working. He founded his first paper, the Cleveland *Press,* in 1878 with an investment of only $10,000 which he borrowed from his brother George. Sixteen months later, he went to St. Louis to found the *Evening Chronicle.* Subsequently he returned to Cleveland, stayed six months, then left for Europe with his adored sister Ellen. From then until his death in 1926 he was in complete control of the Cleveland *Press,* yet during all those years— to quote his own words—"I have not spent as much as thirty days in Cleveland." By the turn of the century the *Press* was worth millions.

"I was always ready," he adds, "to do four men's work in a day, when there was any occasion for it, but I was always seeing to it that such occasions were very rare. I am sure that from the time I was twenty-four, more than half my days have been spent with no conscious thought or attention to business of any sort. The practice of journalism seems to me, even now, to have been an unimportant incident in my life."

In the course of our conversations, Scripps mentioned three reasons why he had succeeded so brilliantly without much steady work. One was that he decided early exactly what he was going to do. It seems to have been the size and proportions of the Roman Coliseum that brought him to this decision. He was wandering aimlessly around Europe, twenty-four years old, dreaming of becoming a great writer; but one afternoon, lying in the sun on a fallen pillar in the Coliseum, he decided to be a great power instead. He would build an empire, a newspaper empire. Others could do the writing. He would stay in the background, unknown, unacclaimed, but with absolute control.

Another reason he gave for his success—almost the same one perhaps—was that he knew exactly what the essence of his genius was: practical judgment. By cultivating that and letting others shoulder both the work and the worry, he saved the energy at the beginning that few ambitious men save until the end of their careers. A third cause of his seemingly offhand success was his intuitive knowledge of men. He made the astonishing statement that in his entire career he had probably not given over five hundred orders to the men employed on his papers. All he did was to choose the men, study them, inspire them with talks and letters to do the best they had it in them to do.

A few surviving aphorisms will suggest the kind of inspiration to be found in those talks and letters:

1. It is possible for a hypocrite, by exercising constant restraint, to appear as good as the most sincere moralist, but it is awfully hard work.

2. Never do anything yourself that you can get someone else to do for you. The more things someone else does for you, the more time and energy you have for the things no one else can do for you.

3. Never hate anybody. Hatred is a useless expenditure of mental and nervous energy.

4. Be diplomatic, but don't be too damned diplomatic. It is rare indeed when circumstances are such that a conscientious man can lose anything by fearless, frank, speech and writing.

E. W. was especially fearless and frank about his illicit love life. He had the bad-boy habit of dividing girls into "nice" and "not nice," and until marriage, was both assiduous and promiscuous in his devotion to the "not nice" girls. One of them who had been his mistress in Detroit came to his office in Cincinnati where he was just getting a good start with the *Post* and tried to blackmail him. He summoned the city editor and directed him to call up the two rival papers and tell them to send over reporters. When the reporters arrived, he introduced his visitor.

"Miss Brown," he said, "used to live with me as my mistress. She was paid for what she did and we parted on good terms. She has come here today threatening to revive that story and asking for money. You are at liberty to print the story. So far as I am concerned, the incident is closed."

The story was run with big headlines, and to the surprise of everybody, it did no harm either to the circulation of the paper or the standing of its editor. Cincinnati's approval of fearless, frank speech evidently outweighed its disapproval of illicit sex relations. When he married at the age of thirty-one, Scripps foreswore such relations, successfully, for the rest of his life.

As startling as the casual way Scripps built his empire, is the promptitude with which he abdicated and began gradually to get out of it. Only twelve years after that day of dreams in the Coliseum, E. W. called in his business manager, Milton McRae, one morning and offered him a limited partnership with a one-third share in the salary and profits. To this he attached one condition: that McRae should run the Scripps-McRae papers on 85 percent of their gross income. He also continued, from his ranch in California, to watch over the empire like a hawk, receiving daily and weekly reports from each paper, and traveling in spurts that mounted up to ten thousand miles annually to keep tabs on them. He would do this traveling in a private car with two secretaries, working all the time. But when he got home he would give his whole heart again to planting eucalyptus forests and citrus groves, building reservoirs, laying miles of pipe to reclaim his private wilderness, grow-ing up with his sons, and above all reading books that had nothing whatever to do with journalism. He estimated that, throughout life, he had spent a good half of his waking hours with his eyes on the pages of a book.

One of his agreements with McRae had been that, if moved to expand the business, each should have as his special territory the region in which he happened to start a paper first. Scripps had observed—and he thought McRae had too—that there was a free field for a lively evening paper in Dallas, Texas. He had also observed and studied an obscure reporter named Alfred O. Anderson, who was working for a small wage on the Scripps-McRae paper in St. Louis. Out of the blue sky young Anderson received a telegram, signed with the imperial letters, directing him to go to Dallas and have an evening paper on the streets at the earliest possible moment. He would find money to his credit in a Dallas bank. Anderson, after catching his breath, knowing what orders signed E. W. meant, made up the first edition of a four-page newspaper, had it printed in St. Louis, took it with him on a train, and had it on sale in Dallas the next afternoon. E. W. delighted to outwit peo﹢ ple. Especially he delighted to outwit this semi-partner, McRae, whose lack of humor he found as distressing as his enormous energy and concentration admirable.

Scripps took a similar delight in outwitting the plans of the Associated Press to form a monopoly of the news-gathering business. They offered to take him in on the scheme but he declined. They then set a zero hour; he could either come in then or remain forever out in the cold. He waited until the zero hour was past, making his preparations meanwhile to establish a news agency of his own. Then he sent an emissary to their meeting, arrogantly demanding that his papers be admitted on an equality with all others. When they responded, as he anticipated, with derisive laughter, he sent out his already prepared tele-grams announcing the formation of the Scripps-McRae Press Association—subsequently renamed the United Press. He regarded this blow against monopoly in the gathering of news as his greatest service to American journalism.

To his serene recollection of the few orders he gave, his employees would add that when he did give an order, it was obeyed instantly or the explosion would rock the build-ing. At home he behaved like an oriental despot. His ranch-house castle was all on one floor, and as you passed from room to room, you would see tacked up beside each door-way in his handwriting:

SHUT THE DOOR. E. W. Scripps.

After breakfast, just before rising from the table, he would issue an order-of-the-day: "Bob, I want to confer with you immediately, and I'll see you again at two P.M. Nackie [his wife], I will drive with you at four. Max, we will talk in my office at ten."

Our talks would last from ten o'clock to one usually, and be subject to renewal afternoon or evening. Upon dismissal, as I staggered from the room groggy with nicotine and sheer exhaustion of the brain cells, he would say "thank you for the conversation," as though I had had some choice in the matter.

I remember his reading me a frankly boastful Disquisition in which he stated that he was one of the thousand richest men in the United States and, with an apology for the "conceit," asserted that he was "two percent responsible for all that is good or ill in the management of this great nation." To prove this, he showed me a letter from Burleson, Woodrow Wilson's Postmaster General, acknowledging that the Administration owed its victory in the 1916 elections to the Scripps papers. So this conceit was not unfounded. But no such trait was ever present in his conversation. He had, with all his imperiousness, a vein of honest humility. I asked him once why he never tackled New York with a Scripps paper. "I'm not a big enough man," he said. "That takes a Hearst or a Pulitzer."

From my point of view he was too big a man—too thinking a man. He was too fond of reasoning and of thoughtful speculation. He cared more about the meditations he locked up in that iron box than those he expressed in his newspapers. His purest passion was for scientific truth. The

press release bureau called *Science Service* that he established in Washington, and the Scripps Institute for Biological Research and for Oceanography which he proudly
showed me through at La Jolla, are, according to my recollection of him, more eminently than the United Press or
the great Scripps-Howard chain of newspapers, the children of his mind and spirit. In that phase of his being his
motives were pure and clear.

As a man of the world, he had two motives which seemed
to me perilously mixed. One was a passionate determination to get rich—to rise into the big employing class se-
curely and forever. *It is more blessed to give than to receive—wages* was a maxim of which he became convinced
in early youth, and his purpose to stay on the upper side
of this transaction was as hard as steel. But at the same time
he was instinctively hostile to men of wealth, and despised
militantly the journalism which consists of "rich men talking to the other rich."

In 1900 his brother James, who was losing money on a
newspaper in Chicago, begged him to come in and take over
the management. They met to discuss it in a hotel room
that looked down on Dearborn Street. While they were
talking, a noise of shouts and scuffling came up from below.
It was a riotous incident in the teamster's strike then in
progress. As they looked down, James muttered: "I wish
I were mayor of this city; I'd teach those men a lesson."

E. W. said: "You want those teamsters clubbed, shot
down, or arrested. I want them to win. That shows we can't
work together. You'll have to go it alone."

Politically E. W.'s papers were independent, and they
have been credited with having "freed the American press

from its slavery to party title and obligation." But they were bound by a passionate loyalty to the workers and the common people—95 percent of the population, according to E. W.'s evaluations. "CP" and "95%" were inter-office abbreviations employed on the Scripps papers to designate this object of their loyalty. They championed every measure designed to improve the status of labor: the eight-hour day, closed shop, collective bargaining, workers' compensation, employees' insurance, anti-injunction laws. They also fought for the income tax, although Scripps regretted this in later years as bad economics.

It was instinctive with him to champion every measure directed against what he called the "wealthy and intellectual classes." He always linked those two adjectives in describing the chief enemy; and both adjectives exactly fitted him. A war like that against himself would defeat, if not destroy, most men. In most times and places it would defeat any man. But in American newspaperdom from 1878 to 1916—and in E. W. Scripps—it produced an enormous personal fortune and one of the most powerful weapons ever wielded in behalf of the underdog.

There was a developing class struggle in America in those years, and the Scripps papers, without getting tangled in the doctrinal formulation of it, took the side of the rising class of wage labor. E. W. stoutly and constantly championed the cause of the trade unions in his papers. But he had the good sense to leave socialism alone, or dismiss it with such remarks as: "Society owes nothing to any individual—only that human being who can support himself or herself is entitled to a place in the world"; or—with more ultimate wisdom: "Class warfare must be perpetual." He seems now to have seen through socialism more clearly than any other critic I met in those days. He surprised me by saying: "Your propaganda will probably in the long run succeed," and then adding this perfect prophecy, "The thing you'll get will be as different from what you are talking about as modern organized Christianity is from the visions of Jesus."

Scripps did, as Steffens predicted, give money to my magazine, although he refused to call it a gift. He called it an experiment. "You come out here next year and show me your financial report," he said, "and I'll know whether I acted from sentimentalism or good sense."

The next year I had my business manager make a report from which the inference was unescapable that Scripps ought to double his contribution. I explained this to him while he looked over the document.

"Max, you make a good speech," he said, "but I knew that already. I heard you over in San Diego. The figures on this paper, on the other hand, convince me that your magazine is a failure. It's a delight to me personally, but it isn't good business. You'll have to find a philanthropist. I'm a businessman."

I did find a philanthropist, and although the story belongs in my biography rather than this portrait of him, I will repeat it here, for it brought our friendship to an appropriately humorous conclusion.

Like most people addicted to property, Scripps had a strong sense of identity with his family. Thanks to his life-long guidance, his sister Ellen had become almost as rich as he was. She lived down by the sea at La Jolla, and he asked me before leaving that afternoon to stop in with him and

meet her. Ellen Scripps was thin and scrawny, and so old
that her skin was yellow and caked in large squares like a
crocodile's. I never saw another walking thing that looked
so old. Her mind, however, was not dimmed except by the
impulses of her heart, which were more pious than E. W.'s
and more benevolent. She believed in church and Sunday
School, and gave large subsidies to religious as well as educational ventures. She believed still more in her brother,
however, and received me with great warmth because of
our friendship. I said good-bye to E. W. at her door and
drove away—but I did not drive very far. I was lurking
behind a bush on her lawn when E. W. took his leave, and
a few moments later I rang her bell. I had come back—
just on an impulse—to ask her if she wouldn't help me
with my magazine. I showed her the figures that had been
so convincing when prepared for E. W., and they became
again miraculously logical and clear.

"How much does your magazine need?" she asked. "I've
pledged almost all I planned to give this year to a little
paper that our church is publishing."

"I only need six thousand dollars right now," I said.

"I'm really very sorry," she said, "I couldn't give you that
much right now. I wonder if it wouldn't be possible for you
to get along if I sent it in three annual installments?"

Many years later, when Jo Davidson made his bust of
E. W., the old man related with gusto how, when he refused to give *The Masses* four thousand dollars and told me
to find a philanthropist, I went down and lifted six from
his philanthropic sister. It added, I think, to his respect for
me.

Three Visits with Einstein

It was Dick Simon and Max Schuster, publishers of my book *Enjoyment of Laughter,* who engineered my first meeting with Albert Einstein. He had written, in collaboration with a young Polish mathematician named Leopold Infeld, a popular account of his contributions to physics, and Simon and Schuster were preparing to make a bestseller of it. A conference of the four of them, two authors and two publishers, was slated for April 20, 1937 at Einstein's home in Princeton, New Jersey. Dick Simon, whose candor is as winning as his sense of humor and closely allied to it, said to me: "Max, we have an appointment with Einstein, and as the publishers of his book we feel we ought to take along someone who can at least put up a show of understanding what it's about."

In that mood and with that confidential mission, I went to a meeting I had aspired to for a long time. My way of accomplishing the mission was to steer the conversation as far away from the book as I could without abandoning the general subject of science. I had taught a course in the Principles of Science at Columbia University many years before, and felt I could still put up a show of knowing something about that. The result was two hours of conversation with Einstein which I treasure among my happiest memories, and which interested him enough at least to give rise to two more conversations, not engineered by Simon and Schuster.

Einstein's wife had died only a month or two before our visit, and we were apprehensive that we might find him distraught or depressed. But Infeld assured us that the loss had made little difference either in his mood or the tenor of his life.

"He lives so entirely in his thoughts, literally working with his mind all day long, that he is almost insensible to pain," is what Infeld said.

We found him in a conventionally ugly frame house, a form of ugliness prevalent enough in America to suggest that everybody lives in his thoughts—or at least not in his eyes. But he received us upstairs in a back room with an enormous plate-glass window looking out so immediately into the trees that the ugly house did not seem to matter. Maybe after all he doesn't live entirely in his thoughts, I reflected. When I asked him, however, whether he had found that window in the house or had it put in, he said:

"No, my wife did that. I didn't like it at first. I thought when I was in a house I ought to be inside."

"It seems logical," I said, though it did not seem any more than that.

Everything about him, the outflying hair, neither mane-like nor properly combed, the absence of a necktie, the rather baglike costume, the ill-cared-for teeth, the furniture too much sat in, suggested a man indifferent to the sense-qualities of the world whose laws of motion he studied with such rapture.

As I have remarked elsewhere, I usually receive from great men in any walk of life, and always with surprise, an impression of femininity. In Einstein this was striking, his gestures being fastidious rather than compelling, and his swaying gait suggesting to my mind a buxom mammy. His hands were fat, veinless, and unwrinkled like those of a baby. It was a strange body in which to locate a mind with an edge so keen and hard it could penetrate all the natural assumptions of life and conversation, and even of what had been physical and chemical science, to an armature of mathematical abstractions which contain hardly a recollection of the concrete perceptions that make them valid.

After a little desultory talk about the date and format of the book, Dick Simon, who is a photographer of genius, asked Einstein whether he would mind posing for a picture or two.

"Oh no," he said, "that is my profession now."

And he related how on a train he had once put off an inquisitive fellow-passenger who asked him what he did for a living by saying, "I'm a photographer's model."

To make the picture, it being a warm spring day, we

went down to a little plot of lawn and garden behind the house. It was there, sitting in two arm chairs, while the sun sifted down through the baby leaves, and Dick circled around taking pictures from carefully chosen points-of-view, that our conversation about the universe began. One or two of the pictures, Dick assured me on the way home, were so fine that I would certainly go down to posterity as having got next, at least, to a great man. But when he reached home he telephoned to break the sad news that I was still mortal—he had forgotten to put a film in his camera. So I had to content myself with writing down very carefully the substance of the conversation he had intended to immortalize.

Einstein had been quoted to me as saying that while he did not believe in an anthropomorphic God, he considered himself a religious man, and regarded the scientist's striving toward rational knowledge of the universe as "religion in the highest sense." I told him that I did not think he was really religious, and I thought it was a mistake for him to use the term.

"For the sake of clear thinking," I said, "the word religion ought to be used only to mean a faith that something in the external world is sympathetic to man's interests."

"That is true of religion in its origin and early development," he said. "It is true of the primitive religion of fear, and the social or moral religion which grew out of it."

In both of these phases, religion does, he conceded, assume that a force, or forces, in the external world are sympathetic to man's interests. But there is a higher religion which is free from fear and has nothing to do with morality. This higher religion he describes as "an attitude of humility toward universal being."

My recollection here is far from verbatim, but the word humility I distinctly remember. It was the *insignificance* of human aims and wishes by comparison with the grandeur of a rationally ordered universe that he emphasized. He seemed to believe it was this religious feeling that sustained such men as Newton and Kepler—and by inference, of course, himself—in their arduous efforts to understand the universe.

I had my doubts about that. A scientist of the factual kind who devotes himself to becoming a world authority on molluscs, say, or caterpillars, often displays without any deification of the subject matter, a similar devotion to his task and to the truth. I said something like this, and maybe had the hardihood to suggest that there was something like professional pride in attributing a more arduous devotion, or a more honorific motive, to those who study the universe as a whole. At any rate, that was the drift of our difference, and in response to his association of religion with humility, I said that a certain humility toward natural fact seemed to me characteristic of science at its best, and "it only confuses people's minds and makes them introduce supernatural ideas into science to call this attitude religious."

Einstein did not dissent very strongly from this; he did not want to introduce supernatural ideas into science; but I do not remember what he said. Our conversation was broken off because the sun was withdrawing its rays from the garden, Dick had taken the last of his imaginary pictures, and Einstein proposed that we go in to the porch, which was hospitably close to the kitchen, and continue the discussion over a cup of tea. By the time we were all seated around a small table waiting for that tea, our conversation had shifted, as conversations frequently do, from the subject of religion to that of causal determinism. Neither Dick nor Max Schuster took any part in it—for the reason, Dick told me afterward, although I question his seriousness, that they could not follow it. Infeld also, though for a different reason which he afterward explained, kept mum.

I have more than the usual diffidence, but the naive generosity with which Einstein gave the gift of attention to anything that anybody said, looking up out of his merry eyes with a childlike expectancy, broke the barrier completely. I told him with the boldness of my youthful days as an "assistant in philosophy" that I thought he talked about the universality of causal determinism with too much assurance. The principle can not be profitably abandoned in performing a scientific experiment, I said, but if generalized it destroys the validity of all scientific judgments. "If a mind is determined in its judgment by antecedent causes, then it cannot be determined by the reasons upon which its judgment is supposed to be based."

Einstein had evidently never thought of that. Indeed I never met anybody who had, although it has always seemed to me the most obvious argument against universal determinism. He grappled with the idea delightedly, however, as though it were some new kind of game we were playing. After some random parries and thrusts, he said:

"We view the situation in one aspect when we say that a

whole process is caused, and in another when we say that a mind is judging on the basis of the evidence."

"But that is merely a dodge," I said. "If you are going to be philosophic, you can't leave the ultimate truth with two aspects."

He assented to that, but countered it with the difficulties involved in the notion of free will. I admitted that this notion seems of no more ultimate use or validity in describing the situation than that of universal cause. A skepticism about the power of the human mind to solve any ultimate problem honestly confronted is all the philosophy I have, and like other negative positions it is not hard to defend.

The argument was long and meandering, and I naturally remember best my own contributions to it. I do remember his surprise when I assured him that it was not moral freedom I was primarily concerned about, but a confidence that judgments and arguments in a discussion like ours are real, and that the conclusions we reach (if any) are valid.

We did not, of course, reach any conclusion—who ever did in the game of free will versus determinism?—but the argument ended in his explaining my position to Infeld in German with great clarity and force. What he said exactly was:

"He means that if a judgment is merely a fact, then it can not also be a truth."

"It sounds so good when you put it in German," I said, "that now I am perfectly sure I am right."

To which he replied with a beaming smile, and proceeded to carry the conversation back to that original question about religion and science. There again I can only remember how glib I was, and I hope this will be put down to his entrancing attitude of inquiry rather than to an egotistical absorption in my own opinions. It happened that I had just published in *Harper's* magazine an essay on Marxism, and to illustrate what I meant by defining religion as involving a belief that the external world, or something in it, is sympathetic to man's interests, I cited the Marxian philosophy of dialectic materialism.

"Though it pretends to be scientific," I said, "the Marxian system is really a religion. Marx declared that the world is made of matter, but proceeded to discover, mysteriously enough, that this world of matter was achieving with dialectic necessity exactly what he wanted to achieve. The whole thing was just a gigantic effort to prove that the external world is in favor of the proletarian revolution and is helping it."

Carried away by my success with that, I went on to assert that John Dewey's philosophy of pragmatism is a similar effort: "Dewey gets the objective facts into harmony with man's will by putting his will into the very process of determining the facts."

Einstein did not answer this peroration. He only looked around the table with a mischievous laugh.

"This man is wicked!" he said. "He is really wicked!"

At the door, when we shook hands, he said: "Hasn't it been a delightful discussion!" And I must confess that I feel ashamed when I see how little of his part in it I put down in my notes or can now recall.

II

Our second meeting came about through the mediation of Infeld, who wrote me on April 22:

> Both Einstein and I were glad of the opportunity of meeting you and thoroughly enjoyed your visit. . . .
>
> If you would care to continue your argument with Einstein I could easily arrange another meeting. I should also be glad of the opportunity to take your advice in several matters concerning the book we are writing.
>
> Let me hear from you.

Of course I was delighted, and I talked with Einstein again in early May. This time I went down to Princeton alone, and to diversify the adventure I stopped off on my way to see the 5000 cows at the Walker-Gordon Dairy Farm. Infeld met me at the station and we found Einstein seated at his dining room table poring serenely over a pad full of equations. It occurred to me that he probably produced thoughts as contentedly and with as little interruption as the Walker-Gordon cows produce milk. As between the two, I thought Einstein had the better of it, but I could not pretend that either represented my ideal of a jovial life. Those cows stand in their stanchions, eating, sleeping or chewing their cuds, all day and all night, all the year around, and their only diversion is to walk twice a day down a long underground chute, coming out in another building onto a turntable, which carries twenty of them round and around for exactly ten minutes. During this time each receives a bath and is milked by an electrical milker. They then march out through another chute and back to their stanchions. It refutes all my theories about life's adventure to say it, but I have to confess that they were among the happiest cows I ever gazed on.

The comparison seems a little foolish, perhaps, and disrespectful, but the two visits occurred within the same hour and I can't help it. Einstein too seemed permanently contented and happy. "He lives entirely in his thoughts"; "he is almost insensible to pain": Infeld's phrases came back into my mind, and I wondered whether, after all, that isn't the safest and securest place to live.

Einstein had evidently wanted to see me again, because my remarks about causation had stimulated him to some intense thinking on the subject. He wanted to tell me his new thoughts. At least he was impatient of our talk until we got on that subject again, and he brought forward his new position with the eagerness of a child showing you something he has made out of a broken toy. It began, almost in the language of Kant, with the statement that the law of causation does not apply to the observed order of phenomena, or can not be proven to. It belongs rather to the conceptual system with which the order of phenomena is explained. Some phenomena, however—and this was un-Kantian enough—can be better explained with a conceptual system which does not universalize the principle of cause, but assumes on the contrary that certain kinds of events are uncaused.

I had heard rumors of this idea, or the dispute about it among physicists, and I asked him whether it was pure speculation or a concept that can actually be made use of. He assured me that it is actually used.

"In certain situations," he said, "we find that the aggregate of a vast number of individual events can be calculated according to the laws of probability on the assumption that each individual event is a matter of pure chance. Our laws concern the aggregates and they prove valid."

These statements, which I think I have quoted almost verbatim, are of interest because they were a complete reversal of the position Einstein had stubbornly held ever since the dispute arose. Just why I should have been chosen to receive the first news of this revolution, I can not imagine. But it is a fact that when we emerged from the house, I found Infeld in a state almost of rapture about what Einstein had said.

"Do you realize how far he has moved!" he exclaimed.

Of course I realized nothing at all, and he explained to me in joyous tones that these pronouncements marked a total change of mind on Einstein's part, a surrender to what he called the "younger" men. When we joined Mrs. Infeld, who had come for us in a car, he communicated the great news to her as though Princeton had just won a football game, or Poland a war, and rather as though he had played the major role in gaining the victory.

"I've been working on him for over a year now," he said, "and here at last is the result."

When I made no answer he added:

"Didn't you notice the other day when you were talking about causation I kept still, I never spoke a word?"

I said—there was something in him which impelled me

to say: "Yes, I did notice that, but I don't see quite how it proves that *you* were the one who awoke him from his dogmatic slumber."

He did not smile or seem to notice the drift of this assertion of my own egotism, but his wife smiled as though she did.

III

On June 6, I received another letter from Infeld: "Could you come out to Princeton either Thursday or Friday or Saturday of next week. Einstein is still here. I need hardly repeat how glad I shall be to see you again."

I came of course, and this time Max Schuster came with me, though not, alas, Dick Simon with his camera—that hope of immortality was lost forever. I took along, however, a copy of *Harper's* containing my essay on Marxism, cheering myself with the thought that I would have at least one very distinguished reader. We met in Infeld's apartment on the ground floor of 28 Vandeverter Avenue. It was again a sunny day, and Einstein came strolling up the street in a few moments, hatless and dressed like a student in an open shirt, an old brown-leather windbreaker, and tennis shoes with no socks.

"What is this, a soviet of best-sellers?" he exclaimed as he came in. He was in a charmingly discursive mood, and I had the modesty this time to let him do the talking, content to admire the sparkle in his eyes, the vigor, the vividness and delightful variety of his thoughts.

I remember Max Schuster's inquiring about the possibility of a book about chemistry such as they had written about physics, and Infeld's saying: "Chemistry is so dull that I don't see how you could find anybody to write about it." Einstein agreed that chemistry is dull—a strange opinion, it seemed to me, since I thought the exploration of the atom had well-nigh obliterated the distinction between chemistry and physics.

We spoke again of the people who employ the prestige of science in order to propagate religious beliefs. I mentioned the books of Jeans and Eddington, and Einstein said—far more boldly than I would dare to:

"Those are bad books. They are not honest books. And yet those men are such great astronomers and famous writers—it is hard to find anybody who can oppose them with the simple truth."

We talked about politics, and I was led to believe that Einstein possessed a remarkably hard and keen political intelligence. He predicted that if Hitler was victorious in his ambition to dominate Europe, America would be drawn into war—"not by an attack, but by the mounting authority of fascism." He predicted an alliance between Stalin and Hitler. Of the "confessions" of the old Bolsheviks in the Moscow trials, then in progress, he said:

"Of course they are not true. It is impossible that twenty men being caught in a conspiracy, would all react in the same way—and that in so unnatural a way as to defile themselves publicly."

To my remark that if the French premier, Leon Blum, had sent the requested munitions to the Spanish republic, there would have been no civil war in Spain, he answered: "That is true, but you have to remember that Blum had a difficult situation in his own country. More than half the French army were fascists. He wasn't wise enough to do it, but he was also not strong enough to do it if he had been wise. You might say that if Blum had been a greater man he both would and could have done it."

"Time works against the democracies," is a remark I recorded. And this: "They should have stopped fascism when, or before, it began. And they should stop it now." He meant stop it by force of arms, and as he had burst upon my political horizon ten years before as an ultra-pacifist and anti-militarist, this revealed a concreteness and flexibility of judgment that delighted me.

Such opinions, advanced in 1937, gave no hint of Einstein's post-war career among the most willing of the liberal tools of the Communist conspiracy. In those later years, he gave his name unhesitatingly to communist fronts, twenty-six of them; he wrote for the Communist magazine, *Soviet Russia Today;* he went to the defense of the "Hollywood Ten" who were jailed for contempt of Congress (most if not all of them identified as Communist Party members). He wrote a letter urging all intellectuals to defy the effort of the government, through congressional investigations, to frustrate an avowed conspiracy to overthrow it—as though any government could ultimately survive which tolerated such a conspiracy. He avowed his belief that the ills of the world can only be eliminated by "the establishment of a socialist economy," and published this avowal in *Masses and Mainstream,* a magazine published by pro-Communists and dedicated to the defense of the Soviet dictatorship. He put himself in a position to be hailed by the Communist *Daily Worker* as "the living symbol of the United Front," the United Front being one of the most dastardly tricks of blandishment and betrayal ever practiced upon mankind.

It is beyond my scope to explain what happened to Einstein to soften him in this way during the decade of the Second World War. In 1937 he was ready to stop the tyrant Hitler by force of arms; in 1947 he was a cushion brought forward to deaden every blow against Stalin's more perfected and more menacing tyranny.

The explanation which fits best with my admiration is that Hitler's specialized and bestial persecution of the Jews, with whom as a people Einstein fervently identified himself, unsettled his judgment of the problem in general human terms. For it seemed, although the inference was erroneous, that in overwhelming the Nazis, Soviet Russia had been a liberator of the Jews. Whatever the explanation, this streak of blind emotionalism in a ruthlessly rational mind may serve as a warning to me, and to all those inclined to hero-worship, not to let our admiration carry us too far. "Let every man be respected as an individual and no man idolized," is a quotation from Einstein himself that may well be remembered in appraising him.

Another subject we spoke of in that third conversation was Sigmund Freud, whom Einstein described as "a very great man." "I think he has invented some wonderful ideas, but whether they are true or not, we in our lifetime will probably never know. The trouble is that in psychiatry verification is impossible. The fault, I think, is in the subject rather than in Freud."

I remarked that I thought Freud lacked the spirit of verification, not only the possibility of it. And Max Schuster interposed, very astutely I thought:

"What Freud lacks is the spirit that led Mr. Einstein to make that remark about him."

"I had a dream once," Einstein said, "that seemed in a small way to verify one of Freud's theories. At Berlin we had a professor named Rüde whom I hated and he hated me. I heard one morning that he had died, and meeting a group of my colleagues I told them the news this way: 'They say every man does one good deed in his lifetime, and Rüde is no exception—he has died!'

"That night I dreamt that I was sitting in the lecture hall and Professor Rüde came in looking very healthy and self-important. I hurried up to him, shook his hand cordially and said: 'I am so glad you are alive!'

"I suppose Freud would say I was inwardly ashamed of my bitter remark about Rüde, and the dream relieved me of that feeling of remorse."

Whatever Freud might say, the incident did, I thought, cast a charming light on Einstein's character.

As he stood up to go, I gave him the copy of *Harper's* with my essay and said I very much wanted him to read it. He clasped the magazine eagerly.

"I will read it. I want to read it very much," he said.

Infeld took it from his hand, and asked:

"Will you take it with you now, or shall I read it first and bring it to you?"

"No, I'll take it with me," Einstein said, and made him give it back.

He had decided to walk home "behind the town," as he

expressed it, "to avoid embarrassments," and after settling some technical questions with Max Schuster about the book, he bade us good-bye. Max and I went to the window to watch him ambling down the street in the old windbreaker and rather baggy pants—a simple and gentle and audacious man. When we turned back, Infeld had picked up the copy of *Harper's* from the table on which Einstein had left it, and was preparing a little speech.

"Now that is perfectly typical!" it began. "He decided to take it instead of leaving it with me; and then after making the decision he left it just the same. He didn't really want to read it. But I will see that he does. Have no fear. I will read it, and I will make him read it. . . ."

At that point in his speech the door opened a crack behind him, a cherubic face appeared in the opening, a hand reached out and snatched the magazine from his grasp, and the door closed again.

No word was spoken, but how we all laughed! And Infeld, after recovering his poise, turned a red face to me:

"Well, that's a tribute to you!" he said. "You don't know what a tribute that is!"

In an obituary essay on Albert Einstein, Bertrand Russell ignored the change I have described in his attitude toward the statistical view of our knowledge of physical reality.

"Einstein never accepted this view," Russell says. "He continued to believe that there are laws, though as yet they have not been ascertained, which determine the behavior of individual atoms."

Little as I know about the subject, it was easy for me to

find in Einstein's *Out of My Later Years* evidence of the change which Russell denies, but which gave Infeld so much joy.

In March 1936, writing on "Quantum Theory and the Fundamentals of Physics," he said: "Probably never before has a theory been evolved which has given a key to the interpretation and calculation of such a heterogeneous group of phenomena of experience as has the quantum theory. In spite of this, however, I believe that the theory is apt to beguile us into error in our search for a uniform basis for physics, because, in my belief, it is an *incomplete* representation of real things. . . . The incompleteness of the representation is the outcome of the statistical nature (incompleteness) of the laws." (*Journal of the Franklin Institute,* Vol. 221, No. 3.)

Four years later, writing about "Physics and Reality," he said: "It is probably quite out of the question that any future knowledge can compel physics again to relinquish our present statistical theory in favor of a deterministic one. . . ." (*Science,* Washington, D.C. May 24, 1940.)

He seems to have wavered, however, for in a concluding paragraph he said:

"Some physicists, among them myself, cannot believe that we must . . . accept the view that events in nature are like a game of chance. It is open to every man to choose the direction of his striving; and also every man may draw comfort from Lessing's fine saying that the search for truth is more precious than its possession."

I suspect it was the emotion which he described to me as religious, rather than a concern for the fundamentals of physics, that made Einstein so reluctant to abandon the deterministic view. In the foreword to his *Mein Weltbild,* published in Amsterdam in 1933, he sang almost a psalm of praise to the idea of universal causal determinism. "Schopenhauer's statement that a man can do what he wants to but he cannot will what he shall want to do, has been an inspiration to me," he exclaimed, "from my youth up."

This kind of "inspiration" is so alien to my nature that I hesitate to make inferences from it. But it does seem obvious that anyone who in youth found it inspiring to live in a world thus fixed and deprived of hazard would stubbornly resist being routed out of it in old age.

The Great and Small in
Ernest Hemingway

Ernest Hemingway will be surprised, I think, to find himself among the people I call great. Our acquaintance, though friendly and of long duration, was casual. But I was very fond of him, and moreover he gave me one of the great surprises of my life—two of them in fact: one when he turned out to be a magnificent writer, another when he hit me in the face with a book.

We met in the spring of 1922 at the Hotel de Gênes in Genoa. We were both attending that first face-to-face meeting of the authentic heads of the great powers which has gone down in history as the Genoa Conference. It was an attempt to get Europe to settle down after the First World War, the First Foolish Peace, and the First Communist

Revolution. The defeated Germans were there, and the triumphant Bolsheviks, and every writer or newspaperman who could manage to horn in. Ernest was sent down by the Toronto *Star* as a special feature writer, an unusual distinction for a young man of twenty-three. I was there with an accreditation card from the New York *World,* and I did send them one story.

My story was a description of the opening session of the conference. I told how after all the delegations were seated, Lloyd George having made his grandstand entrance and the chairman having leafed over his notes and got ready with his gavel, the four chairs reserved for the Russians remained unoccupied. "Two minutes—three—five—ten. The tension began to grow into restlessness, impatience, vexation. The Russians were late. Russians are always late. Well, they ought not to be late when all the great men of the earth have assembled for the express purpose of letting them appear."

Ernest, who sat near me, summed it up more succinctly with a remark about those chairs. "They are the four emptiest looking chairs I have ever seen."

He summed me up in the same article with a phrase which I find considerably less brilliant: "like a big, jolly, middle-western college professor."

One of those lazy-hearted spring days, George Slocombe and Ernest and I motored over to Rapallo together. George was the picturesque correspondent of the London *Daily Herald.* His picturesqueness focused in a bright red dagger-shaped beard and a vast black felt hat of the kind that professional agitators, especially Italian anarchist agitators, were accustomed to wear. His eyes after you found them under that hat, were a mild and gentle blue, his nose small and shapely, his opinions fairly regular, and you said to yourself, "Well, after all, the red beard and big black hat was all there was to it!" But you liked him; he was and is, a "swell guy." Ernest was a swell guy more simply and obviously. Although already looking beyond journalism to a career in literature, he did not begin by putting on the Bohemian manner and trappings. He was gentle and unassuming, dressed in easy-fitting but conventional suits of clothes, and distinguished mainly by a winning laugh, a handsome face and the most beautiful row of teeth I ever saw in man, woman, or child.

Rapallo was only a few minutes beyond Santa Margherita where the Bolsheviks were lodged and where I hung around a good deal of the time. I felt as if the little red-and-white painted Ford car we rode in was a time machine carrying us from the threshold of the revolutionary future back into the previous century. For once in Rapallo we had only to ring a bell at a little gate, climb up an in-going stairway, and there was the inimitable person of Max Beerbohm, exquisitely clad and graciously at leisure, sipping a little Marsala wine on the open terrace of his villa, looking out over the blue water, and feeling quietly happy because he had just finished a series of deft and devastating caricatures of the life of King Edward the Seventh!

He was cordial, most warmly cordial, considering the abruptness of our arrival from so far off in the future and with no introduction and no excuse but a desire to talk with him.

"Not about politics!" was his only demur, and to that we agreed so heartily that before long we were talking politics with candor and abandon.

There is a displacement of the light rays when Britishers

come in contact with warmer-mannered people, which makes it hard for them even to catch sight of each other for a while. This difficulty was increased by the casualness of our get-up and the exquisite neatness of the British gentleman in Max Beerbohm, the faultless fit of his gray suit, the neatly creased gray fet hat, and the trim mustache—also a perfect fit. The air did not clear completely until we got to talking about the revolt of creative artists against commercial journalism. I was pretty glib about this, for as editor of the *Masses* and its successor, the *Liberator,* I had to play up this aspect somewhat at the expense of proletarian revolution in raising money from American millionaires. It was also the subject of a little book of mine that Knopf had published, *Journalism Versus Art.*

"We made the same revolt in England in *The Yellow Book,*" Beerbohm said. And he described how, under the guidance of his friend Aubrey Beardsley, he had made his debut as an artist in that most famous of "little magazines." In him the mood of revolt had persisted, and in latter days he never offered his drawings for publication at all. If they appeared, it was by accident.

"For me they have achieved their destiny when they exist," he said.

I imagine this conversation, culminating in that extreme remark from a man we all admired, had a strong impact on Hemingway's emotions. Although I did not know it then, one of the major problems of his life was how to escape from his money-earning activity as a journalist—how, although married, to fix things financially so that he could devote his time and his pen to literary art. The solution was delayed for another year by the arrival of a baby, but he must have been filled already with the hope and the miseries of it. He was so quiet, however, and so youthfully attentive to our conversation, that I actually thought he was a stranger to such topics.*

After we drove away I stopped the car a moment to jot down a few of Max Beerbohm's remarks. Ernest laughed at me and tapped his forehead.

"I have every word of it in here," he said. I believe this was true, and is one of the main sources of his genius for dialogue.

Ernest was a modest and princely-mannered boy in those days, and his attitude to me, I thought exceptionally friendly. He must have liked the *Liberator,* for he asked me to read a sheaf of narrative and descriptive sketches he was experimenting with. Although I was not deeply impressed I sent them along to my editorial successors, Claude McKay and Michael Gold, for possible publication. Perhaps we were all unperceiving of Ernest's intense and noble effort to "put down what really happened in action; what the actual things were which produced the emotion you experienced." † Perhaps, on the other hand, these first efforts were not too successful. Whatever the reasons, they never appeared in the *Liberator,* and Ernest Hemingway is one of the few distinguished writers of his generation

---

* Charles A. Fenton, in *The Apprenticeship of Ernest Hemingway,* describes the vicissitudes of his transition from journalism to literary art. But Fenton's judgments seem to rest wholly on the *post hoc ergo propter hoc* fallacy. Since after five years of journalism Hemingway achieved a magnificent literary style, the five years of journalism seem to Mr. Fenton to have been proven a good preparation. I think on the contrary, they left him with certain bad habits and he did not overcome them all.

† The quotation is from *Death in the Afternoon.*

that I have to leave out when I list its contributors. I learned afterward that his wife Hadley lost a whole brief case full of those early writings and Ernest had to begin all over again—a lucky loss, I am inclined to think, having seen a sample of them.

At any rate, Ernest was not a genius to me then, but only an alert and vivid-minded journalist whom I liked for his frank way of telling me that he had been scared to death in the war. We lived in the same hotel, and one morning a hot water heater in his bathroom exploded and blew him halfway down the hall. He picked himself up with a firm and smiling composure that impressed everybody, and made me treasure all the more affectionately the fact that he had been scared in the war.

It was in Antibes and Paris, between 1924 and 1926, that our friendship was renewed. I had finished my pilgrimage to Moscow and returned to the west with Eliena Krylenko, the laughter-loving sister of Nikolai, the Bolshevik orator and Minister of Justice. American literary men were flocking to Europe like crows to a cornfield during those years of the debased currencies, and most of them would alight for a few months in the vicinity of the Cap d'Antibes. Antibes, itself, as the base of the Cap, has for its climax a romantic rampart, high and tawny-colored, with anciently impregnable walls rising out of the water, and towers looking beyond Nice to the snowy tops of the Alpes Maritimes. I found Ernest a nest for his typewriter up in a cranny of the rampart, where I too for a time had a hide-out. He was staying three miles away toward the end of the Cap and rode back and forth on a bicycle. We swam together once or twice at Eden-Roc, but it was in Paris the following win-

ter that we became what I venture to call good friends.
Eliena and I had a room on the rue Vaugirard not very far
from where he and his wife, Hadley, were living. Hadley
was a likable though not alluring girl, rather on the square
side, vigorously muscular and independent; I think of her
as a natural born "hiker." We were all warm friends, warm
enough so that Ernest gave me a copy of *Torrents of
Springs* inscribed "To Max and Eliena with love." Some
accident or instinct diverted me from reading it just then,
but I read "Up in Michigan" and other stories in the original edition of *In Our Time,* with startled admiration. I
could hardly believe that these harsh stories, so rank with
the savor of brute fact, so concise, so complete, were written
by the diffident young journalist who had shown me some
disconnected paragraphs in Genoa, three years before.

I was, I must explain, totally ignorant of the ambiance
and prehistory of this startling apparition. I am almost always out-of-date and out-of-touch with what at any given
moment the literary circles are getting excited about. Sherwood Anderson, it seems, was in and out of the bunch that
Hemingway foregathered with on the Left Bank during
this period. I had published some of Sherwood's first and
best stories in the old *Masses* and the *Liberator,* and admired them vastly, but I was unaware that he was, or would
ever be, a talked-of innovator in styles of writing. Of his
presence in Paris or his literary friendship with Hemingway, I had never heard. Of Gertrude Stein and her cult, her
Three Lives, her influence on American writers in Paris, I
also knew nothing. I had seen years before in New York her
silly book, *Tender Buttons*—equivalent in every respect
except sincere passion to the ravings of a lunatic—and had

dismissed her and all her doings with a tolerant laugh. I knew Leo Stein and lunched with him occasionally in Paris because he had a learnéd brain, a prodigious vocabulary, and an interest in the philosophic errors of John Dewey and William James. He was, however, something of a bore, and the fact that he had a foolish sister seemed to me illustrative but incidental.

Owing to this constitutional incapacity to be *au courant* with literary modes and talk-items, I was struck all of a heap by the sharp, short, unelaborated, almost illiterate realism of Hemingway's *In Our Time*. Eliena was working in the Russian Embassy then, and we were both innocent enough of what was going on in Moscow to think she might translate the book into Russian, and I wrote a foreword explaining this new prodigy to the Soviet intelligentsia. I asked her once, in Ernest's presence, what would be the Russian equivalent of "straight talk," and when Ernest asked me why, explained that I was wondering how to characterize his prose style in my introduction to the Russian text.

"I like that," he said.

We never found the Russian equivalent of "straight talk," and in the spring of 1925 the publication of my *Since Lenin Died,* an exposure of Stalin's conspiracy to seize personal power, put a quick end to Eliena's job at the Embassy and the hope that any word chosen by either of us could be printed in Moscow.

Four other incidents involving Hemingway had enough emotional impact to stand clear in my memory of those days and places in Paris. He showed me in his room, the day it came, a letter from Scribner's, who had read *In Our*

Time and wanted to publish his next book or books. That the courtly firm of Charles Scribner's Sons, who had published my *Enjoyment of Poetry* and *The Sense of Humor,* and whom I had abandoned as too genteel for my more revolutionary books, should take on a piece of stark writing like "Up in Michigan" seemed to me incredible. I had forgotten that in bringing out an American edition of *In Our Time* (originally published in France) Horace Liveright had eliminated that shocking story altogether. Still my surprise was not unjustified, for having taken on Hemingway, Max Perkins backed him to the limit, and I guess Scribner's did more toward debowdlerizing American fiction than any other publisher.

I was trying to write fiction myself at the time, being halfway through a novel and having a couple of short stories in my desk. I gave one of them to Hemingway to read, and naturally remember his bringing it back with words of praise.

"I'm not saying I like it because I like you, either," he said, which gave me two grounds for complacence.

In another clear memory, I was sitting with Lincoln Steffens in a café on the Boulevard Montparnasse telling him how much I liked Ernest.

"He's such a simple, unaffected, down-to-earth person," I said, or words to that effect.

Steffens answered, "That's true, Max, but he has a bad streak in him."

"Has he?" I said in surprise, but I did not pursue the subject. I never thought Steff's sententious remarks were quite so wise as he thought they were. I have since supposed he was referring to Ernest's heartless mockery of his old friend Sherwood Anderson in *The Torrents of Spring*, which I read only much later when I heard it described as "the meanest book ever written." I thought it one of the poorest books ever written. It sits like a puddle of escaped water in the careful architecture of Hemingway's writings.

Another Parisian incident I remember vividly is this: I was sitting alone at a little table far out on the sidewalk in front of the Café du Dôme when Ernest happened by. He seemed to be loitering and I asked him to sit down for a drink. He told me he had just waked up remorseful after spending most of the night on Montmartre. My memory is not verbatim here, as his would be, but he said in effect: "You can't help feeling desirous of some of the girls in those dance halls, and I always come home disgusted with myself for having such feelings, don't you?" It struck me as a strange thing for the author of "Up in Michigan" to say, and I answered (this I do remember verbatim):

"No, I don't, Ernest. I enjoy lustful feelings, and what's more I don't think you're talking real."

To my regret, Ernest jumped up suddenly and, waving me back into my own world with a laugh, continued more briskly his walk up the street.

I have no interpretation of that incident—only the vivid memory and a regret that with my brusque remark, for which I had no valid grounds, I blocked a tendency of our friendship to become more confiding than it had been.

On another occasion we were standing, two or three of us, at the counter of a little Tabac around the corner from the Closerie des Lilas. This time it was I who was telling about the night before. I had attended one of the famous parties given by the intemperate and delicate painter, Jules

Pascin, in his apartment on the slope of Montmartre. Besides being the most generous, Pascin was the most candidly interested in the physiological aspects of sex, of all the dwellers on that sacred mountain. He would invite the entire artistic population to these parties, and entertain them, not only with a magnificent dinner—the first big meal many of them would have had for months—but with plenty of liquor and plenty of nakedness, and a general atmosphere of abandon. I don't think Pascin was more interested in sexual experience than anybody else; he was merely free of the slightest reticence about it. This particular party, at any rate, although beautified by a couple of sylphlike ladies who removed their clothes for purposes of decoration, was more swimming in anger than lust. Everybody got to scrapping, and as morning approached the warfare simmered down to a violent altercation between a large drunken hulk of a Bulgarian and a small pale tremulous Britisher who was frightened for his life. They were fighting the First World War over again, and the Bulgar, who could have killed the small Englishman with a blow, was threatening drunkenly to do so.

"As I was the only one anywhere near the size of the big Bulgar," I told Ernest, "it looked as though it was up to me to do something . . ."

"And you didn't do it!" Ernest broke in with gruff and sudden scorn.

"Will you please let me finish my story?" I said, vexed more by the interruption than the reflection on my prowess. I suppose I was intending to boast a little in a properly casual way, and didn't want my boast to take the childish form of "I did too!"

My story was that when the mighty Bulgar, bellowing for a renewal of the war between Bulgaria and Great Britain, found himself laid on the floor with an American sitting on his chest, he merely squeaked in a small infantile voice: *"Mais, vous n'êtes pas gentil, Monsieur!"* He repeated that three times, and not a word or motion else. He didn't even feel of the back of his head where it hit the floor.

I had also in mind to describe the melée which followed. The naked sylphs, anticipating a massacre, leaped right over us on the way to their clothes, and little Pascin, too drunk to know who was who, rushed to the further defense of his British guest by pounding *me* on the back with harmless fists. It was a picturesque mix-up and would have amused anybody polite enough to listen. Why then this crazy interruption: "And you didn't do it!" It brought back to my mind what Steffens had said about Hemingway, and I wished I had asked him to explain it.

From there this story jumps to 1932 when Ernest published his *Death In The Afternoon,* a celebration of bullfights and the "religious ecstasy" of killing—of killing, moreover, as a protest against death. I happened in the same year to pay a visit to Spain, and took a try at watching a bullfight. Like most lovers of beautiful animals, I was angered by the spectacle. I was violently on the bull's side, sharing with specific passion his desire to run a horn through the dressed-up smart-alecks who were tormenting him. In general I think tormenting less witty animals for his enjoyment, or to show himself off a hero, is one of man's poorest employments. Therefore when Ernest's treatise in sentimental praise of bullfighting arrived in my hands I was aroused to express my own conception, both of bull-fighting and of Ernest as the book revealed him. I called my essay "Bull In The Afternoon," and it was published in the *New Republic* in June 1933.

My thought about Ernest was that, being extremely sensitive as an artist has to be, sensitive enough to have been, as he told me, "scared to death" under fire, his reaction had been to overcorrect this trait—to turn himself into a blustering roughneck crying for more killing and largely dedicated to demonstrating his ability to take any quantity of carnage in his powerful stride.

This was a fairly simple and almost obvious inference from the facts I knew, but I did not know then that Ernest had been almost blown to pieces, had had 237 fragments of shell removed from his body, and spent weeks in a hospital in such a mental state that he could not sleep in the dark. He had never said a word to me about his wounds or about this harrowing experience. Indeed I learned of it only recently when reading Philip Young's critical study, *Ernest Hemingway*. In that studious little book, however, I found my intuitive inference carefully reinforced, and my thesis applied, not only to *Death In The Afternoon*, but to all of Hemingway's books, to everything he wrote between *In Our Time* and *The Old Man and The Sea*. "It is a flight from violence and evil which . . . Hemingway's life and Hemingway's work eternally rehearse."

Such surprising things resulted from my anticipation of this thesis, that I want to recall the gist of it in my own words.

"There are gorgeous pages in Ernest Hemingway's book about bullfights," it began, "—big humor and reckless straight talk of what things are, genuinely heavy ferocity against prattle of what they are not. Hemingway is a full-sized man hewing his way with flying strokes of the poet's broad axe which I greatly admire. Nevertheless, there is an unconscionable quantity of bull—to put it as decorously as possible—poured and plastered all over what he writes about bullfights. By bull I mean juvenile romantic gushing and sentimentalizing of simple facts."

That was my beginning; and I subsequently asked: "Why does our iron advocate of straight talk about what things are, our full-sized man, our ferocious realist, go blind and wrap himself in clouds of juvenile romanticism the moment he crosses the border of Spain on the way to a bullfight? It is of course a commonplace that Hemingway lacks the serene confidence that he *is* a full-sized man. Most of us too delicately organized babies who grow up to be artists suffer at times from that small inward doubt. But some circumstance seems to have laid upon Hemingway a continual sense of the obligation to put forth evidences of red-blooded masculinity. . . . This trait of his character has been strong enough to form the nucleus of a new flavor in English literature, and it has moreover begotten a veritable school of fiction writers—a literary style, you might say, of wearing false hair on the chest."

My conclusion, like my introduction, contained a hint of the reasons why, notwithstanding that monotonous twist in his nature, I hold Hemingway in such high esteem. Other poets, I observed, having gone through the "insensate butchery" of the First World War, had come out mourning the tragedy and horror of it. Their bitter words had been "the true aftermath in poetry of the Great War—

not the priggish trivialities of the Cult of Unintelligibility, not the cheap moral of decorum (that shallow cult so admirably exterminated root and branch by Ernest Hemingway in a paragraph of this book), not the new Bohemianism of the synthetic gin period . . . but the confession in blood and tears of the horror unendurable to vividly living nerves of the combination of civilized life with barbaric slaughter.

"Will it be too much like a clinic if I point out that Ernest Hemingway is one of the most sensitive and vivid-living of these poets, one of the most passionately intolerant too, of priggery and parlor triviality and old maids' morals, and empty skulls hiding in unintelligibility? I am not strong for literary psychoanalysis, but I must record a guess that *Death In The Afternoon* belongs also among those expressions of horror."

The meaning seems clear enough, and I cannot imagine, as I read the essay over, how anyone could have inferred that I was talking about anything but prowess, and the need felt by most sensitive children to demonstrate this manly quality. In my autobiography I have told how strong the need was in my case, and described a lonely act of pugnacious daring to which it impelled me. If I made bold to psychoanalyze Ernest, it was only because I had so perfectly shared the feeling I was imputing to him.

Imagine my astonishment, then, when Bruce Bliven, Sr., the *New Republic*'s editor, called me up and asked whether I had intended to accuse Hemingway of sexual impotence! Archibald MacLeish, it appeared, had drawn this conclusion from my essay and had written a letter of outrage—full page, single space—demanding to defend his hero against this "great and irremediable injury." The crux of my crime—my "arch sentence" according to MacLeish's letter was this: "It is of course a commonplace that Hemingway lacks the serene confidence that he *is* a full-sized man." Since I had just reiterated my assertion that Hemingway is a full-sized man, I don't know how this could be construed —even supposing I had been talking about sex—as an imputation of impotence.* But Archie managed to read it that way, and commented: "Of those more personal evidences of virility to which Mr. Eastman so daintily and indirectly refers I have no personal knowledge. I refer him however to the birth records of the cities of Paris and Kansas City where he can satisfy his curiosity in secret."

Bruce Bliven, who was as bewildered by the letter as I, begged me to say something to Archie that would head off his intention to defend Hemingway against a charge that had never been made. "That would really damage him," he said. So we each wrote a letter to MacLeish so contrived as to bring him back to his naturally cool judgment.

"I am both astonished and much distressed," Bruce wrote. "None of us in the office read into the Hemingway article the significance that you found in it. I have asked everyone I could about it, and I do not find anyone who interpreted it as you did. Among those I have consulted are Edmund Wilson, Robert Morse Lovett, Robert Cantwell, George Soule and Slater Brown."

My letter read:

---

* In republishing "Bull In The Afternoon" in a volume of essays, I changed the words *full-sized man,* in that "arch sentence," to *made out of iron,* hoping, at the expense of clear sequence, to avoid the least suspicion that I might be talking about sex.

Dear Archibald MacLeish:

I was shocked and astounded by your letter to Bruce Bliven. Nothing could be more remote from my mind or nature than to sprinkle innuendoes or peddle scandal in my writings. I have a genuine affection as well as a vast literary admiration for Ernest. . . .

You made me mad, but on reflection I realize that some particularly mean recent scandal-mongering must have put you in a mind to misread my article. I beg you to believe that I did not know there was such a rumor in the world.

To this MacLeish replied very courteously, accepting my assurance that I had not intended the injury, although adding: "Nothing I have read in print in my life has ever shocked and angered me as much as your article." By that time, however, he must have communicated his misconception to Ernest, for a letter now arrived from Havana addressed "To the Editors of the New Republic," and containing a couple of ironical jabs which those on the staff would understand:

Sirs:

Would it not be possible for you to have Mr. Max Eastman elaborate his nostalgic speculations on my sexual incapacity? Here they would be read (aloud) with much enjoyment (our amusements are simple) and I should be glad to furnish illustrations to brighten up Mr. Eastman's prose if you considered them advisable. Mr. Alexander Woolcott and the middle-aged Mr. Eastman having both published hopeful doubts as to my potency is it too much to expect that we might hear soon from Mr. Stark Young?

Yours etc. . . .

Ernest Hemingway

After reading this, I wrote the following letter to Ernest, which he never answered:

Dear Ernest:

Your letter to the *New Republic* was all right, if you really thought I said or implied any such thing. But you might have remembered me better than that. I never heard the breath of a rumor that you were sexually or any other way impotent, although I have long been familiar with the news that I am—and gymnastic enough to be syphilitic at the same time. The idea strikes me as a joke. It is humanity's last tribute to those who do something.

I suppose it is fresh to psycho-analyze a man by way of literary criticism, especially one whom you esteem as a friend, but I think there is plenty of cruelty in the world without your helping it along, and I am within my rights to say so with as much force as I can.

The next chapter of this narrative opens four years later, in August 1937, when I was calling on Maxwell Perkins, editor and vice-president of Charles Scribner's Sons. Max was a shy and sensitive soul, so shy that his lips would tremble sometimes when he talked. To offset this, and perhaps also in protest against the genteel traditions of his office, he liked to keep a well-worn felt hat on the back of his head while sitting at his desk. He was an astute and yet generously—even tenderly—sympathetic editor-publisher as many have testified. He had suggested that I make an anthology to be sold in conjunction with a new edition of my *Enjoyment of Poetry,* a book which Scribner's had brought out in 1913, the year he joined the firm, and which he had watched over with affection ever since.

He was sitting behind his desk facing the door, and I was on his right facing the same way. Our mood was mellow, and it was more than a surprise when a big, burly, and also very peppy, Ernest Hemingway strode in and greeted me with:

"Hello, you great big son-of-a-bitch!"

He smiled when he said that, or I chose to think he did, and I answered:

"Hello, Ernest! Big? Why you're twice as big as you used to be!" And I felt his arm to see if it was still hard, notwithstanding his increased bulk.

"What are you doing here? Where are you going?" I asked.

"Over to Spain," he said, "to see what your P.O.U.M.* is doing. Is that your outfit, the P.O.U.M.?"

"I haven't any outfit, Ernest," I said. "I merely try to tell the truth."

"Uh-huh," he said.

"You aren't really running with that Stalin gang, are you?" I asked, and he said very emphatically:

"NO!"

"I'm mighty glad to hear it," I said.

We discussed Andres Nin, my friend recently taken from jail and murdered by the Stalinists, one of the finest men in the revolutionary movement. Ernest said he had heard him highly spoken of everywhere.

"I was sorry I missed you last winter in Key West," I said. "I enjoyed meeting your wife and seeing your house and children."

* A group of Spanish revolutionists who, disillusioned with Stalin's dictatorship, were inclined to do justice to Trotsky's position.

He answered with pleasing sincerity: "Yes, I was very sorry too."

But then suddenly, as though he had forgotten an errand, he came closer and said: "I want to show you something."

He opened a button of his shirt and laid bare some rather coarse and surprisingly dark hair on his chest.

"Is that false hair?" he asked, and he brushed his fingers through it. Then he opened a button of my shirt—we were all three laughing, or at least I still thought we were—and I said: "I guess you've got me there!"

His laugh died and he said:

"Look here, what did you say I was sexually impotent for?"

"Ernest, you know damn well I didn't say that or anything like it. You ought to be ashamed of yourself. We've been friends long enough for you to know I don't deal in dirty innuendoes."

"Yes, you did, and you played right into the hands of the gang that were saying it."

"I never heard it said. I never dreamed anybody ever said it. Didn't you get my letter?"

"Yes, and I thought that was nasty too. Moreover, you tried to kiss my wife in a taxicab in Paris."

"I never was in a taxicab with your wife, and never had an impulse to kiss her."

"Yes, you did, and you go around saying things behind my back. If I had your essay here, I'd show you what you said."

"Here it is," I said, picking up *Art and the Life of Action,* my volume of essays, which happened to be lying on

Perkins' desk. "Show me—show Max, and let him judge whether I said or insinuated that you are impotent."

He took the book and leafed the essay through.

"You've taken it out," he muttered. . . . Then: "Here it is. I'll show you."

"Show it to Max," I said.

"No, I won't, I'll show it to you," he said. "Listen to this," and he read aloud the passage beginning:

"But some circumstances seems to have laid upon Hemingway a continual sense of the obligation to put forth evidences of red-blooded masculinity."

and ending:

"This trait of his character has been strong enough to form the nucleus of a new flavor in English literature, and it has moreover begotten a veritable school of fiction-writers—a literary style, you might say, of wearing false hair on the chest."

"What does that mean," he said,—"some circumstance?"

"It means I haven't an idea what the circumstance is," I said. "That it does not mean sexual impotence is shown by what I say in my very first paragraph: 'Hemingway is a full-sized man whom I greatly admire.' "

"Never mind that," he said, "I'm talking about this right here."

He had been growing more and more truculent, and I was not entirely surprised when he burst out, "You know damn well what you meant," and pushed the open book into my face—insultingly, though not hard enough to hurt.

My response, although angry and instantaneous, was circumspect. I knew that Ernest could knock me out in a half-second in a boxing match, but I can wrestle. I grappled with him, clinging so close he couldn't hit me. After some swaying and grunting I threw him on his back across Max Perkins' desk, and down on his head on the floor. My fingers were at his throat and I had some vague idea, although by that time no wish, to do him violence. More accurately, I think I was wondering how much my "honor" demanded that I should do. I forgot all about the necessity, if that is what it was, of hitting him in the face with a book.

Ernest solved the problem by smiling up at me, the old friendly smile, and reaching up to pat my shoulder. I thought he meant: "Well, you're not as soft as I thought you were," or perhaps: "Okay, both my shoulders are on the floor." The gesture served, at any rate, to restore me to my natural world, a world in which fighting is unpleasant and friends try to understand each other. At the same moment gentle and tremulous Max Perkins leaned down and urged me in my ear:

"Max, please! Please don't do this!"

As I remember it, Whitney Darrow, Sr., was conducting a similar propaganda from the side toward the door, and the doorway was probably filled with the joyously anxious faces of several secretaries and stenographers. It was socially, to say the least, a distressing situation. I got up promptly and with happy relief. Ernest scrambled to his feet too, and we both started picking up books, blotters, pens, pencils—for the desk had been swept clean by our dive across it.

"You don't need to pick up those things, boys," Perkins said. "The girls can do that."

"I'm glad," I said, "because I'm winded," and I returned to my chair.

Ernest, smiling that same friendly smile, came over as soon as I sat down and patted me on the shoulder *again*. But then—once more as though he had forgotten something—he walked off to the space in front of the desk and began shouting insults at me.

"I hit you in the face with your own book," he shouted, "I let you off easy too, see?"

On reflection, I judge he was talking for the audience at the door or in the adjoining rooms, but at the time it seemed to me that these shifts of emotion were simply crazy.

"Ernest, I think you're a lunatic," was all I said. But his rage, or whatever emotion it was, increased with the expression of it. When he arrived at an obscene epithet considered to be the ultimate in the way of challenge to battle, instead of diving in again, I turned to Perkins:

"Max, who is calling on you, Ernest or I?"

Max looked infinitely embarrassed, and in the pause Ernest said:

"All right, I know. I'll get out."

Which, after adjusting his collar and tie, he did.

I said to Max when he was gone: "That was a little remote from our anthology of poetry, wasn't it?"

He answered, with comforting irrelevance:

"Well, anyway, you were on top!"

As I went out, Hemingway, who was now in another office, shouted something about "scratching people's eyes out." It was a taunt, obviously, at my grappling with him instead of standing off and socking him, a taunt that would soon grow up into a full-sized fantasy. A merited taunt, perhaps, but I cannot honestly say that I regret that life-saving "choice of weapons." Max Perkins comforted me somewhat when I called to see him a few weeks later.

"I don't like to discuss the embarrassing thing that happened when you were here before, Max," he said. "But I do want to tell you that I think you acted magnificently. You were Arthurian. You couldn't let a thing like that pass without doing something, and you did just enough."

It might have looked Arthurian, but there was nothing so clear-purposed in me. I was angry, scared and bewildered —chiefly, I think, bewildered: What is a civilized man supposed to do in such circumstances?

I have been able to relate this incident in such detail because, interpreting Ernest's erratic behavior as I did, I had a hunch that he would invent fantasies, and I went home and wrote down exactly what happened and was said.

My hunch was correct, and so far as the hero of this essay goes, the significant part of the story begins here. Eliena and I had dinner that evening in Croton with our neighbors, Eric and Jere Knight, and I naturally regaled them with my adventure. Two mornings later Eric went to town and towards noon I was startled by telephone calls from the *Post* and the *World-Telegram* asking for an account of what had happened at Scribner's. They were printing the story and they didn't want to get it wrong. I outlined the main facts impromptu to the *Post*'s reporter, and to the *World-Telegram* (my special friends), I read over the telephone the gist of what I had written. Hemingway was in bad standing with newspapermen at the time because of his reported habit of knocking down reviewers who didn't like his books. It is not too much to say that the whole newspaper world was wishing somebody would knock down Ernest Hemingway. I did my best to convince the two reporters who called me that I had dismally failed to fulfill this civic duty.

But it did little good. Both papers carried on the front page a hilariously laughing picture of me taken from the jacket of my *Enjoyment of Laughter,* and alongside one of Ernest in a dismal grouch. The *Post's* headline read:

"Unimportance of Being Ernest Hemingway Shown When Eastman Unbeards a Chest. Literary Hair-Pulling Sends Bullfight Lover Asprawl When Max Goes Picador."

Its long story concluded: "Mr. Eastman is planning an article to be entitled 'Enjoyment of Thrashing Ernest.'" The *World-Telegram* was more subdued, but both papers, and indeed every paper in the country served by the principal news agencies, carried the story substantially as I told it. Ernest had a hard time putting his fantasy across, but he possessed the necessary skill. He made an appointment with a reporter from the *New York Times* to meet him in Scribner's editorial rooms, where for obvious reasons, he was safe from contradiction. And as the *Times* was sending him to Spain, he was sure also of a respectful listener. His version appeared the next morning under the headline: "Hemingway Slaps Eastman in Face." Here is the story as it appeared in the *New York Times:*

Mr. Hemingway commented on an essay by Mr. Eastman that had been entitled "Bull in the Afternoon."
Mr. Eastman had written:

"Come out from behind that false hair on your chest, Ernest. We all know you."

The volume containing this essay happened to be on Mr. Perkins' crowded desk. "And when I saw that," says Mr. Hemingway, "I began to get sore."

In what he hoped was a playful manner, he said, he bared his chest to Mr. Eastman and asked him to look at the hair and say whether it was false.

He persuaded Mr. Eastman to bare his chest and commented on its comparatively hairless condition.

"We were just fooling around in a way," Mr. Hemingway said yesterday. "But when I looked at him and I thought about the book, I got sore. I tried to get him to read to me, in person, some of the stuff he had written about me. He wouldn't do it. So that's when I socked him with the book."

"Was he in a chair or standing up?"

"He was standing over there," pointing to a window with a window seat in Mr. Perkins' office. "I didn't really sock him. If I had I might have knocked him through that window and out into Fifth Avenue. That would be fine, wouldn't it? That would have got me in wrong with my boss, and he might have had me arrested. So, though I was sore, I just slapped him. That knocked him down."

"But how about throwing you over the desk?" Mr. Hemingway was asked, "and standing you on your head in a corner?"

"He didn't throw anybody anywhere. He jumped at me like a woman—clawing, you know, with his open hands. I just held him off. I didn't want to hurt him. He is ten years older than I am. . . ."

"How about books and papers being knocked off the desk?" Mr. Hemingway was asked. "Mr. Eastman says—"

"Sure, some books were knocked off. He jumped at me, I held him off, there was a little, a little wrestle. . . .

"The man didn't have a bit of fight. He just croaked, you know, at Max Perkins. 'Who's calling on you? Ernest or me?' So I got out. But he didn't do any throwing around. He just sat and took it. . . ."

Mr. Perkins and other members of the Scribner's staff refused to do more than verify the fact that the affair had taken place, taking the stand that "this is a personal matter between the two gentlemen in question."

Not satisfied with this achievement, Ernest apparently found or prepared a book with a smudge in it, and in a subsequent interview declared that this was "Eastman's nose-print when I slapped him in the face." Stimulated by this bit of documentation, he discovered, according to another reporter, that we had agreed to say nothing about the scuffle and that I had violated the agreement by releasing my version to the press. By the time he reached the *New York Tribune,* he had a story that was really worthy of his talent. Here he had slapped me in the face with such force that I "tottered backward and collapsed on the window seat."

Eastman sat there on the window seat, trembling with rage. He said, "Ernest, you're a big bully." I was laughing at him all the time and I said, "Max, if you were ten years younger I'd knock the hell out of you." He came for me then and I backed up against the desk, still laughing. I said: "Make this guy stop being silly. He's too old." I just held him off. I was trying to keep from hurting him. . . .

Rather in contradiction with his concern for my premature decrepitude, he concluded with a challenge to me to meet him "in a closed room where no one can interfere," and an offer to post $1000 as a purse to go either to my favorite charity or to defray my "medical and hospital costs."

To this, as quoted by the *Tribune*, I answered: "Tell Hemingway I fight when I'm attacked—either by a natural born ruffian, or a self-made one."

The columnists and cartoonists, of course, and even the sports writers, had a holiday with this "battle of the ages" between "Ernie and Maxie," in one version—in another "the Croton Mauler and the Havana Kid." Alain in the *New Yorker* showed a sturdy young man with a chest of hair being examined by an astonished doctor. "Writer?" the doctor exclaims. Ed Reed in "Off the Record" drew three babies in a creche, one of them similarly decorated and another sneering: "He swiped his dad's toupee—he heard that nurse likes he-men." "Everybody knows that when Ernest goes swimming he takes his own seaweed with him," was a commentator's remark that sticks in my mind, along with Westbrook Pegler's casual allusion to Hemingway as "one of the most talented of our fur-bearing authors."

A farcical note was introduced into the general hilarity by the Communists, for whom Hemingway on the way to Spain was a shining hope (a false hope, as it turned out), and I, having just earned an international denunciation by Stalin as a "brigand of the pen," was enemy number one. The *New Masses* chose to regard Hemingway's pushing a book into my face as a "political gesture." And I thought I sensed the influence of the party line when Malcolm Cowley chose that moment to send to the *New Republic* an essay beginning: "Chief among Hemingway's virtues as a writer is his scrupulous regard for fact, for reality, for what happened."

Though on reading this I wanted to underline the words *as a writer,* I cannot say that I thought Cowley was wrong. He seemed to be probing with those phrases for the thing I had called "straight talk," or "talking real," when it first commanded my admiration. Even when a more recent critic speaks of Hemingway's "stubborn honesty and personal integrity," I don't wholly disagree. There is a difference between a poet's honest loyalty to the reality of what he describes or imagines, and an honorable man's loyalty to factual truth when another's vanity is involved. Both these virtues require discipline, judgment, self-culture, undivided and unforgetful exercise of will, and in one at least Hemingway has risen very high.

Which brings me back to my initial purpose—to take a hand at defining the something that is great about Ernest Hemingway. For me it begins in his passing through and triumphing over the subtly influential, and yet basically degrading, baby-talk cult of Gertrude Stein, who is generally credited, and who credited herself, with molding his style. When I called Hemingway "a full-sized man swinging the poet's broad axe" I was thinking of this. I had in mind Walt Whitman's "Song of the Broad Axe." I had in mind Walt Whitman whose "this is no book—who touches this touches a man" sums up pioneer America's revolt, not only against feudalism and the genteel tradition, but against all those mincing refinements which separate the pen-and-ink life from life in the world. And I was thinking of Mark Twain too, who lived a full life before it occurred to him to become a writer of books. In the *Old Masses* and *Liberator* days, I coined the word "literarious" to describe the particular thing, or this one of the many things, against which "the *Masses* crowd," both artists and writers, were in revolt. In retrospect, when they are noticed at all, those two magazines are usually identified with Greenwich Village and the mood of Bohemian monkeyshines that is conveyed by that name. In reality "Greenwich Villageism" was one of the things against which we were in revolt. And although Hemingway's early contributions seem to have got lost in our editorial office, I think his style has more kinship with what was being attempted there than with the tedious babble which enabled Gertrude Stein and her circle to pose as the intrepid vanguard of literary culture in the twentieth century.

I do not mean to deny what Ernest himself has testified, that her teacher-like comments on his manuscripts were of critical value to him. She did, after all, have a flair for conveying the quality of an act or person in some perceptive metaphor. Although floating in a sea of mediocre prose, there are examples of this in her *Three Lives.* They are even to be found in that still more tedious book *The Making of Americans,* which she, with touching modesty, described as "the monumental work which was the beginning, really, of modern writing." That she could create a vivid sentence once in a while bears out his testimony that she knew how it was done; it is more than many good teachers of "writing" can do. Moreover, Ernest was just crossing over then from commercial journalism, the craft of writing in such a way as to please everybody a little and not offend anybody at all, into the realm of literary art—

the poet's reckless saying of things the way he thinks they ought to be said. Her obtuse disregard, not only of all readers, but of the very terms of communication, would naturally have allured him at such a juncture. To read the two of them, however, you would think that Hemingway was "molding" Gertrude, or trying to with little success, rather than Gertrude molding Hemingway. The choppy short sentences and endless strings of "and's," the self-admiring repetitions, borrowed, by the way, from Matthew Arnold, and carried by Gertrude to an inane extreme—or should we say *insane,* since it descended often into actual echolalia—all these rather infantine parlor tricks became in Hemingway's more skillful hands an art of quick, harsh, brutish realism that made *In Our Time* a uniquely awakening book.

Ernest must have been working on *The Sun Also Rises* while I was in Paris, for it was published in 1926. On the whole, as a sequel to *In Our Time,* it disappointed me. That monotonous staccato relieved only by an and-and-and legato, which had been so impressive when employed in a short story to convey exactly what happened in action, became tiresome when employed in a long novel to describe a landscape or characterize a person or an idea. On this larger canvas it began to appear that what Hemingway was doing stylistically was to renounce the riches of the language. Instead of a fertile innovation, the thing began now to seem retrograde, an effort to write mature things in the language of a schoolboy. I still think Hemingway's short stories, and the story parts of his novels, are his great achievement. The style of the short story has reached a new kind of perfection in his hands. But in all his work he gradually freed himself from what was confining in this after all rather tricky way of being forceful and realistic. By the time he arrived at *Death In The Afternoon,* realism no longer demanded that he refrain from using a grown-up vocabulary and his brains.

In short, when his teacher, the monumental Gertrude, discovered that Ernest was "yellow," and, still more devastating, "ninety percent rotarian," a process of graduation must have been under way. And when—once more with the accustomed modesty—she acknowledged that she and Sherwood Anderson had "formed" Hemingway, and apologized for spending so much of her time on the job with the remark that "it is so flattering to have a pupil who does it without understanding it," the graduation must have been about complete. For me those wild parting shots from Gertrude Stein merely indicate the speed with which Ernest was travelling away toward his greater destiny.

He does not belong in any little Bohemian circle of specialists in admiring themselves as an "avant-garde." He is not concerned to beat all rivals in the race to be modern, thus to outslide them all in becoming out-of-date. He lives in the ages; he is immune to fad. He lives outdoors on the earth and is intolerant of hot-house culture. He is intolerant of New York, where he could have daily adulation as our leading "literateur" if he wanted it. What he wants is the rough flavor of life as men live it who have something on their minds besides gossip about Art with a capital A. I can best explain the quality of my admiration for Ernest Hemingway by recalling the praise of Aeschylus in the initial pages of my first book, *Enjoyment of Poetry.*

With the participation of that poetic hero in the campaign of defense against the Persians, and in the battles of Salamis and Marathon, it seems as if Nature had achieved her aim. There experience was at its height, but purpose was unshaken. The little library and piazza poets and esteemers of poetry in these days of Art, will do well to remember the great Greek, who died the most renowned literary genius of his age but had carved upon his proud tomb only this boast, that "The grove of Marathon could bear witness to his good soldierhood, and the long-haired Mede who felt it."

There is a little of Aeschylus in Ernest Hemingway, in his character and his fierce code of courage and hardihood —a little of Prometheus bound. There is a little of Homer too, and of his translator, George Chapman, who wrote:

> Give me a spirit that on life's rough sea
> Loves to have his sails filled with a lusty wind
> Even till his sailyard tremble, his masts crack,
> And his rapt ship run on her side so low
> That she drinks water and her keel ploughs air.
> There is no danger to a man that knows
> What life and death is—there's not any law
> Exceeds his knowledge.

That, apart from his short stories, is the thing I admire in Hemingway both as a man and a writer. Philip Young adds inflexible will power to it, when he tells us that Hemingway built himself up deliberately from a "fright which seems once to have been nearly incapacitating" to a point where veterans and professional soldiers of World War II declared him "quite simply the bravest man they had ever seen." That he got these qualities mixed up in his mind with being exaggeratedly masculine and going around spoiling for a fight is just too bad. In order to be brave, he thought he had to turn himself into a bruiser, and he seems to have held the thought so firmly that it actually nourished the hair on his chest. At least so I judge from a photograph in my possession of a much younger Ernest posing playfully in the nude on a beach at Marquesas Keys. It was sent to me, amid the epistolary downpour following our "battle of the ages," by a lusty mutual friend of ours with some verses which I regret cannot be quoted here. I have testified that Ernest brought heavier chest-hair into Max Perkins' office than I did, and I note that in advertising a subsequent book he issued a picture of himself sleeveless at the typewriter with a grizzly forearm whose virility I could not even approach. But the fact visible in this earlier picture is that in those days Ernest's forearm was not grizzly, and he looked more like a statue of Apollo than a hairy ape. He was masculine enough, well formed, adequately equipped with both primary and secondary sexual characters, but by comparison with what he seems to have become in later years, delicately unsuggestive of a fur-bearing author.

Theodore Roosevelt had a code in which courage and hardihood received an emphasis similar to that which Hemingway gives them. Indeed these two Americans were in remarkable ways alike. Substitute rough-riding for bullfighting, the Spanish-American War (the best one open to him) for World War II, and the jungles of the Upper Amazon for the Green Hills of Africa—you have a similar pattern. They both believed in "the strenuous life," and both felt they were getting it in running down and shooting wild animals. But Teddy's code was not narrow; it included a variety of noble virtues. He was as much concerned as Hemingway not to be a "mollycoddle," but he did not think this was the whole duty of man. There is no reason why an intense moralist like Hemingway should concentrate on that one virtue either. But if he had to, in order to build a rampart between himself and the little library and the piazza poets above mentioned, I cannot be deeply sorry about it. He has cut a swath through contemporary letters like the spoor of a great animal—leading back perhaps to the jungle, but reminding us of the fragility and foolishness of much that we cherish as so very "modern" and "monumental."

Our last meeting was friendly and I would like to describe it here. In Havana in 1946, Eliena and I were loitering at the Bar Florida, watching the sober, slender, delicate-handed creator of daiquiris making them for his clients. He made them as though he were playing a violin. Glancing in the mirror behind the bar, I saw standing four feet behind me a thick, stern-faced character with big glasses, beetle-black eyes and graying black hair. Something familiar about him . . . yes, it must be . . . but so heavy-glaring, sad, brutal, unillumined . . . Ernest Hemingway. A kind of Ernest Hemingway.

My heart jumped a little. But I measured the space between him and the open door behind him: he was in a position, if tackled, to be thrown through the door to the sidewalk on his back. This calculation insured me against the bewilderment which had been so painful when he insulted me before, and I was untroubled when I turned around and said: "Hello, Ernest."

He stared at me while I waited as one waits for a radio to warm up and say something. Finally he said: "Hello, Max," and we shook hands.

"You remember Eliena," I said, and made room for her between us.

He greeted Eliena more warmly, and smiled when she said: "Are you really Ernest? I looked and looked and simply couldn't believe it was you."

"How have I changed so much?" he asked.

"You used to have blue eyes!" she said.

It summarized the change in him, she told me afterward. But his eyes looked so opaquely black, so like discs of obsidian, that it sounded ludicrous and we all laughed.

"Will you have a drink?" he said.

And so we stood there a while, sipping a cocktail and talking about our mutual friends, about the beauties of Cuba, about his being in France and running into Ross Sander's son, about his own son—then a soldier. A man with a camera came up and spoke to him, then backed off. Ernest took off his big glasses.

"Now I look more like I used to," he said smiling.

We spoke of Waldo Pierce, Dos Passos, Hadley, Bill Smith, Gerald Murphy. Ernest thought they were all awfully nice. He seemed awfully nice himself, although every little while he would stare beyond us in an unseeing way that suggested inward tension to my perhaps too diagnostic eye.

"I'll be seeing you around," he said when we parted.

My Friendship with Edna Millay

In his *Shores of Light* Edmund Wilson relates with delightful candor how in youth he and his close friend, John Peale Bishop, fell "irretrievably" in love—both at once—with Edna Millay. He describes this as a common experience, an "almost inevitable consequence of knowing her in those days." To be as candid, I shall have to confess that I tried to fall in love with Edna Millay, believing it for a time to be my romantic destiny, but regretfully failed. Long afterward, we became close and even intimate friends, but I never experienced the "intoxicating effect upon people" which Wilson says "created the atmosphere in which she lived and composed." It seemed to me that her frequent effect upon people was to make them a little tense and self-conscious as though because she was there, life, which had been flowing along naturally enough, had become an enacted drama.

She was not voluptuously beautiful like her sister Norma; she had the legs and, at times, the expression of a maiden aunt. But her eyes were of an incredible wild gray-green out of the forest, and they had bewitching crinkles around them. Her torso was shapely, and her voice as thrilling as a violin. She could indeed in moments of high animation *become* beautiful, almost divinely so, as Wilson suggests, but then all the more she seemed—to me at least—in some estranging way remote. Her determination to be a poet, and not some man's woman or even some child's mother, was absolute—and absolutely necessary, I'm afraid, if a woman is to rival men in creative art. Perhaps it was this that made simple people shy and a trifle constrained in her presence. You felt the strength of character behind that decision, and strength of character is always a trifle alarming.

I first met Edna Millay at some small party in Greenwich Village. She and Norma did one of the little folk-song-and-dance acts they had brought to New York from the rural village in Maine where they were born and reared. The act was skillful—their harmonies perfect, their rhythmical sense exact—but I did not find it pleasing. They seemed a little schoolgirlish, almost simpering, to me. It set me against Edna and her writings for a long time. I remember Floyd Dell's bringing a few fragments of her poetry to the *Liberator* office one day, and my saying:

"Why should we publish fragments of poetry? Why doesn't she send us a poem?"

"Maybe I'm prejudiced, Max," he said, "but I feel as I would if I had offered you some unpublished fragments of Swinburne."

Why Swinburne exactly, I cannot guess, but it is true that Floyd was prejudiced. He was at the time, as I learned afterwards, in love with Edna to the point of distraction.

At any rate, I remained stubborn about those fragments and, to my present regret, they never got into the magazine I edited. I too was prejudiced perhaps, for in 1912, when Mitchell Kennerley published my thin first volume of verse, *Child of the Amazons,* he happened to bring out simultaneously Edna's famous schoolgirl poem, *Renascence.* In the excitement about *Renascence,* neither he nor anybody else gave even a left-handed lift to my book; it dropped directly and by mere force of gravitation from the printing press into the waste basket. I do not think this prejudiced me against Edna's poems: I merely remember that it happened, and feel sure that any properly "psychological" biographer would say so. It is a fact, anyway, that I did not read a single one of her earlier poems, the poems of the "Greenwich Village gamine" period, until she had outgrown it. Elizabeth Atkins, her enraptured eulogist, accuses me of "imitating" a poem of hers called "I Think I Should Have Loved You," but until preparing the present essay I had never read it, and I cannot imagine what poem of mine she thinks it resembles.

This early insulation from the Millay cult, both personal and literary, enables me to speak of her more judiciously, perhaps, than some of her later critics have. Winfield Townley Scott, discussing her *Collected Poems,* in the *Saturday Review,* confessed to having outgrown poems which once had him "babbling in the streets by night."

And John Ciardi, in an essay in the same magazine at the time of her death, described how in adolescence "we were moved, we were filled, we were taken" by verses which now seem no more important than our first cigarette. "One finds himself less inclined to criticism than nostalgia. At least it will be so for all of us who were very young and very merry and aren't exactly that any more, but who once long ago opened those little black books with their titles pasted to the binding, and suddenly found the wind blowing through everybody's hair and a wonderful girl running to us through the wind." John Crowe Ransom, though not so nostalgic about his youth, seems equally filled with pride in the fact that he is grown up, and adds to it a boastfulness about being "intellectual" and "male" so reiterative as almost to cause the reader to blush.

I approach the question of Edna's character and her poems without any of these obsessions. That she was a rage in the teens escaped me, as I have said. That her "reading appearances were triumphs"—though not "of trailing gowns and far-flung gestures," as Ciardi asserts, for there were no gestures and the gowns hung straight down and stopped at the floor—also left me unmoved, for I did not entirely like the way she read her poems. They are melodic and she read them so slowly that for me the melody was lost. I also find it possible to be a man without inferring that women are thereby proven inferior. And as to the "lack of intellectual interest" which, according to Ransom, sums up her limitations—"it is that which the male reader misses in her poetry"—it was certainly not true of her nature, and I find it less true of what she wrote than of most lyric poetry. I agreed with Thomas Hardy when he said that, next to our skyscrapers, the poetry of Edna St. Vincent Millay was the thing he admired most in America. And I do not think anything has happened among us to alter that judgment.

To me, I had better confess, the whole "modern" movement in poetry has been a decline. Its going indoors, its abandoning under pretext of using contemporary plain talk the effort toward intense and perfect utterance, its consecration of the mental blur, its pouring out of metaphors without regard to their aptness, its loftiness above song, its conception of artistic creation as progress and of itself as the vanguard of a movement of reform, its living of poetry instead of living life, its strewing a poem with obscure references that no man occupied with life has time to look up, all these traits which may almost be summed up in the single word pedantry—a quality to be seen at its most tedious in T. S. Eliot's recent *On Poetry and Poets* —will be condemned as a blemish, I think, if our culture recovers its health. To me then, the growing-up of which the modern critics are so proud seems to have proceeded in a downward direction. They were wiser and more manly in their adolescence—a time of "tremendous vitality," according to Ciardi, and "passionate living"—than in this premature decrepitude which he describes as a "development toward the ambivalent consciousness and the pessimistic intellect."

It is important to distinguish the "intellectualism" of which these literary moderns boast from thinking profoundly, or knowing how to think. It is almost the opposite thing: taking delight in the unregulated mixture of ideas, images, and feelings in a mind stocked with knowledge and yet impassioned. It came in as a vogue with the rediscovery of John Donne—"the poet of intellectualized persons," as Ransom describes him, and he was indeed a master of this kind of poetic art. It is a magnificent experience to read him, to enter into his mind and puzzle him out, but it is remote both from trenchant thinking and from song. How remote it is from thinking as it is employed by those who desire to attain knowledge or understanding may be inferred from a glance at the first three names on the list Ransom gives of Donne's followers, the "intellectualist poets" of our time: Ezra Pound, whose learning is phony* and whose mind when exposed in prose is without edge or depth; Allen Tate, who can rarely say clearly even in a prose essay what he is driving at; William Butler Yeats, who was the dupe of every unscientific notion afloat among the quacks and crackpots who gathered around him. "Intellectual power," Ransom thinks, is characteristic of these poets, and he adds—for in all this he is still talking about Edna St. Vincent Millay—that their "field of reference is too wide to be commanded by the innocent female mind."

If these "intellectualist" poets were employing their intellects for purposes of understanding, they could hardly fail to know that their "snooty" attitude toward Edna Millay is not a critical judgment of her poetry, but a part of their recoil against the entire poetic idiom to which she belongs.† It is the focal manifestation of a major turn in

---

* On Pound's learning, the reader will find delight in consulting Robert Graves, "These Be Your Gods, O Israel!" in *The Crowning Privilege*. Graves strikes me as the one critic of poetry bold and unobsequious enough to fulfill the real function of criticism in this obsequious age.

† On the question of poetic idiom, Frederick A. Pottle's *The Idiom of Poetry* will tell the reader all I have in mind.

the cycle of taste—focal because she was the most prominent, and is in my opinion one of the greatest poets of the preceding cycle. I know nothing in American literature to compare in scope and grandeur of intellectual grasp and eloquence with her "Epitaph for the Race of Man." Brief though it is, this is the only poem in the language since Milton that can be compared in mental boldness, with Dante and Lucretius. And its brevity is intrinsic. With the top-hamper of superstition and ideological wish-constructions swept away, how much is there to say about man and the universe? How characteristic that these brain-proud exponents of the New Criticism have none of them an adequate remark to make about this great poem, its epic wealth of imagery, its perfected dreadfulness, the virile courage of the mind that dared at last to speak it out.

I have to say then, still only getting started on my memoir, that Edna had as clear, hard, alert and logical a mind as I have encountered in man or woman. She surprised me continually too with her large and accurate knowledge about many things—about nature, about language, about everything relating to her art. She had in these fields the instincts and discipline of a scholar. Far from being "indifferent to intellectuality," to quote another of John Crowe Ransom's naïvely revealing phrases, she was, for my taste, a little too austerely addicted to mental as well as moral discipline. She had a trace of the schoolmarm about her. It was this quality—surprisingly associated with her boldness in the enjoyment of sensual pleasures—that made it impossible for me to fulfill my dream of falling in love with her.

That dream shone down upon me all of a sudden out of a blue sky while I was climbing a mountain in Italy in spring. I had lost, or destroyed, the first great love of my life, and had come to Europe in self-distrustful loneliness —adventure-thirsty, however, as in emotional freedom I always am. The spring was 1922 and the mountain was twenty miles down the coast from Genoa, where I had gone to attend the famous post-war conference of the Great Powers. Edna's *Second April* was published in that year, and whether I had that volume with me in Genoa, or had read elsewhere some of the maturer lyrics it contained, I do not know. But I had achieved an understanding of the true reasons for her great fame. Somebody told me that she was "batting around" Paris; I had been batting around Paris, too, and was going back there again. The idea of loving someone more like myself than my lost love, a companion of my ambition as well as of my mind and body, had always intrigued me. And so much the better if she was famous—for I like to admire those whom I love. I like to love those whom I admire. Thus I found myself loving Edna Millay as I made my slow way up that mountain path, and composing a sonnet which I thought I might send her.

"I climbed a sunny-shouldered hill with you," it began, and what happened in between I don't remember, but this is how it ended:

> Above the clash, the rancour, and the rage
> Of this embattled and empuddled age,
> Above all wounds and weapons it could send,
> You have held high and beautifully strong,
> And flowing rose-and-silver in the wind,
> The bold clear slender pennant of your song.

I remember that as one of the happiest days, and one of the happiest loves, of my life—a love like Dante's for Beatrice, never spoken to or touched. It was a little briefer than Dante's but it filled my heart until I got back to Paris. There I did find Edna "batting around," meeting her I do not know quite where, but probably on Montparnasse at the Café du Dôme, where all the American bohemians, writers and artists and small-income expatriates, were spending their handfuls of francs. We dined together, making conversation successfully, and after the coffee, I asked her to come to my room on the rue des Beaux Arts and read me some poems. I was not, alas, falling in love with her, but still only hoping that I might. She did come, and as my room was infinitely narrow with only the bed to sit on, we sat, or rather lay, on the bed together with our heads propped against a pillow. She read to me, after one or two less personal poems, a sonnet which defends, or pays its respects to, a love that is momentary and involves no complications. But by that time I knew that my dream had flown. Though we were almost in each other's arms, we were not together. We were still making conversation. Some fixed vacuum between us held apart the atmospheres we breathed. Another fifteen years would pass before, short-circuited by a slight but completely spontaneous gesture, her voluptuous magnetism would leap to me, and I would feel in full warm stream the "intoxicating effect" that Edmund Wilson speaks of.

Disappointed of my romance, I did not linger in Paris, but resumed my pursuit of a more impersonal dream—my pilgrimage to Moscow. For that was my larger purpose; I had only paused at Genoa. I was on my way to find the truth about the new socialist society being born in Russia, when that irrelevant bright light beamed across my path on the Italian mountainside.

I spent almost two years in Russia, and another on the Riviera before I saw Edna again. She had married in the meantime my dearest friend, Eugen Boissevain, an incomparable companion. He and I had shared an apartment on St. Lukes Place, sharing also the services of a divine cook named Annie, and had lived an excellent life together for the two years before I set out for Russia. Thus it seemed now almost as though Edna had moved into my family. But in Moscow I too had married—a still more incomparable companion, and one with the same rare habit of taking life straight, or taking it with laughter in the place of prayer. We all four became the best and most unrivalrous of friends. I don't believe it would have been possible to say which one liked which other best. For a year Eliena and I played with the idea of buying the farm next to "Steepletop," Eugen and Edna's place at Austerlitz, and only gave up when the seashore at Martha's Vineyard clasped us in its arms. We spent weeks and weekends together in their farmhouse in the foothills of the Berkshires, others in our little house with a tennis court at Croton-on-Hudson, and one long memorable holiday swimming and basking in the nude on a lonely beach at Martha's Vineyard.

It was during those years that Edna wrote her greatest poetry. *The Buck in the Snow* came out in 1929. It was enthusiastically welcomed in England, although reviewed with a note of disappointment in America, the reason for this being, I think, that she had been silent long enough to

become a myth, and it was the myth of a more lightly tuneful and less warmly thoughtful poet than she had grown up to be. There was more passion and less wit in these larger and freer rhythms. There were more thoughts and not perhaps so many bright ideas. I suppose it was a question what one had originally perceived as the essence of her genius. For those to whom it was her very great lyrical cleverness—that delicate skill as a grammatical engineer, which people who do not write poetry always admire so much and take for the very fluid of inspiration—for them, no doubt, the new warmth and thoughtfulness seemed a decline. And those super-modern critics who "babbled in the streets at night" over her immature verses—partly, one cannot help thinking, because that was the fashion—were off already on the trail of a new fashion. As one who remained, by the grace of God, in the earlier fashion, I can say that the title-poem of *The Buck in the Snow* seems to me one of the perfect lyrics in our language, a painting of life and death unexcelled, indeed, anywhere. It is completely her own; no one else that ever lived could have written it.

White sky, over the hemlocks bowed with snow,
Saw you not at the beginning of evening the antlered buck
    and his doe
Standing in the apple-orchard? I saw them. I saw them
    suddenly go,
Tails up, with long leaps lovely and slow,
Over the stone-wall into the wood of hemlocks bowed with
    snow.

Now lies he here, his wild blood scalding the snow.

How strange a thing is death, bringing to his knees, bring-
    ing to his antlers
The buck in the snow.
How strange a thing,—a mile away by now, it may be,
Under the heavy hemlocks that as the moments pass
Shift their loads a little, letting fall a feather of snow—
Life, looking out attentive from the eyes of the doe.

Epitaph for the Race of Man was also composed during
the years of our close friendship, as well as the sonnet
sequence *Fatal Interview*—another classic that the poet's
adolescent admirers, in belittling her mature poetry, have
managed largely to ignore. Neither of these magnificent
works of genius is once mentioned by Horace Gregory and
Marya Zaturenska in their *History of American Poetry—
1900-1940*. This pretentious volume, supposedly a standard
work of reference, sums up Edna St. Vincent Millay with
the remark that "Her virtues are those of an effortless,
seemingly artless charm of youth, and of lightly touched
and quickly dispelled sorrow," and voices the prophecy
that her verse will probably "introduce other generations
of girls and young women to the phenomena of an adolescent self-discovery in terms of poetry." Unless it be personal pique, only the general decline of critical taste
throughout the whole period can explain this astonishing
fact.

Many who felt the heartbroken passion contained in the
serenely controlled forms of *Fatal Interview* were puzzled
by the idea that they were composed "when the author
was living quietly with a husband of eight years standing."
Elizabeth Atkins showed a manuscript containing this
quoted phrase to Eugen, and reports that he responded "in

a deeply bitten marginal comment" that the assumption it makes is a lie. I never discussed this question with either of my friends, but I can join my testimony to his that, passionately and admiringly as they loved each other, "living quietly with a husband of eight years standing" is far from a description of Edna's mind during those years. Nor would the corresponding phrase be a description of his. He never ceased to adore her and care for her with a unique devotion, less like a husband's than that of a nursemaid toward a child of whom she is enamored. But he was a man, and men are a nomad sex. He was, moreover, in principle opposed to possessiveness in marriage on either side. Freedom of emotional experience had been a cardinal item in the private marriage vows taken by him and Inez Milholland in the heyday of the feminist movement in America. Glorious Inez died too soon, alas, for their youthful dream of a new kind of partnership to undergo a crucial test, but I have no reason to suppose that Eugen offered to Edna a less openhearted love. That she, on her side, felt no need to be possessed or circumscribed will be obvious, I think, to anyone who lives a little with her poetry.

A memoir, if it is forthright, has to be fragmentary, for small bits of things stick vividly in one's memory out of all connection with other things. We were playing one of our very realistic games of charades at a party at our house in Croton to which a smooth-haired young man from Yale (I think) had been invited. The word to be enacted on our side was Bathsheba, and in the final scene Edna was to play the part of Bathsheba bathing on a rooftop and he of David passing by.

"This high table will be the rooftop," he said excitedly. "I'll enter from the side door, and you'll be up there in a bathing suit. . . ."

"Bathing suit!" Edna said. "You don't take baths in a bathing suit!"

The young man played his part of David, blushing somewhat, but with heroic fortitude.

Edna and I were talking one evening about the highly colored notions that prudishly conventional people have about those who take sex, so to speak, in their stride. The narrowing down, in American usage, of the words moral and immoral to apply only to the minute question whether one obeys a formula or his own selective good taste in sexual relations seemed lamentable to us both. But what would the psychoanalysts do if people were direct and simple about such things?

"There wouldn't be any psychoanalysts," she said. "They're all pathologically inhibited—that's why they think sex is at the bottom of everything." And she told me that once at a party she was sitting alone nursing a bad headache when a young doctor approached and said that he had been watching her and thought he might be able to help her if she would allow it.

"If you would come into the library with me, where we might talk privately?" he suggested.

"I'll be glad to," she said, out of curiosity rather than the hope of relief.

When they were safely isolated and ensconced in two large chairs, he got up and closed the door, then came back and requested her permission to ask a few questions. After a long and roundabout approach, he finally brought out, with much hesitation and several false starts, a momentous remark:

"I wonder if it has ever occurred to you that you might perhaps, although you are hardly conscious of it, have an occasional erotic impulse toward a person of your own sex?"

"Oh, you mean I'm homosexual!" she exclaimed. "Of course I am, and heterosexual too, but what's that got to do with my headache?"

One of Eugen's traits which I associated with the Dutch side of his nature—for his mother was Irish—was a strong property sense. He cared intensely, and sometimes irritatingly, about everything that belonged to him. One hot summer when Eliena and I were visiting them in Auster-litz, and we were all four sleeping in the front part of the house with double doors wide open, Eugen going into the bathroom found a slit in one of the little white guest towels that hung there. Someone apparently had used it carelessly to wipe the blade of a safety razor. He assumed that I had been the one and "called me down" with excessive intensity. At least I thought so, for I was sure I had not done it, and my reaction was bellicose. He was equally sure I had done it, and the conflict remained unresolved. . . .

In order to finish this story I have to digress now, and tell the reader that in the Russian language there are no definite or indefinite articles, no "the's" or "a's," and therefore when familiar objects like the lamp or the teapot are mentioned, it seems to an English ear as though these objects were being personified. "Shall we bring teapot?" "Shall we light lamp?" Eliena and I, as we gradually stopped talking Russian, used often to employ in English this whimsically affectionate way of speaking about our inanimate companions. And now my story continues. . . .

Just as we were all dropping to sleep with that fading animosity hanging around us, I said into the darkness:

"Eugen!"

"Yes," came the gruff answer.

"I'm sorry about little towel!"

It was the omitted article, I am sure, rather than my contrition toward Eugen—at least it was the two combined—that affected Edna so deeply. She jumped out of her bed and running across to me in her filmy nightgown clasped me in warm arms and embraced me with joyous affection. It was then, and from that time on, that the barrier between us of her self-captaincy and my diffident reserve got broken down. I felt finally the "intoxicating effect" that Edmund Wilson speaks of, and realized—alas so late—that my dream on the mountainside in Italy had not been wholly utopian.

Although we came close, and a shaft of love entered our friendship, there remained some quality in her that troubled me. Austerity, I think, is the name of it, a certain rigidity about scholarly matters and matters of taste and moral principle. I am not referring to what Edmund Wilson calls her "tough intellectual side," for that I adored. And I am not using the word moral in the sexually overloaded sense. In the matter of sexual relations we all four believed in freedom restrained by intelligence, not convention—a freedom that many imagine was attained in America only during the roaring twenties, although an indelicate flaunting of it was all that distinguished that decade from other times when adventurous minds have been mature. It was in asserting the exact letter of an ideal principle or a piece of information or an exercise of aesthetic judgment that she was something of a puritan or martinet. She drove herself, and drove other mortals, too hard. She drove them with inferences from absolute standards rather than judgments based on the flux of the actual and potential. Her letter (numbered 254 in her collected letters) to a member of the firm of Harper's who had suggested that she append some notes to her poems explaining the motive and occasion of them will serve as an example. She answered as though the poor man had violated a fixed principle of aesthetics. In the preface to my *Poems of Five Decades* I pointed out that seven hundred years ago Dante, in publishing his love poems, had set the style for such a book. But Edna takes a sideswipe at me too in that letter, asserting as though it were eternal law her extreme taste for reticence. In another letter (numbered 253), she answers, as though she were sitting straight in a sewing chair, a mild proposal from Harper's of some new way to make money out of her books. She does, to be sure, conclude this rather irate rebuff with a smile: "Trusting that for one year more it may be said of me by Harper & Brothers that although I reject their proposals I welcome their advances." But in another example of this trait that I am going to describe, there was no easing of her austerity, no smile at the end, although one was more particularly called for.

I refer to her relations with the Academy of American Poets, an institution organized, at first somewhat naively, by a blue-eyed young woman named Marie Bullock with a view to promoting poetry in the United States. Mrs. Bullock had a dream in her eyes, and she had energy and address and contacts with wealthy people. Her rather high-sounding institution—of which, after some kicking against its seeming swankiness, I became a chancellor—has conferred thirteen $5,000 fellowships on poets chosen by the chancellors, and is now using a fund of $50,000 to subsidize books of poetry which publishers admire but dare not take the financial risk of publishing. In other ways, it has been an unqualified boon to American poetry, and this I think every poet and poetry lover in the country now acknowledges. But in her first eagerness to make sure of achieving her aim, Marie Bullock drew up some truly formidable "terms" on which the stipend of $5,000 was to be paid to the lucky poets. A by-law stated that each one should "at least three (3) times the year of his fellowship and each time within thirty (30) days prior to the time fixed for the payment of his next quarterly installment of the stipend, communicate with the secretary of the corporation in writing as to the general nature of his activities in connection with the purposes of the fellowship." The Certificate of Incorporation contained a clause even better calculated to throw a scare into the poor poet:

> The following persons shall be eligible for fellowships: poets of proven merit, either natural born or naturalized American citizens, not possessed of a regular income in excess of five thousand dollars ($5,000), lawful money of the United States of America, per annum. No holder of a fellowship shall engage in any gainful occupation for the whole or any part of his time other than such occupation as may be approved by a majority of the chancellors of the corporation as not incompatible with poetic production.

I never read these documents until Edna called my attention to them in an indignant letter in which she declined to serve on the Board of Chancellors. It was a withering letter, I must say.

> This is not a "reward for poetic achievement." This poet must sing for his supper. The pen with which he has written poetry of conspicuous merit must now be employed in writing letters to a secretary of a corporation, explaining "the general nature of his activities."
>
> Is this mature artist being treated as if he were a talented child of undeveloped capacities? No. He is being treated worse than that. For this is not the sum of his onerous and humiliating obligations. Not only three times during the year, but every day of the year, during "the year of his fellowship," he must be circumspect that he engage himself in no "gainful occupation" "for the whole or any part of his time," which might in the opinion of a board of judges be "incompatible with poetic production." In return for his freedom, his freedom from poverty, this "poet of proven merit" must conduct himself, throughout the period of his fellowship, precisely as if he were a prisoner on parole. . . .
>
> I think of what Shelley said, in "An Exhortation":
>
>> Yet dare not stain with wealth or power
>> A poet's free and heavenly mind.
>> Spirits from beyond the moon,
>> Oh, refuse the boon!

Her letter, although addressed to me, was sent to all the chancellors and also to Marie Bullock. In a covering letter to me she was full of fun, and in one to Mrs. Bullock she tempered the ferocity of her eloquence with the pleasant question: "Can you not, in some way, persuade the Board of Directors to bestir themselves, repeal a few articles, drop a few lawyers out of a few high office windows, do something to make more simple and more acceptable this marvelous and shocking award?"

Mrs. Bullock revealed her magnanimity, or her flexible intelligence rather, by bestirring herself exactly as Edna suggested—except only that the lawyers received a slightly more considerate treatment. The offending "terms" were removed both from the by-laws and the Certificate of Incorporation, and only a legitimate stipulation retained that the recipients of the awards should not be "engaged in any gainful occupation incompatible with poetic production." By the time I got around to answering Edna's letter, these changes had been made. But the story does not end there, and for that reason I want to quote my answer.

Dear Edna,

I did receive your letter to me in the character of "chancellor" although belatedly and in a warm country where I was on a moral holiday.

I felt humiliated by it because I so impulsively agreed with everything you said and yet I could not remember ever having seen either the by-laws or the certificate of incorporation of the Academy of American Poets. I have certainly never been called upon to do any of the dreadful things or make any of the austere judgments suggested in your quotations from these documents. All I have ever done is:

(a) vote for a poet who is to receive $5000;

(b) vote for a chancellor who is to replace some other chancellor whose term of office has expired;

(c) attend a nice little cocktail party for my old friend, Ridgely Torrence, and hear him read a poem—with surprising simplicity and very well.

Now that I have come home I find your letter has already borne fruit; at least the worst features that you object to have been removed.

The truth is, Edna, that the Academy of American Poets consists of Mrs. Bullock, whose sincere zeal for poetry is a lovely and engaging thing. She is anything but the austere paternalist or disciplinarian that some of those sentences you objected to suggest. I don't really know how they got in there. I honestly think her sole motive was to make sure she was helping poetry and not prose.

By 1950, the Academy of American Poets had functioned four years without ever a restriction being put upon any of the poets it endowed, without ever a chancellor doing anything but write his name on a ballot sent him by mail with a return envelope already stamped. In that year the vote was cast for Edna St. Vincent Millay. Edna, moreover, was in dire need of money, Eugen having died the previous August, and her own condition and temperament making creative work, and above all remunerative work, impossible. The Academy held one of its glamorous money-raising banquets at the Ritz Hotel. The famous British General Wavell was among the distinguished speakers, and an immense throng was there to see and hear him. Mrs. Bullock naturally wanted to announce the award at that dinner, and I, of course, knowing its value to Edna not only in money but publicity, was eager to have this happen. To Mrs. Bullock, however, it seemed rash to announce it without an assurance that it would be accepted, for Edna had never acknowledged the changes she had made in the by-laws. Discussing the problem with her at the speaker's table, I offered to stand sponsor for Edna, I was so confident she would be gracious and sensible about it. But Mrs. Bullock was not satisfied and I finally undertook to call her up in Austerlitz and make sure. It took me the better part of an hour to get in touch with her, for her receiver was down and a neighbor had to drive over and request her to hang it up. And when I reached her she was adamant. She would have nothing to do with the Academy of American Poets, no matter the changes they had made at her bidding.

"It is true, Max, I do need the money desperately, but I can't take it. I could not be happy if I betrayed my ideals in this thing. There's no use arguing."

We did argue for another quarter of an hour, but it came to nothing. To her some abstract principle was still involved; to me there was no concrete sense left in her position. I returned to my cold dinner at the speaker's table with feelings unpleasantly mixed: admiration, on the one hand, for her unshakable firmness of character; on the other, an offense to something in the depth of me for which I can think of no nobler name than common sense. I could not disagree when Leonora Speyer, who heard me report her answer to Mrs. Bullock, said: "She's a goose!"

A more deeply self-damaging result of the puritanical streak in Edna was her disastrously conscientious attempt, in the crises of World War II, to write popular propaganda in the form of poetry. She gave all that she received for this poetry, and the manuscripts of it, to buy ambulances for the Red Cross. She was tremendously sincere—sincere enough, had it occurred to her, to go to work in a munitions factory, or wrap packages, or knit socks for the soldiers. That would have been a better gift to the war effort than bad poetry. But it would not have been the sacrifice of self that New England's rigid moralism demands. Edna may have imagined her name to be so renowned that her poetry, diluted to newspaper copy, would be an important help in "rousing the country," but I find this hard to believe. Her statement, "I have one thing to give in the service of my country, my reputation as a poet," strikes me as one of the most aberrant products of the modern brain-disease of propaganda. It was righteousness on the rampage, the sense of duty gone mad. And it ended, naturally, in a nervous breakdown.

"For five years," she wrote, explaining her illness to Edmund Wilson, "I had been writing almost nothing but propaganda. And I can tell you from my own experience that there is nothing on this earth which can so much get on the nerves of a good poet as the writing of bad poetry."

In sending us her beautifully titled book, *Make Bright the Arrows,* she wrote on the fly-leaf an inscription that was painful to read: "To Max and Eliena, who will not like the many bad lines contained in this book, but who will like the thing it wants so much to help to do, and who will like the reaffirmation of my constant affection and love. . . ." Many American writers—most of them—have at times diluted the purity of their art in order to make money; Edna's sin, we can say at least, was of a nobler-seeming kind. But it was a sin no less. She acknowledged later that this debauch of self-sacrifice had been a mistake, and regretted it sadly. But then it was too late. She never recaptured her lost self. She never wrote a great poem after that. . . .

Now I feel that I have to qualify what I have been saying, or define it more carefully. When I spoke of a certain asperity—or did I decide upon the word austerity?—in Edna's assertion of what she believed to be right or true, I did not mean to disparage her noble conception of the poet's role. She believed with Shelley that the poet should take his stand on the side of liberty and justice in the social and political struggles of his day, and of all days. She was greatly and courageously earnest in this—enough so to travel to Boston and risk imprisonment and the loss of her then monumental popularity by marching in the "mob protest" against the execution of Sacco and Vanzetti in 1927. Her presence in that hazardous and disreputable action is perhaps a better answer than I have made to those extremely literary critics who dismiss her as a bohemian play-girl and reduce her role in American literature to "adolescent self-discovery." None of them, I am sure, can boast of having shown up at Beacon Hill on that heroic occasion, or ever demonstrated their boasted "maturity" in an equivalent fashion. Delicate as her verse was, and lyric rather than dramatic, Edna Millay stands beside the poets to whom you raise your eyes after reading their books—poets who were minds and muscles in the world and not mere versifiers.

Perhaps it was inevitable that a combination of lyric waywardness with such a moral code should express itself sometimes in austere or puritanical forms that held me a little at a distance. Perhaps it was my own softy-ness, my wish at all costs to have things run smoothly, rather than any excessive sharpness of edges in Edna, that I was depicting with that word austerity. At any rate, it is not her consecration to the struggle against Nazism that I have been meaning to criticize, only her terrible mistake—worse than austere, fanatical—of sacrificing to it the integrity of her art.

And I must mournfully add that a good while before that stern revel in self-mortification, and quite possibly among the predisposing causes of it, the springs of her lyrical genius had ceased to flow. *Conversation at Midnight,* a book of unkempt and inconsequential prose mixed with poetry which was published in 1937, marked the end of her life as a great poet. I do not know all of the causes of this. She seemed to be mysteriously sick a great deal of the time, and notwithstanding her moralism she had nothing of the soldier in her. She cultivated for all it was worth the privilege of being sick. She lived largely upstairs in her bedroom, and would fly up there from the slightest annoyance—a noisy guest, an untimely call from a neighbor or a passing friend. The last time I stopped by at Steepletop I had rather angrily to ignore a sign nailed up on a tree by the gateway: "Visitors received only by appointment." Edna was a self-spoiled child. She had, in early girlhood, when dedicating herself to poetry, decided that she was a specially delicate-fibered, somewhat supernal being, and this did not help when she was called upon to triumph over pain. She babied herself and Eugen babied her; the most was made of every reason why she should not spend her energy. Often a good deal of energy is consumed in trying too diligently to conserve it. Valetudinarian would be too ponderous a term to describe her attitude; one felt on entering Steepletop that some very fragile piece of china, inestimable in value, was in unstable equilibrium upstairs, and that even the air-waves, if too much agitated, might unbalance it. Eugen, to be sure, could disturb the air-waves all he pleased, and being an obstreperous, athletic, noisy-laughing person, he disturbed them a plenty, but he did stand guard over his frail treasure, his "child," as he sometimes called her, like a dedicated dragon. No poet ever lived a more sheltered life. But I doubt very much whether that state of affairs increased the output of poetry.

There was, at any rate, a cruder cause of the decline not only in the quantity, alas, but the quality, of Edna's poetry —one which I dread to mention, but since it affected our friendship as well as her poetry I cannot leave out. She and Eugen, in the first flush of their love, had gone in too romantically for rural solitude. The theory was that she would write poetry and study the stars, while he would run the farm and the business of promoting and selling her poetry—a thing he did, by the way, with masterly skill and success. Thus they would be happy with nature and each other, and the world would not be too much with them. The metropolitan world, particularly, would not be with them at all. Many in love have dreamed this dream, and have realized it for a while. In the long run, however, for those who grew up on a diet of stimulating diversions, of social and egotistical fun, of "something to do" in the long evenings, the reality is very different from the dream. The romance becomes a discipline. Something has to be done to keep up the poetry of it. What Eugen and Edna did was to stimulate their hearts and dull their cerebral cortices with alcohol. That is an inner short cut to a condition not remote from poetic exhaltation, a heightened consciousness without the drive toward action. It is, as everybody knows, a great deal of fun, and Eliena and I enjoyed that fun with Eugen and Edna many times. But knowing the price to be paid, we were sad to see it settling into a habit indispensable to their enjoyment of living.

I once said to Edna: "If I lived the year round at Steepletop, I would miss the social stimulation that I need after my work is done."

"The rising of Cassiopeia," she exclaimed, "is stimulation enough for me!"

Inwardly my answer was: "Edna, darling, you are stimulating yourself with your fifth cocktail while you make that romantic remark." But that is one of the many, many answers that throughout my life I have refrained from making.

I did subsequently, however, in a letter on some other subject, remark to Eugen and Edna that they were drinking too much. They acknowledged in a prompt answer that it was true, thanked me for having the hardihood to say it, and assured me that they were reorganizing their life-pattern—very soon—in such a way as to correct it.

They never did correct it; their life-pattern went from bad to worse. There is no doubt that chemical stimulation blunted the edge of Edna's otherwise so carefully cherished genius. It also caused our four-sided close friendship to dwindle away, for the old gay conversations came to depend upon a preludial pepping-up which required more alcohol than Eliena and I could, or cared to, as a matter of daily habit, take. Our back-and-forth visits gradually ceased, and we drifted apart. We drifted so far apart that in 1949, when Eugen died in Boston under an operation for ulcer of the stomach, I knew nothing about it for several months.

I telephoned Edna when I learned of it, and suggested that Eliena and I come up to Steepletop to see her. She said:

"Yes, but please don't plan to spend the night, because I break down sometimes, and I don't want you to see me when I do."

This left so little room in which to renew our friendship that I inferred she did not really wish, under the heart-breaking circumstances, to renew it. I might have gone alone and I sometimes wish I had, but the mood of indulgence revealed in what she said awakened in me a sense of the thing I liked least in her character. I did not want to see her disposition to baby herself declining into self-pity. I was a coward perhaps—or was I wise to preserve a beautiful and heroic memory that had already gone far into the past?

Santayana in a Convent

Ever since my young manhood, when he confirmed me in my still diffident opinion that Greek wisdom is wiser than the wisdom of the church, I have felt a kind of companionship with George Santayana—his close presence, at least, on the intellectual road I was traveling. I have read many of his books with studious admiration, and he read at least six of mine and wrote me thoughtful and inspiriting letters about them. In one of those letters he dreamed up an "often remembered" image of me as a boy who produced in his lecture room at Harvard a sonnet on the Stoics and Spinoza. I was never in his lecture room at Harvard and never produced a sonnet on the Stoics and Spinoza, but I did not tell him this, as I should have had there been a two-way tie between us. I was content to be a misty item in the flux of his experience. Nevertheless companionship, intellectual and imaginative companionship, is the only name for the riches I received from his presence in my span of history and from his books.

I never met Santayana personally until the eighty-eighth year of his life when I paid him five or six visits in the "Convent of the Blue Nuns" up the hill behind the Coliseum in Rome. The "blue nuns" are a group of pious Irish girls in pale azure hoods, and the institution they run, high-walled and imposing, is properly described as Calvary Hospital. Within its walls the building has the form of a cross: one wing is the convent where the "Nursing Sisters" live; the stem of the cross is the actual hospital where they serve the sick; the other wing is a guest house, or "Ospizio," where they offer a haven to the healthy. Although he was rich enough to buy a chateau, Santayana's home for his last ten years was a single bedroom in this Ospizio. It had no private bath. A shirred screen made of pale flowered print hid his bed and wash-stand. The screen was low enough to reveal a crucifix hanging above the bed. The rest of his life equipment was mostly a desk, a chaise-longue, a few chairs, and a litter of books. Two high windows looked down over lawns to a street where defending and attacking armies marched in and out of Rome during the Second World War. Those armies did not disturb Santayana much. He read the papers and current magazines and kept youthfully up to date on what was happening, but he was not overly concerned.

At the age of twenty-nine he had gone through an inward revolution, a retreat into the world of ideas comparable to a religious conversion. "A surrender of all earthly demands and attachments," he called it. Within a brief time his father had died, his adored sister, Susana, had married, he had learned of the death of a boyhood friend whom he loved as a "younger brother . . . a part of myself," and he had found himself "harnessed for life like a beast of burden." That was his way of saying that he got a job teaching philosophy at Harvard! These sorrows, combining with a temperamental distaste for physical existence, caused a separation of the inner self from the outer which, he says, "rendered external things comparatively indifferent." They still were comparatively indifferent when I saw him, although not absolutely so.

I do not like to intrude on the private lives of famous men, and I felt rather out of character as I approached the big door of the convent. But I had so much in my head about Santayana that it seemed a pity to miss my one chance to look into his eyes. If the reader has patience— and if he has not, what is the use bothering about a philosopher—I will give him a little sketch of what I had in my head as I approached that door. . . .

I think it was the year after my graduation from college that I first met him in a book. He was over forty then, and had stopped writing poetry which nobody read, to set down a few thoughts *about* poetry—and about religion and love. His thoughts were crystal clear, and more beautifully written than any new thing I had seen. But like so many clear things, they were a little cold. His ideal of love was never to attain or even touch the beloved; better indeed if the beloved, like Dante's Beatrice, has died and exists only in idea. Poetry too, in his book, was not a celebration of life's

real and solid values, but a momentary and rather precari-
ous "harmony in the soul" attained in defiance of real life,
which is lived in a general scene of "stagnation and conflict."

As I was then engaged on my own book, *Enjoyment of
Poetry,* which makes an enthusiasm for real experience primary in the very definition of this art, I did not nestle down
very deep in his *Poetry and Religion.* But I was taken prisoner by its beauty of style; I escaped with an effort. Since
then, Santayana has published twenty-nine books and he
has taken a great many people prisoner with his beauty of
style. Some of the books bear such titles as *The Realm of
Essence, The Realm of Matter, The Realm of Spirit.* Need-
less to say, they are highly intellectual books and contain
what may truly be called a system of philosophy. Our
American intelligentsia has been rather overawed by this
philosophy. The number of people, even very learned ones,
who would venture to tell you just what it consists of, is
small indeed. There is universal agreement on one point
only: that it is beautifully written. And since that places
Santayana alone with Plato, Hobbes, Schopenhauer, and a
very few others, a certain amount of awe would seem to be
his due.

Nevertheless it has seemed to me that a little irreverence
would help in understanding Santayana—irreverence toward philosophy, I mean. I don't think systems of philosophy, except as intellectual adventures, sublime works of
art, are worthy of a serious (or humorous) man's obeisance.
Our knowledge of the world is particular and piecemeal
and will continue so forever. Attempts to bind it into a general whole require loops and dodges in the mind's pro-

cedure that, brought into plain view, can only be described as foxy. Therefore, I have not entered wholeheartedly into any of those Realms of Being that Santayana fences off. The phrase itself is a blandishment; there are no realms, except as dying echoes of the kingdom of heaven and the kingdoms of this world. Omitting those echoes, however, I have found his teaching both simple and sensible. He agrees with Democritus that the dynamic principle in whatever exists is matter; but he notes that matter produces spirits and that spirits have ideals. The way to happiness for each spirit is to pursue the ideal that is appropriate to its individual nature. He stresses the distinction between serene happiness and a mere succession of pleasures, and builds much moral wisdom, as did Democritus himself, upon his basis of materialism. To me, as I have said, it helped to crystallize my own early notion of a system of "Beatitudes" that would derive from the teachings of Socrates and Plato and Aristotle. These Greeks did not give enough place to the ideal of sympathy, but they went at the question of moral ideals in a simple, downright, this-worldly way that seemed to me correct. . . .

With this solemn headful of thoughts I passed through the old vine-covered walls and approached the great dome of the convent. I supposed that I would have a hard time getting in. A genius of detached meditation must have to protect himself against curious intruders. The Blue Nun surprised me when she said with a casual gesture:

"Down the long corridor, the last door on the right."

The door was open and the great man sitting at his table, dressed in loose flannel pajamas, bedroom slippers and a worn brown bathrobe, engaged in translating a poem of

Propertius. He got up with lively courtesy as I entered. I mentioned my name and reminded him of our correspondence.

"You must forgive me," he said, "I have no memory for recent things, but I'm very glad to see you."

His smile was almost a laugh, and we sat down and plunged into a conversation that could not have been more cordial if he had remembered me well. After a time he began to look at me with surprised attention:

"Oh, I do remember who you are! You were on the opposite side of the barricades from me, but I liked you. Your colleague, Upton Sinclair, on the other hand, I not only disagreed with, but I didn't like him!"

It was not entirely flattering, after all the wonderful and wise and mostly non-political books of mine he had read so thoughtfully! But it was a good beginning for a conversation—for six conversations as it turned out. And I made them more fruitful by reading in the intervals the two books of memoirs he had then published, *Persons and Places* and *The Middle Span*.

Our conversation was about poetry and religion at first. We differed less about poetry than I had thought in the early days. I was able to remind him of a letter in which— speaking of my book, *The Literary Mind*—he had said, "I agree with the *gist* of your definition of poetry . . . I agree also that aesthetic feeling involves the inhibition of action and transitive intelligence." I had this sentence by heart because I had waved it in the face of a professor of Aesthetics who tried to quote Santayana *against* my views of poetry and art. Santayana really makes more of that inhibition of action than I do, for to him it is a dive off the deep end of existence into the Realm of Essence. I think of it only as a damming of the stream of experience, a "trance of realization," almost better anchored than science to the existing world.

About religion we had more to say because we disagreed. Although a materialist, Santayana considered himself devout and worshipful. He loved the rites and ceremonies of the Catholic church. He loved its dogmas, knew them to the last detail, and dwelt on them with unreserved emotion. But he did not think they were true. He thought they expressed in a symbolic way ideals that were needful to spirits in finding their way through a material world.

"The churchly ideas have no authority," he said. "Lately I've been making much of that word 'authority.' Only material facts, at bottom only the facts of physical science, have authority."

I remarked that it seemed a little old maidish to me to perform solemn rites and bask in adult emotions concerning events you do not think happened and persons you consider unreal.

"It is like playing at life with paper dolls," I said.

"That's because you were brought up a Protestant," he answered. "You can't sense the tradition that hallows those legends and gestures. As a boy in Spain I grew up among them. The world I grew up in was a Catholic world."

He seemed content to leave me out of that world; there was no effort to open a door. And I was content to stay out. I do not think going through the motions of religion without genuine belief is a peculiarly Catholic phenomenon— or even a peculiar phenomenon. The peculiar thing about Santayana was his candid confession, or rather bold celebration, of it. He made a sincerity of being insincere. He was religious without a religion.

"I wonder how the Blue Nuns like this kind of religiousness," I said, and he laughed not ironically.

"They pray for me," he said, enlarging his eyes. "I asked them only please not to pray that when I die I go to heaven. Send me rather into limbo where I can enjoy a little conversation with my friends. That I really think they understood."

Santayana had a great deal of fun out of life, in spite of —or was it because of—his detachment from it. Sometimes the high theologians of the Vatican would come in and try to convert him to a literal belief in these dogmas that he loved. His friend and amanuensis, Daniel Cory, told me that once in the heat of a discussion, one of them quoted a passage from St. Thomas Aquinas. When he had finished, Santayana said:

"While you are using that argument you might just as well get it right," and gave him back his quotation, corrected—and in Latin!

Santayana emphatically denied that any such thing ever happened, and I believe him, but it makes a good story and a significant one. He vastly surprised me with his taste for fun. Not that his books lack humor of a subtle kind, but he had written me a letter about my book, *Enjoyment of Laughter,* that made me think he cherished a meditative grouch. I couldn't quote that letter then; I could only remember how it had surprised me. But I can quote it now, and it surprises me still more since I have the image of him laughing. It began with the assertion that he couldn't understand a word of the book!

"I can understand *your own* words, and no doubt I should see a part, at least, of your reasons for making the distinctions you make in the kinds of the comic. My difficulty is with the comic universe itself. *There* is where everything eludes me in so far as it is supposed to be *comic* and in so far as this comic is supposed to be a part of the *good*. All these jokes seem rather ghastly. And the *enjoyment of laughter,* rather than a painful twist and a bit of heartache at having to laugh at all, being your whole subject, I say I don't understand a word of your book. . . ."

Can you wonder that I was surprised to find him possessed of a merry laugh that took charge of his whole face, and was ready to go into action on the most trivial provocation? I expressed my surprise and he answered:

"Don't you know I'm a follower of Democritus, the 'laughing philosopher'? A good many of my friends think I laugh too much. They think I'm a little silly. But I think laughter is very important. It's one of the two things I demand of a friend—the ability to laugh and the ability to worship."

I left the subject there, for I did not like to try to remind him that he had written me letters about my books. But I must say it puzzled me, and does still.

"I wonder what a materialist can mean by worship," I said.

"I mean adoration of the ideal, of something beyond and apart from yourself."

In that quick easeful way he would answer every question I asked. I never knew a man whose thoughts flowed out of him so like a liquid—nothing stiff or contained, no guards put up against inconsistency or misunderstanding.

They came out of him that way, and couldn't come any other. In his books you sometimes feel this as a fault. You say to yourself: "This man writes too damn well!" But in conversation it was a delight, and made him winning at the first encounter, and if you kept on going to see him, lovable.

He had one disproportionately long canine tooth that might have belonged to a devil, and his eyes were a bit demonic, the irises black as a black beetle, and so placed that, when he was alert, you could see the whites all the way round. They were Bob Hope eyes, only serious. But the attention they expressed was warm and genuine and you felt in the end that there was something childlike rather than satanic in the way they startled you.

If America were more intellectual, George Santayana would have been regarded throughout my life, I suppose, as her most distinguished writer. I don't know who could beat him. But he was a philosopher, and most of his twenty-eight volumes give the cerebral cortex a workout for which the average United States reader is ill prepared. One of his former students at Harvard told me the boys used to wear heavy overcoats to his lectures, he carried them to such icy pinnacles of abstract speculation. At the age of seventy-two, however, he descended from those pinnacles and captured the world with a best-selling novel, *The Last Puritan*, a feat theretofore unknown in history. And he subsequently wrote three small autobiographical volumes as knowingly delightful in their comments on concrete men and women as though he had passed all his life in the cozier valleys where they live.

Notwithstanding these signs of earthy alertness, Santayana was commonly thought of as looming above, rather than occupying a place in American literature. His Spanish parentage and citizenship gave force to this notion, although he lived from his eighth to his forty-ninth year in and around Boston and to quote his own surprising assertion, "hardly ever read a Spanish Book."

"England is where I feel naturally at home," he told me. "I should have settled there but for my fear of absorbing all the British prejudices. Other prejudices are not so tempting to my nature."

The fact that he spent his last years within the walls of a convent reinforced our sense of Santayana's remoteness from the usual ways and interests of Americans. You would expect a male recluse to get him to a monastery, instead of a nunnery, in retiring from the world. But in truth there was no retiring from the world.

"My retreat has always been moral only, not disciplinary," he assured me, "and it took place in 1893."

He explained on purely financial grounds his coming to the Blue Nun's hospice to live.

"The reason was that my money from America was about to be cut short, and I succeeded in making an arrangement with the head of this Order to pay in Chicago, where they have a large hospital, an equivalent of my dues here. This was arranged; and I was for three years with 30,000 lire which I happened to have on hand for pocket money. Later I found that the treasury had stopped my nephew's payments to Chicago, and he and I had much trouble for leave from the government to pay up what was due, after the war."

The nuns made him comfortable. Their prayers for his

soul's future pleased his emotions without unsettling his opinions. Besides he was getting old. He believed with Epicurus that luxury is bad for the spirit's health. It seemed as good a place as any in which to live the last, and he insisted, the happiest, years of life, and, when the time came, to part from it with pleased composure.

Notwithstanding his explanation of its beginnings, there was conceivably a significance in Santayana's spending so long a period in the companionable care of the Blue Nuns. It runs to meet the fact that he played leading lady in the Harvard theatricals of 1884, and two years later danced as a ballerina in the Hasty Pudding play. It calls up the fact that when he was a boy and his brother read Shakespeare aloud, he liked *Julius Caesar,* but found *Romeo and Juliet* "inexpressibly silly." It chimes with his earnest, though not unsmiling, proof that angels—although they do not exist—are of the male sex.

Santayana has an eloquent dissertation on love in his *Reason In Society,* but there is not a sign in his memoirs that he ever experienced this emotion toward a woman. I doubt if any other memoirist has devoted so much energy of understanding to his friends as Santayana did. He paints them with a lingering and loving hand. But they are all, except only his mother and his adored half-sister, Susana, men. He remarked to me that all his good friends, with the single exception of Robert Bridges, the English poet-laureate, were men younger than himself. They were thinking men, and the life of the mind is what drew the friends together, and yet the friendships were highly charged with emotion. Of a boy, Edward Bayley, with whom for a few weeks he used to walk home from school, he writes:

"The bond was established, silently of course, but safely. Even the fact that we never saw each other after that year and hardly a letter passed between us, made no difference in our friendship. Strange enchantment! Even today, the thought of that youthful comradeship, without incidents, without background, and without a sequel, warms the cockles of my heart like a glass of old port.

"There is a sort of indifference to time, as there is a sort of silence, which goes with veritable sympathy. . . . Clearness and depth in the heart, as in the intellect, transpose everything into the eternal. . . . Never was trust more instinctive, more complete, or more silent, at least on my side, for sixty years."

Had Bayley been, by permission of destiny, a girl, or had Santayana been what at moments he came so near to being —Plato!—only one change would have occurred in this passage. Instead of "sympathy," the key word would have been, as it should be, love.

I am not trying to psychoanalyze Santayana. I am not one of those voluble doctors who can tell you all about the "unconscious" of a famous writer by glancing through his books, but will charge you fifty dollars an hour five hours a week for a hundred and fifty weeks to arrive at some little preliminary inkling about your own. I am only calling attention to what Santayana deliberately and frankly said in his memoirs about himself—a source of light on his philosophy that for some reason none of those puzzled by it has yet thought to exploit.

As a young man, being witty, vivacious, and a born gentleman, he was quite a success in Boston's intellectual society—especially in the somewhat scandalous circles surrounding Mrs. Jack Gardner, who shocked the Bostonians almost to death with her bohemian goings-on, but revived and silenced them with the gift of a sumptuous museum of art. Santayana never "took a shine" to any of the luscious and bewitching girls he must have met in those gay circles.

"I never courted any of them," he says in the language of the 1880's—for that is how long ago it was. "I liked to sit next to them at dinner, when conversation became more civilized in the midst of light and flowers, good food and good wines. The charm of the ladies was a part of that luxurious scene and polite intoxication; for me it was nothing more. But people could not understand that this could be all. . . ."

Ostensibly he was explaining, in this passage, that he did not want to marry an American woman because he regarded himself as "involuntarily uprooted," and not at home in our soil. But certainly no one who had felt amorous toward those women would have explained this judicial decision in just such terms. When he adds, "My real affinities were with three or four elderly ladies. . . ." and therewith concludes the whole subject of his relations with women up to his fiftieth year, there is no need to draw inferences. He is presumably withholding his most intimate experiences in this sphere, and there is no sign in his dissertation on love that he was without such experiences. But he is also telling us in plain language that he was not, even at the height of his young manhood, possessed of any strong interest in women as women. His half-sister Susana, he had already told us was "the greatest power, and certainly the strongest affection, in my life."

And so all in all he has pretty plainly stated—I am sorry I lacked the nerve to ask him point-blank—that he was never passionately attracted to a woman. He liked women to be elderly; he enjoyed them as table companions.

There is a discourse on friendship immediately following the one on love, which to my thinking points up this fact.

"Friends," he says, "are generally of the same sex, for when men and women agree, it is only in their conclusions; their reasons are always different. So that while intellectual harmony between men and women is easily possible, its delightful and magic quality lies precisely in the fact that it does not arise from mutual understanding, but is a conspiracy of alien essences and a kissing, as it were, in the dark. . . . The human race, in its intellectual life, is organized like the bees: the masculine soul is a worker, sexually atrophied, and essentially dedicated to impersonal and universal arts; the feminine is a queen, infinitely fertile, omnipresent in its brooding industry, but passive and abounding in intuitions without method as passions without justice. Friendship with a woman is therefore apt to be more or less than friendship: less, because there is no intellectual parity; more, because (even when the relation remains wholly dispassionate, as in respect to old ladies) there is something mysterious and oracular about a woman's mind which inspires a certain instinctive deference and puts it out of the question to judge what she says by masculine standards. She has a kind of sibylline intuition and the right to be irrationally *à propos*. There is a gallantry of the mind which pervades all conversation with a lady, as there is a natural courtesy toward children and mystics; but such a habit of respectful concession, marking as it does an intellectual alienation as profound as that which separates us from the dumb animals, is radically incompatible with friendship."

For me this only proves that Santayana was never in love with a woman. In love he would have learned that women have often much of the masculine in them, just as men—himself notably—have much of the feminine. Santayana's criticisms of other philosophers is masculine in a high degree; it is logical, methodical, lucidly annihilating. But when he comes to bringing forth a philosophy of his own, the parturition is "mysterious and oracular" to such an extent that logicians find it almost impossible to follow. He himself confesses: "Abstraction is difficult for me. Unless I can move with a certain volume of miscellaneous notions in my mind, I lose interest and direction. I could never play chess. . . ." And is there any admirer of Santayana's prose who would deny him "the right to be irrationally *à propos?*"

One need not be a Freudian to recognize the illumination these facts cast upon Santayana's reasonings about the universe. I believe that without considering them it is impossible to appraise his claim to be a moral philosopher —that is, a man wise in the search for life's best values. They must be supplemented, however, before the picture is clear, by one or two other things he frankly tells us.

He was born in Spain of parents who did not love each other enough to stick together. Indeed, his mother, he says, did not love erotically at all, but "to men as men, even to her two husbands, seems to have been cold, critical and sad as if yielding to some inevitable but disappointing fatality." When little Jorge, a prodigiously sensitive child, was seven years old, his mother packed up and went to live in Boston, leaving him alone with a rather preoccupied father. Whether to make it better or worse, an "Uncle Santiago" and his kitchen-dwelling wife and daughter moved in to live with them. Describing this awful moment, Santayana says: "I didn't feel deeply or understand what was going on, but somehow the force of it impressed my young mind and established there a kind of criterion or standard of reality. . . . That crowded, strained, disunited and tragic family life remains for me the type of what life really is: something confused, hideous, and useless."

Most young boys, so wounded in their spirit, would have found the cure in a subsequent love affair. But for one to whom *Romeo and Juliet* was "inexpressibly silly" no such cure apparently could be had. Santayana's reaction was to recoil from reality altogether. It seemed thereafter "axiomatic" to him, he says, that "the real was rotten and only the imaginary at all interesting." It became his firm opinion that existence itself is "profoundly ugly and wrong." And recalling this opinion in old age, he added that, with a slight allowance for youthful exaggeration, "it is still what I think."

That there might be something "wrong" with Santayana, and not only with existence, seems not to have occurred to his mind. And yet, I think his further confessions tend to bear this out. For they are confessions of an almost total amnesia extending through the years of his growth up to manhood. He was up-rooted and brought over to Boston to rejoin his mother at the age of eight and a half, and he described his memory of events and feelings from then up to the age of sixteen as "for the most part a blank."

"And yet I know that my feelings in those years were intense, that I was solitary and unhappy and attached only to a persistent dream-life fed on books of fiction, architecture and religion."

Whatever griefs and dismays lay behind the curtain which memory, so often merciful, drew over those years, we may be sure, I think, that existence in general was not to blame. Existence can be right and beautiful as well as ugly and wrong, as is quite obvious to common sense. It is existence as experienced by a man limited in passion as he was, and injured as he was in childhood, that Santayana rejects wholesale and despises. For me, after much reading of him and a half dozen thoughtful conversations with him, that seems to be the point at which a study of his ideas should begin.

With such emotional limitations, and an injured childhood, a person of medium force would probably have limped through a rather apologetic life. Santayana stood up firm and bold, grappled with the universe and bent it —so far as twenty-nine books can do so—to his spirit's needs. That is the story of his life and philosophy as I see it.

This is hardly the place to discuss Santayana's system of metaphysics, and yet I think I can make its main point clear if the reader has a little curiosity. It is a system for getting free of the world without leaving it. You must, first, make a sharp distinction between things and the characters they take on. A flower has beauty, for instance, and it fades. The flower continues to exist, but not its beautifulness. Still the beautifulness can be talked about, reasoned about, investigated, described. So may all the characters that things put on or take off—and even imaginary characters may be so dealt with. These characters Santayana calls "essences." They are infinite in number; they are changeless; and though they do not exist, they have a sort of "being," or you couldn't talk about them. If you call the place, or no-place, where they have this being a "Realm"—allowing yourself that one slight self-deception—you will find it a much richer realm to dwell in than that in which things have the misfortune to exist.

For the Realm of Essence, you see, contains all the characters of existence, and then some. These characters are independent of time. And best of all, although this advantage is not usually mentioned, there is no compulsion on you to entertain any particular one of them in preference to another. You can pick and choose. There is, for instance, an essence called "sliminess," but nobody who dwells in the Realm of Essence—"dwells in the eternal" as Santayana likes to say—is compelled to bother with it. Existence, on the other hand, if you get thoroughly wound up in it, is liable to spring one of these repellent essences on you when there is no escape. What is worse, she will put one on right in your presence when you are looking the other way, or trying perhaps to think about something sublime. Existence is not only "ugly and wrong," but "cruel and nasty," as Santayana says in another connection.

Starting with that opinion, or that emotional recoil from the rough ways of a changing world, Santayana built himself a refuge in the conceptual apparatus with which change is described. This is the gist, as I see it, of his doctrine of essence. It is a brilliant invention, an escape without exit, an ascension into heaven without departing from the earth. It has value for those who are too honest to deny that life is, and must be, lived by the body, and yet too squeamish to take life on those terms and make the most of it.

Santayana's religion as well as his philosophy, his holding to the Roman Catholic faith without believing in it, is to some extent explained, I think, by this recoil from reality. He did not learn any religion at all from his parents.

"My mother," he says, "like her father before her, was a Deist: she was sure there was a God, for who else could have made the world? But God was too great to take special thought for man: sacrifice, prayers, churches, and tales of immortality were invented by rascally priests in order to dominate the foolish. My father, except for the Deism, was emphatically of the same opinion. Thus, although I learned my prayers and catechism by rote, as was then inevitable in Spain, I knew that my parents regarded all religion as a work of human imagination; and I agreed and still agree with them there. But this carried an implication in their minds against which every instinct in me rebelled, namely that the works of human imagination are bad. No, I said to myself, even as a boy: they are good, they alone are good; and the rest—the whole real world—is ashes in the mouth."

There was surely no such implication as that in his parents' opinion. What seemed bad to them was works of imagination put over on the innocent public as objective truth. This seemed at times a little bad even to Santayana. Indeed in one place he says that the attribution of literal truth to religious mythology makes it "odious." But that does not enter into his mature opinion. His mature opinion is that science itself, even physical science, has no pictorial or literal truth. It conveys the relations of material things only by way of symbols. And religion does the same thing for spiritual relations. It expresses them in "obviously mythical and poetical images; but how else should these moral truths be expressed at all in a traditional or popular fashion? Religions are the great fairy-tales of the conscience."

That the symbols of science are exact and verifiable, or at least strive to be so, and the fairy-tales of religions are so made that they can be twisted and turned any way the parson or priest (whether "rascally" or super-benign) may wish to twist and turn them seemed unessential to Santayana. It must have been because his real motive was not to clarify moral relations in a real world, which with all its faults is to be cherished as the best we have, but to escape from that world and dwell among unreal symbols. These symbols were *excused* for their flimsiness by a possible meaning, or any number of confused meanings, they might have in the real world. But they were *loved and adored* for their very flimsiness—for the fact that they are not, like existing things, "ugly and wrong."

Such, at least, is the natural conclusion when Santayana's memoirs and his speculations are brought into the same field of vision. We see in both a man lacking the lusty taste that most living things have, and must have, for the strong flavors of bodily and real existence.

I sent the earlier parts of this essay to Santayana when they were finished, and I sent them with some trepidation because I was not sure he had intended the reader to infer as much about his amatory experience as I had in reading his memoirs. My inference was most explicit in speaking of his early feeling for the boy, Edward Bayley, a feeling which he called "sympathy" although its name was so obviously "love." His answer I thought fully confirmed what I said on that subject:

> Dear Mr. Eastman,
>   Your letter and two articles have naturally interested me, especially where you catch the spirit in which I write, which is not always. But in speaking of my school friend Bayley you are very sympathetic. As to the use of the word "love," I leave the discussion of it for the time when I shall have read your views on my "system" of philosophy, when I shall have radical criticisms to make. . . .

I had promised to write more, but unfortunately had not done so before September 1952 when Santayana died. Thus I will never know why he did not use the word *love,* nor have the benefit of his criticism of my criticism of his philosophy.

He did, however, take one random shot at me in closing his letter, and came so wide of the mark that I wonder whether a further exchange would have had much value.

"Your trouble with me on major matters," he wrote, "is that you do not understand that I am a pagan. Perhaps you don't care for Greek and Roman classics. That seems to blind you to *normality.* America is not normal, not natural, but forced, Protestant."

In view of what Santayana's admiration of the ancient Greeks had once meant to me, and the intemperance of my own admiration for them, that remark seemed almost fatherly in its failure of understanding. In answering him, I did not try to defend America or Protestantism—which does not interest me much more than Catholicism—but I said in my own behalf:

> You are quite wrong in thinking that I don't under-stand you are a pagan. It was as a pagan that you meant so much to me in my early life. A sentence from one of your books: "The Greeks were able to think straight about morals," has come to my mind as often in the forty or so years since I read it as any other sentence I can remember. My own feeling is that I am more pagan than you, and that is why I find it hard to reconcile myself with your Catholicism. This may be, of course, because I was myself, in birth and early environment at least, a Protestant. My paganism bears that flavor as yours does the flavor of Catholicism.

The big difference was, it seemed to me, that in becoming a pagan I had ceased to be a Protestant, while he persisted in being, in spite of his unbelief, a Catholic. Although I recognize the totally new ideal of universal sympathy that came with Christianity into the western world, I do not like churches or church services, no matter what the sect. Even in the sublime and unsurpassable grandeur of some of the great cathedrals of Europe, although humbled and overwhelmed by man's achievement, I feel myself a stranger. I am one who wandered in from out of doors. But in Greek temples—in the Parthenon—I feel spiritually at home. The Greeks thought straight about morals because they did not mix morals with other-worldly super-stition. And their temples were akin to the earth and the sky and the mountains because the air in them was not heavy with that baleful mixture. Their religion was not devout; they had no word, I think, for *sanctimonious.*

Such at least has been my way of idealizing them, and I was full of such thoughts when, after my last conversation with Santayana in Rome, I visited the ruins of the ancient Greek world in Sicily. Syracuse was one of the stateliest cities in that ancient world, almost as impressive to the eye as Athens. It stood on a high crown of land jutting into the sea, and at its topmost point a statue of Athena, the goddess of wisdom, held up in the sun a spear which provided the first gleam of home to sailors returning from far countries. Beside the statue stood a magnificent Doric temple in which the goddess was worshipped—one of the most beau-tiful, perhaps after the Parthenon the most beautiful, of all the works of Greek architecture. It was never destroyed but was coated over so to speak, by a Christian cathedral of mediocre design and messy ornamentation. The vast columns of the classic temple are still visible or semi-visible, embedded like fossils in the walls of the medieval church. To me this was a sacrilege, a crime against beauty and against the few relics that are left of the "rational ideal of human life," to quote Santayana, that was aspired to by the ancient Greeks. And to me it symbolized in a startling way the thing I had found distasteful and bad in San-tayana himself, an unresolved conflict, or rather a false reconciliation, between his heroic championship of the life of reason and his equivocal, half-hearted, and half-minded allegiance to the dogmas of the Church of Rome. His bold Greek wisdom, which had seemed to shine so clear upon my youth, had been, after all, mixed up and coated over with elaborated relics of that life of superstition from which the Greeks had so astoundingly liberated their minds. . . .

When Santayana died, a final volume of his autobiography was published almost immediately, having been held up, he told me, for fear of libel suits by a long lost, but conceivably still surviving, lower-class mistress of Lord John Russell. In that volume I found, almost like an arranged surprise, his own comment on that temple of Athena which he too had visited in Syracuse.

The transformation excited my architectural fancy. To turn a Greek temple into a Christian church all you need to do is to wall up the peristyle, leaving a window in the upper part of each space between the columns, and then pierce arches in the side walls of the cella. Your interior then occupies the whole or nearly the whole of the temple platform; place an altar where the statue of the god had stood, and you have a complete church: even a great church, if you are prudent enough to retain a narthex before the inner door, and an ambulatory behind the altar. This was not done as I could wish in Syracuse, but the great columns were not walled up so as to be wholly concealed, and the line of the pediment remained visible, if not uninterrupted. The transformation had not been the work of one artist, but of many bishops; yet it allows enough to subsist of the ancient temple to make evident the continuity of worship and the identity of civic function in this edifice for three thousand years.

Some of my more worshipful readers will perhaps like Santayana's reaction better than mine to this architectural and religious hybrid. Even assuming that he was a believing Christian and that by worship he meant communion with a living God, I should still think his taste as barbarous as that of the "many bishops" who produced such a crossbred monster. But since his religion was void of belief, and he really stood, as a "pagan" and a "materialist," for a development of the Greek view of life to its logical conclusion, I do not see how anyone can be moved by his stress on "the continuity of worship." It was not the continuity, but the discontinuity, that he was stressing when he reminded me that he was a pagan. In his dynamic beliefs—if anything about Santayana may be called dynamic—he *was* a pagan.

I have the impression, although I can not pretend to have verified it with prolonged study, that in Santayana's earlier writings these dynamic beliefs played a stronger role. In *The Life of Reason,* as I remember it, morality was founded—and this was a veritable revolution in American thinking—upon natural impulse. To live reasonably was to find, each of us, a way of harmonizing our impulses. For each of us there was an ideal, and our best happiness lay in pursuing it; but the ideal had its cause and only justification in those irrational organic drives with which nature had endowed us. This gave our minds a vital function in the battle of existence; it counseled noble action. But in his later work, *The Realms Of Being,* with its root in the doctrine of essence, the mind has little engineering work to do. It seems merely to play over a process of material change and evolution, at best only enabling us to withdraw from and forget it. Critics have pointed out this contradiction, and Santayana has replied that there is only a change of emphasis, that the later doctrines are all to be found in the earlier books. When I spoke to him, however, of *The Life of Reason,* he said instantly (and I think I quote verbatim):

"I don't like those books any more. My later books are better."

He showed me the mountainous manuscript of his political book, then still to be published, *Dominations And Powers.* I remarked with envy as I leafed it over that it must have been fun to sit there with no contemporary cares, no journalistic intrusions, and write down the conclusions of a lifetime about politics. But he shook his head.

"It was a great effort to finish it before I die," he said. And then with a smile: "I don't like to make efforts!"

It is indeed an effort, and by comparison with his other books not, I think, a very successful one. Though it contains astute thoughts and speculations, it is, as a whole, diffuse, pointless, and inconsecutive. So much so that I at first thought the effort had been merely to tie together with a string of ideas those loose notes on politics that had piled up during a lifetime. But when I expressed this opinion to Santayana's once close friend, Bernard Berenson, he corrected me. The book's lack of order and impact, he asserted, was due to a change of perspective in the midst of its composition. Santayana had liked the regime of Mussolini, and his book in its original design took form from his approval of Italian fascism. But fascism had collapsed and Mussolini's corpse had been strung up by the heels in Milan before the book was done. It then became a sermon, and a very long one, without a moral. I was ready to believe this, because in one of our conversations

Santayana had praised Mussolini's government quite emphatically, and yet, I find no mention of Mussolini or of fascism in his book. It says astute and devastating things about the communists and kindly understanding things about the United States, but about this other edifice which tumbled to ruin within sound of the author's ears, it remains strangely silent.

"Mussolini's government was a good one," Santayana said to me. And he further spoke with tolerance of the murderous methods by which it established its tyranny over the minds and movements of men.

"A few dissenters had to be locked up on an island," was his way of dismissing this tale of horrors.

The frailty of his political philosophy is not unlike that of his metaphysics, with its artifice of the "realms" of being. He imagines that man's life in society can be divided into "spheres" called economic and spiritual, and authoritarian control conceived as confining itself within the economic. But every vital activity of man in modern society has economic aspects and conditions. "Economic control is not merely control of a sector of human life . . . it is control of the means to all our ends," as Friedrich Hayek conclusively remarked. Thus Santayana's utopia is not only unattainable on earth, as he, like Plato, frankly confesses; it lacks solid meaning.

This too—and the corresponding affability toward fascism—I find myself explaining on the ground of his recoil from reality as a whole. A tolerance of bloody gang-rule, if it will only leave Spirit alone, is hardly surprising in a man for whom existence itself is "ugly" and "rotten." That opinion of existence survives, at any rate, in a most candid form in this book, *Dominations and Powers*. And there survives also, with pitiful explicitness, the injured child.

"In human nature," the aged philosopher tells us, "generous impulses form amiable interludes like tearful sentiments in a ruffian. Dig a little beneath the surface, and you will find a ferocious, profound, persistent selfishness." "If the child does not retain deep in his heart, the sense that his parents are his natural enemies, it is probably because he has no depth of heart to retain anything in. They *are* his natural enemies. . . . If occasionally—perhaps in the mother—one ray of real sympathy breaks through the everlasting cloud of anxious fondness and admonishing supervision, it seems . . . as wonderful, as incredible, as dream-like, as if the winds, or the sea, or the wild animals had spoken and answered him intelligibly."

A philosopher to whom man's life presents itself in these baleful colors may say penetrating things about many subjects—even, when he forgets his obsession, about "the homage that life pays [in play and ceremony] to its own gracefulness and generosity." But he can hardly give us moral or political guidance. For that he would need a robust discrimination between what is ugly and rotten and what is not.

I must add, though, that I never come to a professional philosopher in search of the wisdom of life. They dwell too much with Being in the Abstract to be of great help to us in the concrete personal details of it. Santayana, of course, was especially unbothered by these mazy details. Although I visited him five times in two successive years, and we talked each time for two genial hours, he never asked me where I came from, or how I happened to be there, or where I was going. It did not matter. Perhaps I compensated for it by feeling a special kind of affection for him—such an affection as one might have toward a very young and unsophisticated person: beautiful-mannered and miraculously endowed and yet naively simple and trustful. In his attitude to his philosophy, especially, he reminded me of a child who has built a wonderful castle out of blocks. He knew where each block belonged, and if you asked him a question, he would lead you around and show you just where it was and how perfectly it fitted in. There was even a block called doubt, but it occupied a carefully appointed place. About the structure as a whole, its equilibrium and validity, he had a confidence that some critics have found unpleasantly dogmatic. I found it entirely captivating. Who wouldn't be cocksure when he had erected such an elaborate edifice and made it stand up!

He built a world of philosophic ideas for the dreamy and squeamish, for those who recoil from a material world yet will not deny its authority. He built it in language as beautiful as any to be found in the history of such buildings. And he fulfilled the task with absolute self-reliance. Every line of his books was written with audacity and yet modesty, a tactful yet unyielding determination to be true to himself. That quality made this man of limitations great. And it made of his bedroom in the Eternal City, where he awaited decay and death serenely and without illusions, a gay place of pilgrimage. To me the conversations there were far more inspiriting than the long, dull, unconvincing exercise in wishful thinking with which, according to Plato, Socrates entertained his friends before drinking the hemlock.

The Magics in Pablo Casals

In 1952 Casals was teaching at a summer music school, or at least blessing it with his presence, high up in the Swiss Alps at Zermatt, and I was in Switzerland "roving" for the *Reader's Digest*. I went up to Zermatt and camped in the hotel where the school held its sessions and where he lived. I had a personal introduction to him and he received me with warmth, but in answer to a remark about the beauty of the scene, he told me that the unaccustomed altitude made him dizzy. He drew his hand over his brow, and I had the impression that it made him *very* dizzy. Instead of bothering him with my talk, I asked permission to sit among the musicians in his classes.

In ten hours of "personal interview" I could hardly have

received a more vivid revelation of the man than I did in hearing him talk to those pupils or colleagues, some of them famous, who had come to drink, so to speak, at the fountain of perfection. He would illustrate what he was saying about some passage in their work by playing it over on his own cello. It was as though a father in heaven had leaned down from the clouds and said: "This is how it should be done," and no mortal could say a word but only listen.

He seemed also at times to be saying, "This is how life should be lived," for his words would apply, consciously and quite often, to problems remote from the exquisite playing of the cello. He is by common consent the greatest cellist that ever lived. Fritz Kreisler went farther and described him as "the greatest man who ever drew a bow." But he has this still rarer distinction, that he stands morally as well as musically on a height to which men all over the world look up. He is a Catalonian, and like so many Catalonians, a fierce patriot of liberty. When Franco's forces swept into the north of Spain, Casals abandoned his lovely seaside home outside Barcelona, left a fortune equal to his fame behind him, and took refuge in the French-Catalan village of Prades on the north slope of the Pyrenees. There he lived in the two small second-story rooms of a gatekeeper's lodge with a view on a barnyard, vowing never to go home until Spain was free. And there, in 1950, his admirers organized a "Casals Festival," and musicians and music lovers from all over the world flocked to the little village to hear him play, and make music with him, and dwell for two weeks in his presence. These festivals, repeated annually, soon acquired a fame like that of

the Wagner festivals at Bayreuth or the passion play at
Oberammergau. The music was played in the ruins of an
ancient cathedral on the mountainside—appropriately, for
there is an element of devoutness, if that means consecration to high ways of life, in everything that Casals does.
People who bought records of the music played at the
second festival in 1951 were surprised to receive as a bonus
a record with a cello solo by Casals on one side, and on the
other—pressed into the vynolite in his handwriting—these
words: "The core of any great enterprise or activity must
be character and kindness." A strange thing—an incon-
gruous thing perhaps. But there is evidently a strong
magic in it, for pilgrims to the Casals festivals come home
in a state of exaltation as though they had climbed the
sacred road to Delphi and met Apollo himself in his temple
on the mysterious mountain.

Casals does not, I must say, look much like Apollo. He is
a dumpy little man, with chubby hands, big round eye-
glasses, and a head that is glassy bald. At first glance he
looks more like a peanut vendor than Apollo. Only after
watching him closely—not watching, but enjoying him—
did I begin to see in his features the union of overpower-
ing sensitivity with the strength to handle it—tremendous strength and determination. That and his spontaneous modesty, the natural absence of any posture of
priesthood, or even teacherhood, in discussing music and
life with those cello-playing pilgrims, made me understand
the state of rapture in which my musical friends come
home from the festivals.

"You must excuse me," he said to a noted Italian cellist
after a critical comment on his playing, "You must excuse

me—remember I have lived more than twice as long as you have."

"If you were half my age," the young man answered, "I would be grateful for any word of criticism from you."

"Be impulsive—be fanciful," I can hear him saying. "Let the music flow out of you as freely as though you were talking. But remember that freedom is not disorder. . . ." A long thoughtful pause. "That is something that has wide application in our times." Another pause. "Hold yourself at the same time within the bonds of the rhythm to the last fraction of a second. Be spontaneous and yet be controlled. That is what you have to learn."

And most often I remember this: "The main thing in life is not to be afraid to be human. If something is so beautiful it makes you want to cry, I'll tell you what to do. . . . Cry!"

It is not to my credit as a journalist, but I was rather glad to gather my impressions of Pablo Casals in this impersonal way—by watching him talk instead of talking to him. Rich with these impressions, I motored down the Alps and across southern France and visited his home in Prades and the old roofless cathedral where the festival concerts were held. The scene was mystically beautiful; all the flowers were in bloom; all the birds were singing; the moon rose boldly in the sunset, getting ready to shine all night. I was happy in the nearness of a great man, but I had no story for the *Reader's Digest*.

I don't know who gave me the address in Perpignan of Casals' close friend and informal amanuensis, Jose Maria Corredor, who has since published a book about him. Corredor was already gathering material for that book and was absorbed in the creation of it. But he stopped his work when he heard of my need, and shared with me everything he had, all the tiniest notes and memoranda on his desk, everything he could remember, as though it were my story and not his book that he was writing. From him I borrowed the guiding lines and many of the colors for a story-portrait that I am going to include in this book, although I cannot describe Casals as my friend, much less my companion.

He was born in the little town of Vendrell in Catalonia, 30 miles from Barcelona. His father was the organist of the village church, and Pablo sang in the choir. He also made music, almost from babyhood, on any instrument that happened to be around the house—piano, flute, guitar, even the violin. His muscular coordinations were as phenomenal as his instinct for music. Impressed by them, his musical father arranged an apprenticeship for him with the village carpenter. But his mother, though she had small understanding of music, knew that her son was a genius, and decided to make it known to the world. Using some arduously saved pesetas, she took Pablo to Barcelona where he could study at the municipal school. There he got, or she got for him, a night job playing the piano at a popular café. In due course he persuaded the proprietor to let him play a program of classical music one evening a week, and as he was only twelve years old, and played well, this made a sensation in musical circles. "El Nen," as they called him —Catalan for *niño*—became quite famous in a local way. His fame increased when he took up the cello, a "foreign" instrument, which he will tell you he knew to be his own the moment he drew a bow across its strings. Thanks to this knowledge—and yet more, he insists, to his mother's force of character and tact—he arrived at seventeen in Madrid and was invited to play before Maria Cristina, Queen Mother of Spain. The queen was captivated, not only by the music he made, but by something shining out of his eyes for which she could find no more specific name than "goodness." She granted him a pension to continue his studies and practically adopted him into her household, where he became the playmate of the future king, Alfonso XIII. In acknowledging a debt of gratitude for this royal patronage, Casals was always careful, Señor Corredor told me, to explain that the feeling was "strictly personal." It did not prevent him from growing up a republican and a libertarian to his finger tips. And the same thing seems to have been true of his mother, who, after a two years indulgence in this life of luxury and high privilege, announced abruptly one morning:

"It's time for a change!"

Next to Bach's music and the cello, this bold and wise mother seems to have been the dominant force of attraction in Casals' early life. He loved her, and his admiration equaled his love. Some of her admonitions to her children were more like the lectures of Epictetus than the things one is apt to learn in church. "Never let any external circumstance alter your purpose or disturb the calmness with which you pursue it," was an aphorism that Casals remembered throughout his life.

The particular change she had in mind just now was that Pablo should, like all aspiring musicians, "study abroad." The Queen's councillor, Count Morphy, gave him a letter to the director of the famous conservatory in Brussels, considered the greatest school in the world for stringed instruments, and promised him a pension from the court throughout his course of study. The director, after reading Count Morphy's letter, sent Pablo immediately to the cello class of the famous Professor Edouard Jacobs. Pablo slipped into the classroom and sat down modestly in a back row. He didn't look like much. Indeed he didn't look like anything at all, for while all authentic musicians in those days wore their hair almost to the shoulders, his was cropped short. When Professor Jacobs asked him what he would play, he said simply:

"Anything you like."

The professorial eyebrows were raised.

"Well, well, you *must* be remarkable!"

The class roared with laughter as the professor asked ironically:

"Can you play the so-and-so, for instance?" naming a little known and difficult composition.

Casals said, "Yes."

"And the so-and-so, perhaps?" naming one still more difficult.

Again Casals said, "Yes."

"Very well then, I suggest that you play the *Souvenir de Spa*. And now, young gentlemen, prepare yourselves for a treat from this young man who can play anything we like!"

Although he had to use a borrowed cello, Casals played this most obscure and difficult composition without a flaw and with a brilliance that left the class, and the teacher also, transfixed.

Recovering his breath, Professor Jacobs invited him into the adjoining room and urged him to join his class, promising him without further examination the annual prize for the current year. But Casals had not liked this priggish reception. It offended his ideal of civilized conduct—of character and kindness. He said he didn't care to stay.

The decision cost Jacobs a lifetime of regret. And it cost Casals his pension, for Count Morphy insisted on his remaining in Brussels, and he very politely explained that he didn't want to.

He went instead to Paris, he and his mother and now also his two younger brothers. They arrived there penniless, ignorant of the language, and without friends or letters of introduction. His mother at least had her wish for a change—a plunge, indeed, from regal ease to penury. The father sent them his small savings, the mother took in sewing. He boasts that she once sold her hair, which was long and lustrous, for a few francs to tide them over a crisis. He himself got an ill-paid job as second cellist in the Marigny Follies. But he had to walk back and forth twice a day from a tiny flat in the outskirts to the center of the city—once for his lessons, once to earn the money to pay for them—carrying a cello on his back. "We learned by direct experience what misery is," he would say in recalling those days. But the lesson was too costly. He fell sick, and they had to abandon the glamorous idea of an education abroad and go back to Barcelona.

There the good luck returned. Pablo's old music teacher was just moving to Argentina, and Pablo, at eighteen, fell heir to his teaching and his services in a church. It was not long before he was reconciled with the queen, and played again in Madrid. At twenty-one he was famous throughout Spain and Portugal. At twenty-three he returned with his mother and two brothers to Paris. He had saved enough for all three to live on now, and he had a letter from Count Morphy to the famous French conductor, Charles Lamoureux, who was preparing a series of winter concerts. The famous man grumbled when Casals presented the letter—he didn't like to be disturbed when at work. Casals offered to withdraw, but Lamoureux took a look into the eyes of his visitor, and grumbled again:

"No, go ahead and play, young man—I like you."

Casals tuned his instrument with special deliberation, remembering his mother's counsel of purpose and calmness. Finally he began to play, and with the first few notes Lamoureux turned in his chair. He had a physical infirmity which made it an effort for him to rise, but when Casals finished, the great conductor was standing before him.

"You shall play in my first concert!" he said.

Casals' debut in Paris with the Lamoureux orchestra was an event in the cultural life of the French capital. But it was in Vienna that he won his place in the history of music. Vienna was then the center of the musical world and he was so nervous when he came before the audience that his hand was tense when he lifted the bow. To limber it, he tried to do a little twirl he had learned when playing drum major as a child. The bow flew out of his fingers and landed in the middle of the orchestra. While it was being solemnly passed back from row to row, he had time to summon once more into memory that maxim: "Never let any circumstance . . ." His hand was steady when the bow reached him, and he played with a mastery never before equaled by him or by any other cellist.

There is a selflessness, a lack of vanity, in Casals' devotion to music that has hardly a precedent. He would rather conduct an orchestra than win glory as a virtuoso. As a conductor, moreover, he enjoys the rehearsals more than the final show. It is "making music" that he loves, and he loves to teach people how to do it. As a child in the choir at Vendrell he never could restrain himself from telling the tenors and sopranos what to do with their voices. And while he was growing to world fame as a cellist, he used his earnings to the amount of six hundred thousand dollars to create and train a "people's orchestra"—the first in the world—at Barcelona.

To make its music available to all the people, he formed a Workers' Concert Society with dues of one dollar a year, and gave concerts for its members at reduced prices. Casals also satisfied his love for simple people, his wish not to let fame and fortune divide him from them, by going back to Vendrell for two or three weeks every year to live again with his old friends, the carpenter, the blacksmith, the shoe store keeper. On these visits his special joy was to get together with the local musicians and give a popular concert in the public square.

Once, when climbing Mount Tamalpais after a concert in San Francisco, Casals barely saved his life by jumping aside from a rolling boulder. It struck the first finger of his left hand, apparently smashing it for good. To the astonishment of his companions, his first words were: "Thank God, I shall never have to play the cello again!"

What he meant was: "I can devote my whole life to making the greatest of all music!" For to him the greatest music is a social achievement—it is the music of a well-trained orchestra, disciplined in mutual good will and the purpose of perfection. "Honesty to the limit" is another ideal he holds before an orchestra, and he means it both of social conduct and of music. His musicians feel toward him the veneration that churchmen feel toward a loved priest or pastor. Years ago when he was only growing into manhood they said of him in Barcelona: "He turns a café into a concert hall, and a concert hall into a temple."

Today all Catalonians, and to some degree all freedom-loving Spaniards, feel the same way toward Pablo Casals. He has become the symbol of their hope of liberation from a dictator. In the successive disasters that have befallen European democracy in his lifetime, he has taken his stand stubbornly and reckless of the cost to himself, on the side of freedom and the rights of the individual man. His popularity in the old Russia and his income from concerts there were enormous, but when after the October revolution of 1917 the Bolsheviks established the Cheka and began executing dissenters, he declined all invitations to tour that country.

"My only weapon is my cello," he says. "Not a very deadly one perhaps, but such as it is, it fights on the side of freedom."

When Hitler attained to power and began persecuting Jews and labor unions, he declared the same boycott against Germany. When Mussolini took over Hitler's policy of anti-Semitism, he extended his cello's protest to

Italy. His action when Franco seized power in Spain was but the continuation of a policy of protest against tyranny, international in its scope.

His life as an exile in Prades was more like that of a Franciscan monk than a world-famous musician. Everybody in the village felt free to drop in on him for advice or help, or just to give him the news of a birth in the family or the high marks a small boy had made in school. As it was with Buddha, peasants from miles around flocked in to converse with him, bringing bouquets of flowers. Whoever came was greeted with a smile and a "Please sit down!" There was no theory of democracy about this; Casals loves people and they make him happy.

One afternoon, long after he had become world famous, he was visited in Paris by a friend and fellow-student from the provinces. They chatted together for several hours, but at five o'clock a pupil who had been practicing in a neighboring room came in, exclaiming at the lateness of the hour: "But sir, you have a concert at eight and you have not had your nap."

The visitor, in great embarrassment, apologized profusely. "You have a concert, and here I've done nothing all afternoon but talk about myself and my little problems."

Casals saw him quietly to the door, took a leisurely farewell of him, and said: "You have done me a great favor. Before you came I was nervous and worried about my performance this evening. Now I am happy because I know that all goes well with you and your family."

Midst of his many visitors, Casals finds time to answer in longhand all the letters he receives—to answer them and file them away in folders he makes out of the sheets of old newspapers. Señor Corredor told me that after one of the Prades festivals he answered six hundred letters in his own hand. Moreover, he has kept every letter that was ever written to him. Some visitor would drop in and mention "that letter my father wrote you a couple of years ago." Casals would get up from his chair, go to his filing system, and be back in a very brief time with the letter in his hand. He made almost a life mission of helping the Spanish refugees, giving them both intimate counsel and material aid.

There must be a limit to this system of loving kindness. But up to the date of my story, Casals had managed to live in the modern world, with all its frenzied multiplication and speed-up of the forms of social communion, almost the life of an early Christian believer—a life dedicated to the love of the neighbor.

To balance this statement, I must add—and I learned this from a discerning pupil in Zermatt—that, although ready to give himself so lavishly to those who need him, Casals is not gullible. He is not an "easy mark." He is not blinded by good will. He has, on the contrary, an almost uncanny way of knowing exactly what everybody in a roomful of people is up to. "Nobody ever fools him," his pupil said. He takes only a few friends deep into his heart. They are the ones he calls "good." Goodness includes opposition to violence, tyranny and totalitarianism in all its forms.

But it also includes self-discipline. Like all Catalans and most musicians, Casals is loaded like a bomb with explosive emotions, but he never blows up. He never behaves like a prima donna. He behaves "like a Greek philosopher"

—until he draws a bow across the strings. Then those pent-up emotions have their day. The ease and spontaneous freedom of his movements seems miraculous, as though some supernal power had taken possession of him, but life-long possession of himself is the real secret of it. He has pondered every note of every composition he plays. He studied the Bach suite for cello, which no cellist before him had tackled, for twelve years before he ventured to play it in public. He is still studying it. He thinks of himself in the presence of all great music as a student. He will announce with delight that he has found a new way of fingering some passage that he has been playing for fifty years.

When a pupil complained to him that she had forgotten a piece she had known well and played many times, he said: "That's fine! Everything should be new every time you play it."

As remarkable as the high firm way in which Casals employs his powers, is their survival in him at so advanced an age. He was an old man when I saw him in 1952. His seventy-seven years seemed a load to lift when you saw him get up or sit down. But when he took that cello into his hands, the weight of those years dropped mysteriously away. A being inside of this aging body was still young and in total command. "Why he's playing it *better* than he used to!" was the astonished remark of a famous musician who attended a festival—rather to honor Casals than to hear him.

And to this judgment practically everybody in the musical world agreed at that time. Few living in other worlds can realize how much it meant. If a gymnast at seventy-five were to run down a spring-ramp and turn a double somersault over the backs of four elephants, that would be world news. But the coordination and control of nerve and muscle, the sheer flexibility and power, would hardly be more remarkable than that of Pablo Casals at the same age.

My story ends here. I only know, as everybody does, that Casals moved in 1956 to Puerto Rico and married a young lovely girl. The festival followed him there, and has been held three times in the milder climate of that southern island. This year, however, his admirers persuaded him, after it had been held there, to return to Prades and let them gather again in the old surroundings. And after that, notwithstanding the altitude and his eighty-one years, Casals attended again the *Cours Musicaux de Zermatt,* and continued explaining to his young colleagues and disciples how the cello is played—and life lived—if you want to do it well.

Problems of Friendship with Trotsky

Although Trotsky's eyes were a rather pale blue, reporters were always calling them black. Not only Frank Harris, with his genius for remembering what didn't quite happen, but John Reed, a keen and careful observer, made this mistake.

"To look at he is slight, of middle height, always striding somewhere. Above his high forehead is a shock of wavy black hair, his eyes behind thick glasses are dark and almost violent, and his mouth wears a perpetual sardonic expression. . . ."

So Reed described him in a dispatch from revolutionary Petrograd in 1918.

"There's something fatal about it," Trotsky commented. "Those black eyes figure in every description of me, although the eyes nature gave me are blue."

I, for my part, can testify that in Prinkipo in 1932, nothing less dark or violent was to be seen on the horizon than Trotsky's pale blue eyes. His mouth, in repose, might be described as cherubic. He could *be* sardonic; he could cause an oratorical opponent to shrivel in the air with a single shaft of sarcastic logic. This seemed a black art, and its Mephistophelian character was emphasized by that wavy black hair and a short, pointed beard. It was, however, a trait of mind and social attitude, not a physical trait.

I came rather close to Trotsky during the year and nine months that I spent in Russia in 1922 to 1924, for he agreed to tell me his life story and let me make a book of it. We never finished the book, but I published half of it with the title, *Leon Trotsky, The Portrait of a Youth*. Nine years later Eliena and I spent twelve days with him and his wife and retinue of bodyguards and secretaries on Prinkipo Island in the Sea of Marmona where he found refuge after Stalin had driven him from Russia. It was there that he and I got really acquainted. It was not on my side a pleasant process—or rather it was pleasant while superficial, but harshly unpleasant as the acquaintance deepened. This was no great surprise to me, for although I took Trotsky's side in the conflict with Stalin, and fail to see how any understanding revolutionist could have chosen otherwise, I was far from enamored of him personally. I hero-worshipped him and do still, especially after reading Isaac Deutscher's glowing account of his revolutionary deeds,* but I did not, even in Moscow while writing my own little book about his youth, feel any affection for him. I used to say this frequently when coming home to Eliena after an hour's conversation with him at the War Office, but I could not explain why. He was not egotistical; he was forever wandering from the main subject to expatiate with thoughtful penetration about the lives and qualities of his friends. Yet to me he was not a friend. With all those intimate talks about his infancy and youth—about all infancy and youth, all growing into life and grasping it—we never came together. Therefore it was not with happy excitement, but with an under feeling of reluctance, that I accepted in 1932 his urgent invitation to "come and spend several weeks with us in Prinkipo and we'll work and go fishing together."

Although it happened twenty-five years ago, my impressions of Trotsky at that time are entirely fresh for I wrote them down then and saved them. I wrote them at two separate times: one in the evening after the first three days of our visit, the other on the train to Jerusalem the morning we left. I present them here as they were written in 1932.

I. After Three Days

Trotsky seems the most modest and self-forgetful of all the famous men I have known. He never boasts; he never speaks of himself or his achievements; he never monopo-

---

* I refer to the first volume of his biography, *The Prophet Armed;* the second is not yet published.

lizes the conversation. He gives his attention freely and wholly to anything that happens or comes up. With all the weight of worldwide slander and misrepresentation he struggles under today, the peculiar position he occupies, he has not so far breathed a syllable suggestive of preoccupation with himself or even the ordinary, quite human touchiness that one might expect. As we work on his book, if I pay him a compliment, he says some little thing, "I am glad," and then passes hastily to another subject. After all, I agree with his colleague, Lunacharsky, although I did not when I came here, that there is "not a drop of vanity in him."

Like many great men I have met he does not seem altogether robust. There is apt to be a frailty associated with great intellect. At any rate, Trotsky, especially in our heated arguments concerning the "dialectic," in which he becomes excited and wrathful to the point of losing his breath, seems to me at times almost weak. He seems too small for the struggle. He cannot laugh at my attacks on his philosophy, or be curious about them—as I imagine Lenin would—because in that field he is not secure. He is not strongly based. I get the impression of a man in unstable equilibrium because of the mountain of ability and understanding that he has to carry. In what is he unequal to the load? In self-confidence? Is it the Jew's inferiority complex after all? Is it that he has never played, never loafed and invited his soul, or observed that the sunshine is good whatever happens? When I remarked that fishing with a dragnet is interesting work, but not sport, he said:

"Two plusses—it is interesting and it is work! What more can you ask?"

I wonder if that is the mood in which he will go fishing —intense, speedy, systematic, organized for success, much as he went to Kazan to defeat the White Armies.

He seems to me over-sure of everything he believes. I suppose that is what Lenin meant in his testament when he warned the party against Trotsky's "excessive self-confidence." But I suspect that his weaker point as a political leader would be that when that cocksureness breaks down, he is non-plussed. He does not know how to cherish a doubt, how to speculate. Between us, at least, to *confer* is out of the question.

His magnanimity, his freedom from anything like rancour, is amazing. I see it in his portrayal of his enemies, but also in smaller things. Yesterday we reached a point of tension in our argument about dialectic that was extreme. Trotsky's throat was throbbing and his face was red; he was in a rage. His wife was worried, evidently, and when we left the tea table and went into his study still fighting, she came in after us and stood there above and beside me like a statue, silent and austere. I understood what she meant and said, after a long, hot speech from him:

"Well, let's lay aside this subject and go to work on the book."

"As much as you like!" he jerked out, and snapped up the manuscript.

I began reading the translation and he following me, as usual, in the Russian text. I had not read three sentences when he suddenly, to my complete surprise, dropped the manuscript and, looking up like a child proposing a new game, said:

"I have an idea. What do you say you and I together write a drama of the American Civil War!"

"Fine!" I said, trying to catch my breath.

"We would each bring something to it that the other lacks. You have a literary gift that I lack, and I could supply a factual knowledge of what a civil war is like!"

This man has the childlike charm of an artist. Perhaps my feeling of his weakness, of his being inadequate to his load, derives from the fact that his character as a man of action is the result of self-discipline and not of instinct. He has made out of himself something more, or at least other, than he is. I do not know. I merely record these two, or rather, three impressions: an utter absence of egotism, instinctive magnanimity, and something like weakness, as of a man overburdened with his own great strength.

II. Ten Days Later

It is fortunate that I recorded the above impressions immediately, for now, after twelve days in Trotsky's home, my mood has changed to such an extent that I could hardly write them down. I feel "injured" by his total inward indifference to my opinions, my interests, my existence as an individual. There has been no meeting either of our minds or feelings. He has never asked me a question. He has answered all my questions, as a book would answer them, without interchange, without assuming the possibility of mutual growth. My pointed criticisms of his policy—that he has not thought out the implications of the problem of nationalities on a world scale, that he never should have let

Stalin make "socialism in one country" the issue, thus jockeying him into the defense of a negative slogan—were met with mere lordly-hasty rejection. I was an amateurish creature needing to be informed of the technical truth which dwelt in his mind.

On the disputed question of Trotsky's "vanity," I still agree with Lunacharsky. His failing is subtler than that and more disastrous. He lives instinctively in a world in which other persons (except in the mass, or as classes) do not count. In youth he stood prodigiously high above his companions in brain, speech, and capacity for action, so that he never formed the habit of inquiring—he was always telling. His knowledge and true knowledge, his view and the right view, were identical. There is no bragging or vanity in this, no preoccupation with himself. Trotsky is preoccupied with ideas and the world, but they are *his* ideas and *his* view of the world. People, therefore, who do not adulate, go away from Trotsky feeling belittled. Either that, or they go away indignant, as I am.

Opinionated minds are usually far from wise; Trotsky is opinionated in the highest degree, but with wise opinions. Cranky people are usually old and barren of fruit. Trotsky is cranky, but young and fruitful.

I want to dwell on the manner in which his arrogance differs from vanity, or self-centered egotism. It is not a conscious thought, but an unconscious assumption that he *knows,* and that other people are to be judged and instructed. It is a postulate laid down in his childhood, as I said, and by his instincts. That, I now suspect, is why he is weak and indecisive and lacks judgment when frustrated. That is why he became almost hysterical when I parried

with ease the crude clichés he employed to defend the notion of dialectic evolution. The idea of meeting my mind,
of "talking it over" as with an equal, could not occur to him.
He was lost. Similarly in the party crisis when the flood of
slander overflowed him, he was lost. He never made one
move after Stalin attacked him that was not, from the
standpoint of diplomatic tactics, a blunder. Trotsky is much
concerned with the task life imposes of making decisions.
He told me once that in youth he passed through a period
when he thought he was mentally sick, because he could
never make up his mind about anything, but that as Com-
mander of the Red Army he often astonished himself by
the prompt assurance with which he gave orders to generals
and colonels trained for a lifetime in military science.

It was in revolt against an inferior father's stubborn will
that Trotsky developed the "excessive self-confidence" that
Lenin warned against. What he needed, when that self-confidence cracked, was a father—an authority to defer to.
That is what Lenin supplied. If you read Trotsky's *History
of the Russian Revolution* carefully—as carefully as I, the
translator, did—you will find that, although he praises
others, he never attributes fundamental importance, either
of initiative or judgment, to any Bolshevik but Lenin and
himself. (That comes near, I must say, to being the objective truth about the October revolution, yet I think a diligent search might have discovered exceptions.)

Trotsky's idea of our collaborating on a play was, he confessed later, a scheme for making money. He is spending
$1000 a month, according to his wife—his secretary tells
me it is nearer $1500—keeping up the establishment he has
founded here and in Berlin. There is, here in Prinkipo, be-

sides the secretary and stenographers, a bodyguard of three proletarians, one continually on sentry duty at the door; there is another secretary in Berlin, an ingenious system for transporting books from the library there and getting them back on time. Besides that, Trotsky is supporting a sick daughter and her child in Prague. He does not live in luxury; there is practically no furniture in his villa; it is a barrack; and the food is simple to an extreme. He merely keeps up the habits of a War Minister after he has become the leader of a tiny proletarian party. His secretary, Jan Frankel, a Czechoslovak, confided to me his anxiety approaching despair because Trotsky, still living like a commissar, ignored completely the problem of financing his new party and his own gigantic labors. This was not a newly developed trait in Trotsky; he was always, even in his poverty-stricken days, incapable of hanging onto his earnings. Even the small change in his pocket would dribble away, thanks usually to some transparent form of *chantage,* in the course of a short walk down the street. In his present situation, however, it is a calamity, for it makes him overestimate the revolutionary integrity of certain dubious characters who chip in generously to the ever dwindling treasury of his "Fourth International." * Money, of course, is beneath the contempt of a revolutionary idealist—gold, according to Lenin, was to be used for public urinals in the socialist society—but while we are on the way there it deserves a little steady attention.

The lack of comfort or beauty in Trotsky's house, the absence of any least attempt to cultivate the art of life in its

---

* Mark Aldanov thinks it was by this route that Stalin's assassin crept into Trotsky's confidence—a speculation that does not seem to me improbable.

perceptual aspect, seems almost despicable to me. A man and woman must be almost dead aesthetically to live in that bare barrack, which a very few dollars would convert into a charming home. The center of both floors of the house is a vast hall—not a hall exactly, but a room twenty feet long and fifteen feet wide with great double doors opening on a balcony which looks outward to the richly deep blue sea and downward to this bright red-cliffed island that crouches in the sea like a prehistoric animal drinking. In these vast rooms and on these balconies there is not an article of furniture—not even a chair! They are mere gangways, and the doors to the rooms on each side are closed. In each of these rooms someone has an office table or a bed, or both, and a chair to go with it. One of them, downstairs, very small and square and white-walled, with barely space for table and chairs is the dining room. The garden surrounding the villa is abandoned to weeds and these are running to seed. "To save money," Natalia Ivanovna explains. Through sheer indifference to beauty, I should say. Trotsky talks a good deal about art in his books and lays claim to a cultivated taste, but he shows no more interest in art than in that garden. I brought home one day from Istanbul photographs of the rarely beautiful sarcophagus of King Tobuit of Sidon that is in the Museum of Antiquities.

"Do you want to see one of the most beautiful works of sculpture in the world?" I said to Trotsky.

He grasped them hastily and handed them back to me almost with the same gesture. "Where were they found?"

"They were dug up in the ruins of Sidon."

"Who dug them up—Schliemann?"

I said, "No . . ." but by that time he was out of the door and on his way down to dinner.

His sole reaction had been, it seemed to me, to avail himself of the chance to reveal his acquaintance with the name of Schliemann. He had, at least, no interest whatever in the sculpture.

Although it is not so in his books, he seems in personal life to lack altogether the gift of appreciation. I think it is because no one ever feels appreciated by him that he fails so flatly as a political leader. He could no more build a party than a hen could build a house. With all his charming courtesy and fulfillment of every rule of good manners, including a sometimes quite surprising attentiveness to one's comfort, his social gift, his gift of friendship, is actually about on the level of a barnyard fowl. His followers, the followers of the great brain—the greatest political intelligence, I think, that we have today—make pilgrimages to him, and they come away, not warmed and kindled, but chilled and inhibited. Those of them, that is, who have individual will and judgment of their own. Hence he has no *influence*, properly so called. He does not sway strong people, but merely directs the weak.

Trotsky is playful and proud of being so, but I notice that his humor consists almost exclusively of banter. A perpetual poking of fun at the peculiarities of others, their nationality, their profession, their circumstances or tendencies—good-natured, smiling and charming, to be sure, but not varied with an occasional smile at himself, or any genial recognition of the funny plight of mankind in general. And when you take part in the game, when you poke fun at him, he does not laugh, and his smile is never so cordial as when he, himself, lands a blow. I feel it is a little mean and picayune to make this hypercritical observation of Trotsky at play, for he can be delightful indeed, if you are firm enough on your own feet to accept his banter and give it back; but as a student of laughter—and of Trotsky —I can't refrain. To me it is all the more significant since it is a superficial trait.

As to his angularity, his cocksure terseness, that quality which led Lunacharsky to describe him as "prickly," I could not honestly be silent. It is a failure of instinctive regard for the pride of others, a lamentable trait in one whose own pride is so touchy. But he also disregards, when his own schemes are involved, the personal interests of others. And he is not forthright about it; he is devious even with his friends. As Trotsky's gift for alienating people has a certain historic importance, I am going to set down here the otherwise rather inconsequential details of an episode which alienated me.

I functioned for some time as a sort of unofficial literary agent for Trotsky in the United States. I got my pay in royalties in the end; I am not pretending to have been extravagantly generous; but I did, when he first arrived in exile, do quite a mountain of unpaid work for him. In the fall of 1931, however, he sent me an article to translate and sell for him, offering me twenty percent of what I got for it. He said he hoped for a large sum, as much, perhaps, as two hundred dollars. I translated it and took it to George Bye, a popular literary agent, who sold it to *Liberty* magazine for $1500. Of this George took ten percent for the sale and I, ten percent for the translation. This seemed not quite fair, and George, who was very generous, agreed in the case of future articles to let me have fifteen percent for the translation and take only five percent for the sale. This arrangement was reported to Trotsky; we sold two or three more of his articles, and he was delighted.

All went well until an article about Stalin arrived while I was absent on a lecture trip and the translation was delayed a few weeks. During those weeks Trotsky, impelled by his book publishers to give an interview to the press, gave out the substance of the article. After that it could not be sold at a high price, but George persuaded the *New York Times* syndicate to pay a hundred dollars for it and give it the wide publicity that Trotsky, whatever the money payment, so much desired.

The delay, and the small fee, and his own costly mistake in giving out the interview, irritated Trotsky beyond measure. He decided to throw me over and deal directly with George Bye, trusting him to find a translator. I suspected this, because a long letter from George was lying on his desk the day I arrived in Prinkipo. I said nothing about it, but I noticed the next morning that the letter was gone. As he had never heard of George Bye, or had anything to do with him, except through me, this piqued my curiosity, and at the risk of impoliteness, I decided I would force him to be frank. To my seemingly casual question about the letter I had seen, he answered nervously: "Oh yes, when you told me you were going to Palestine and might not come to see me until afterward, I thought it might be best to get in touch with the agent directly."

I said: "It is all right for you to deal with George Bye directly, if you want to, but please remember that I have a contract with him giving me five percent of his commission, and if you deal directly with him without mentioning this, it will deprive me of a part of my earnings."

He was not impelled either by friendship, or by a recognition of my unpaid services to make any response to this. He was angry about that Stalin article. I was by this time heartily pleased with the prospect of not being interrupted every week or so with a too-long article to translate, but I ventured to remind him that George Bye did not have a Russian translator at his elbow. He merely said very sharply:

"No, it is absolutely impossible when you are traveling around Europe. The fate of that Stalin article showed me how impossible it is. I prefer to deal directly with a responsible agent."

My breath was taken away by the harsh, irascible tone in which he said this. If I had been at home when the Stalin article came, and had translated and sold it immediately— say to *Liberty*—for a high price, it would have been in print and ready to publish when he gave away the substance of it to the press. The result would have been an explosion in the editorial rooms and a refusal to have anything to do with "Trotsky articles" in the future. I tried to say this, but he cut me off again sharply.

"No! Such delays are impossible. It is quite impossible to have the translator in one place and the agent in another."

In short, I was fired—and being in my heart glad of it, I took it in silence, and we changed the subject.

We both loved languages, and one of our pleasantest diversions was for him to dictate to me, in his horrendous English, answers to his American and British correspondents, which I would take home and bring back the next day polished off and typed on my portable machine. That same afternoon he drew out an illiterate inquiry from some woman in Ohio about her relatives in Russia, asking me if I knew who she was. When I answered, no, he said, "I guess there's no use answering." I agreed and crumpled the letter, or started to crumple and throw it in the wastebasket, but he stopped me with an outcry as though I were stepping on a baby's face.

"Is *that* the way you treat your correspondence? What kind of a man are you? That letter must be filed!"

I straightened the letter out, laughing at my mistake and passed it over to him, remarking, however, that it didn't seem to me very important to file a letter that wasn't worth answering.

There followed a certain amount of playful banter on that subject, and we went on with our fun, entirely friendly and good-natured.

The next day, however, I got to worrying, as everybody in the household did, about Trotsky's money problems. (In that respect, at least, he was a faithful follower of Karl Marx.) Realizing that if he sent articles to George Bye to be translated by anybody with a Russian accent who happened along, he would spoil his last chance of getting the needed $1500 monthly out of the American press, I ventured to raise again that question on which he had been so crisp. (Trotsky was a hero, you must remember, and moreover, he had been through such nerve-shattering experiences at the hands of the implacable avenger of excellence, Stalin, that no one could hold a grudge against him.)

"I feel a little embarrassed to resist you in this matter," I said, "because my own financial interests seem to be involved, but I can't help warning you that if you leave to a commercial agent the choice of a translator, you can easily lose in a month the position you've gained as a writer available to the American press. Of course, you can get statements on questions of the day published because you are Leon Trotsky, but that is a different thing from being a highly paid contributor to American magazines."

That was, at least, what I set out to say, but he interrupted me halfway through with an exclamation impatiently snapped out:

"No, no! I prefer not to send my articles to a man who grabs up his correspondence and throws it in the wastebasket!"

He imitated my gesture of the day before, but now without the slightest playfulness. He was still angry, I suppose, about the low price he got for that Stalin article. You would have to have in your memory, as I had, the painstaking drudgery of my two years' effort to protect his financial interests and teach him to get what was coming to him from the American press, to appreciate my indignation. Had he been anybody but Leon Trotsky, I would have given a red-hot expression to it and walked out.

Instead, I sat still until there came a brilliant inspiration. It was one of the few times in my life when I thought of the right thing to say.

"Lyef Davidovich, I can only answer you in the words of Lenin." And I quoted, in perfect Russian, from the famous testament: "Comrade Trotsky is apt to be too much carried away by the administrative aspect of things."

At this Trotsky relaxed and dropped back into his

chair, laughing genially and completely, as though to say, "Touché!"

In a moment, however, he was forward and at it again, insisting now that I had been negligent about other articles —"the one on Hitler, for example." This was an article that, after several high-paying magazines refused it, George had finally sold to the *Forum* for three hundred dollars. There was nothing else to do with it and nobody was to blame.

At that point I gave up. Repeating once, and more insistently, my warning that a single article published prominently in a bad translation might ruin his chances, I added that I would let him know as soon as I was settled somewhere, and he might send me his articles or not, as he pleased. What he will do I have no idea, but that he will do anything out of consideration for my interests, or my legitimate stake in the enterprise, I regard as *ausgeschlossen*.

By "gave up," I mean that I abandoned the attempt at friendly conversation with Trotsky. I abandoned it about practical, as I had previously about theoretical, questions. I got away as quickly as I politely could, pleading the need to get back to the West in time to correct the proofs of the second volume of his history. To the end Trotsky kept insisting that we stay for several months at least, so that he and I might continue to "work together and go fishing." He was, so far as I could judge, blandly oblivious to the unwarmth and unfruitfulness of our relation.

The problem of Trotsky's character weaves so intricately in with the story both of the success and the failure of the Bolshevik revolution that it will never lose interest for historians. I hope a little light is cast on it by this memorandum, so immediately set down, of my visit to him after the story ended.

On my way home from Prinkipo, I met in Paris one of Trotsky's greatest admirers and closest friends—the closest, I think, after Christian Rakovsky—and we spoke of the subtle contradictions in Trotsky's character. To my hesitant and groping effort to say that he seemed to me to lack a feeling for others as individuals, his friend said shortly:

"*C'est tout-à fait vrai. Il n'a pas d'humanité. Elle lui manque absolument.*"

Notwithstanding this startlingly extreme confirmation of my impression, I feel that I left out of my memorandum something which, in justice to Trotsky, ought to have been included; a confession, namely, of my own failure of regard for the interests—indeed the most vital passions—of another. It was far from tactful of me to descend upon this intellectually lonely exile with a headful of fresh hot arguments against the religious belief by which he had guided his life to triumph and to this tragic end. It must have put him on edge against me. Perhaps that underlay some of the responses which I attributed to more trivial causes and to the general traits of his character. I find in our subsequent correspondence a letter in which, as though to heal an unmentioned wound, he took pains to mention that he had sent a certain manuscript direct to George Bye only because he had been given to understand that I was away from home.

I think Trotsky earnestly wanted to be regardful of the interests of others, but except in small matters and in the

case of his wife, toward whom the most exquisite consideration seemed to be instinctive, he did not know how to do
it. He lacked the gift of mutuality. He could apprehend,
and discuss at times with keen penetration, the currents of
emotion prevailing in other people, but he could not flow
with them in a warm common stream.

Differing with Sigmund Freud

I was living in Europe in the mid-twenties and had published in London a book on Marxism which contained a chapter entitled, "Marx and Freud." To my delight and excitement, Freud wrote me a letter about my book, calling it, generously, *"wirklich bedeutsam, wahrscheinlich auch richtig,"** and then adding—as though not to be too generous—"I enjoyed it far more than former works of yours."

In thanking him, I said: "I'm sure you won't mind my quoting from your letter in advertising the American edition," and he wrote back, very stiff and caustic:

"I will thank you for *not* mentioning any of the remarks

---

* "Really important, probably also right."

in my letter in public. I seem thus far to have failed to ac-
custom myself to the American life forms."

I replied that I had not mentioned his remarks in public,
but only asked permission to do so. And I think I inti-
mated, as mildly as possible, that the American life forms
are such as to make the difference between these two things
usually quite readily perceptible. It may well be, however,
that I merely wish I had said this, for my dominant feeling
was one of mortification rather than resentment. Freud was
not only in many things my teacher, but by proxy at least,
my Father Confessor. More than one of his American apos-
tles had given me psychoanalytic advice in time of trouble.
I was not in a position, except so far as honest pride demanded it, to sass him back.

It all sharpened in me a long-cherished desire to set eyes
on the great man. I knew I had a certain claim to his attention, for as a result of one of my sessions with his American
apostle, Dr. Smith Ely Jelliffe, I had studied Freud's works
very thoroughly and published, in *Everybody's Magazine*
in 1915, the first popular exposition of his theories and
methods of healing. Thus, happening to be in Vienna in
1926, I sent a note around and asked if I might call.

Bergasse 19 was a big roomy house full of books and pictures, the whole mezzanine floor padded with those thick
rich rugs in which your feet sink like a camel's in the sand.
I was not surprised to see hanging beside Rembrandt's
Anatomy Lesson, without which no doctor's office would be
recognizable, a picture of *The Nightmare*—a horrid monster with a semi-evil laugh or leer, squatting upon a sleeping maiden's naked breast. Freud's early specialty had been

anatomy, and he had in him the hard scientific curiosity suggested by Rembrandt's picture. But then he had too, in my belief, a streak of something closely akin to medieval superstition. He liked to talk about "*the* Unconscious," personifying the mere absence of a quality—and that, the quality of awareness!—and making it into a scheming demon for which anatomy certainly finds no place. Freud's discovery that impulses suppressed out of our thoughts can continue to control those thoughts, both waking and sleeping, and also our actions and bodily conditions, was certainly a major event in the history of science. But what a lot of purely literary mythology he built around it! Mental healing always did and always will run off into magic.

With such thoughts I sat there whetting my curiosity until the door opened and he came in.

Well—he was smaller than I thought, and slender-limbed, and more feminine. I have mentioned my surprise at the feminineness of all the great men I have met. Genius is a nervous phenomenon and, except for the steam-roller variety that has come to the front in the totalitarian states, it involves delicacy. An operation had altered Freud's features a trifle when I met him, so that his nose seemed flatter than I expected and bent slightly to one side. It made him, when he threw his head clear back and laughed softly, as he frequently did, seem quaint and gnomelike. His voice was a little thin too, as though he were purposely holding back half his breath in order to be mischievous.

"What did you want?" he said in English as we shook hands.

"Not a thing," I said. "I just wanted to look you over."

"You want to quote my commendation of your book. But why should I support you? Can't you stand up on your own legs?"

"I'm trying to," I said. "And that isn't what brought me here at all. Still, I do wonder why, if you think I got it right about you and Marx, you want to make a secret of it."

He made no answer and was not troubled by the silence this caused. It was a hard silence, a sort of weapon in his hand, and I made it worse by saying:

"There *is* one thing I always wanted to ask you. I don't see why you talk about unconsciousness as though it were a thing. The only *thing* there, when we are unconscious, is our brain and body. Wouldn't it clarify matters if you stopped using the noun and stuck to the adjective—instead of saying '*the* Unconscious,' say 'unconscious brain states'?"

"Well, haven't you read our literature?" he said tartly. "The Unconscious is not a thing, but a concept. It is a concept that we find indispensable in the clinic."

"It is a dangerous concept," I said, "because people inevitably think of it as a thing."

"Well, then, let them correct their thinking!"

It wasn't very pleasant, and I tried to say with a smile: "You're perfectly sure you're not resurrecting the soul?"

"No, there's no soul," he said. "There's only a concept which those of us engaged in practical work find indispensable.

"Perhaps you're a behaviorist," he went on. "According to your John B. Watson, even consciousness doesn't exist. But that's just silly. That's nonsense. Consciousness exists quite obviously and everywhere—except in America."

He enjoyed that crack at America so much that he began

to laugh and be genial. In fact, he began to lecture me in a fatherly way about the relations between the psychic and the physical. He talked fluently, and I am a good listener, and we were soon very friendly.

"You mustn't confuse the psychic with the conscious," he said. "My old psychology teacher here in Vienna, Theodore Lipps, used to warn us against that. Psychic entities are not necessarily conscious."

My answer, of course, was: "Then the unconscious is not merely a concept after all, but a thing, an 'entity,' just as I thought!"

However, I did not make this answer until I got home and was putting down our conversation in a notebook. I was too far on the underside of my inferiority complex to catch a great man up like that. Perhaps it is just as well, for the contradiction, left standing, is very neat and pretty. It shows Freud in the very act of being both a scientist and a demonologist. Freud would not let his discoveries be a contribution to psychology. They had to be psychology— "Freud's psychology." And there had to be quite a little of the infallibility of the Pope in his pronunciamentos.

He had now become so genial, however, that he even said a good word for America—namely, that she had produced John Dewey.

"John Dewey is one of the few men in the world," he said, "for whom I have a high regard."

I said that I had taught and studied under Dewey at Columbia, and thought very highly of him too, though the World War had divided us. "The war was a watershed in America."

That remark interested him, and he kept returning to it

afterward. Indeed, he had a way of calling the conversation back to where it had been going, not letting it get lost, that reminded me of Plato's Socrates.

For instance, I said that the war was a watershed in America, dividing radicals from liberals, but not in Europe because in Europe everybody was in it whether he wanted to be or not.

"Officially," he put in with a sly inflection. And then he exclaimed: "You should not have gone into the war at all. Your Woodrow Wilson was the silliest fool of the century, if not of all centuries."

He paused for my answer, which got stuck accidentally in my throat.

"And he was also probably one of the biggest criminals— unconsciously, I am quite sure."

I said that Woodrow Wilson's literary style was a perfect instrument of self-deception, and that delighted him. He asked me if I had read *The Story of a Style,* a psycho-analytic character reading of Wilson on the basis of the relative predominance of certain types of words in his speeches. I said I had, and we agreed in praising the in-genuity of its author, William Bayard Hale. We were a long way from my remark about the watershed, but Freud called me back to it.

"I would like you to say some more about that watershed business," he said.

"Well, take Dewey, for instance. He went over on the war side, and wrote a book against Germany, and it seemed for a time to change his whole way of thinking. Most of our intellectual leaders who did that stopped thinking al-together."

"Why?" Freud asked.

"You know why people stop thinking," I said. "It's because their thoughts would lead them where they don't want to go."

That amused him again, and the whole of his gentleness came back, including the delighted little crinkles at the corners of his eyes. He put his head way back finally and laughed like a child. Sometimes a child at play reminds you of an odd little old man; there was something of that odd little old man in Freud's ways. He waggled his head and hands about all the time, looking up at the ceiling and closing his eyes, or making funny little pouts and wry faces, when he was trying to think of a word or an idea. I never ceased feeling that underneath it all was an obdurate hard cranky streak, but I also never ceased feeling its great charm.

He was curious about the support I gave to the Russian Bolsheviks.

"You believe in liberty," he said, "and there you get just the opposite."

I gave him our glib explanation: the class dictatorship is transitional—a method of moving toward a more real and universal liberty.

He made gestures like a man fighting with cobwebs or doing the Australian crawl.

"That is all up in the air," he said. "People who are going to produce liberty some time in the future are just the same for me as people who are going to have it ready for you in the celestial paradise. I live in this real world right here. This is the only world I am interested in."

I told him the very thing I admired about Lenin was his

way of taking the real world exactly as it is, and yet trying to do something with it.

"The Bolsheviks," I said, "have a hypothesis and they're trying it out."

That appealed to the scientist in him, and he became both serious and mild.

"It *is* an intensely interesting experiment," he said. "Really, it's all *terra incognita* to me. I don't know anything about it."

"What are you politically?" I asked.

"Politically I am just nothing."

He settled down in his chair and squinted at me.

"What are you going to do when you get back to that America of yours?" he asked.

"What makes you hate America so?" I queried.

"Hate America?" he said. "I don't hate America, I regret it!"

He threw back his head again and laughed hilariously.

"I regret that Columbus ever discovered it!"

I laughed with him, and rather egged him on, no doubt, for I am not touchy about our national faults.

"America," he went on, "is a bad experiment conducted by Providence. At least, I think it must have been Providence. I at least should hate to be held responsible for it."

More laughter, and then I asked: "In what way bad?"

"Oh, the prudery, the hypocrisy, the national lack of independence! There is no independent thinking in America, is there?"

I said there was a new and lively spirit among young people.

"Mostly among Jews, isn't it?"

"The Jews are not so free from prudery and hypocrisy," I replied.

He seemed to change the subject.

"You didn't answer my question; what are you going to do when you get home? Have you any definite plans?"

"None except that I am going to write."

"I'll tell you what I want you to do. I want you to go home and write a book on America, and I'll tell you what to call it. *Misgeburt*— What is that word in English?"

"Abortion?"

"No, not abortion."

"Monster?"

"Well, that will do. You write a book about the monstrous thing that America turned out to be. . . ." He paused. "The word is 'miscarriage.' *The Miscarriage of American Civilization*—that shall be the title of your book. You will find out the causes and tell the truth about the whole awful catastrophe."

He was standing up now.

"That book will make you immortal. You may not be able to live in America any more, but you could go and live very happily somewhere else!"

I had risen too, and he extended his hand.

"Now I want to see that next book of yours without fail. So please remember to send it to me, and I'll read it with happy memories of this conversation. . . ."

A very gracious dismissal! How suave and charming—on the face of it.

As I went down the steps, my thoughts recurred to his

similarly gracious letter about my book: "Really important; probably also correct. . . . I enjoyed it far more than
former works of yours!"

Are those—I thought—the European life forms? Is
Freud a little vain and cranky with too much peering into
other people's complexes? Is it perhaps our rather hard-
headed skepticism about some of the more mythological of
his reported discoveries in "the Unconscious" that caused
this extreme feeling? His American friend and translator,
Dr. A. A. Brill, told me that this feeling dated back to his
visit to this country in 1909 and the meager recognition he
received from scientific circles then. It seemed a strange
thing for an admiring disciple of Freud to say so casually
and calmly. For was it not to deliver mankind from just
that kind of displaced emotion that this hero of self-knowl-
edge was born into the world?

That visit in Vienna was but an incident in a one-way
companionship which had begun with a deep plunge into
Freud's books in 1914 and has never ended. When my account of it first appeared, I received a letter from Freud's
sister, Anna Bernays, saying—very politely—that although
I had met her brother, it was evident I did not know him.
On the other hand, two distinguished psychoanalysts, one a
former close colleague of the master, congratulated me on
the justness of the impression I had gathered so quickly.
The contrast intrigued me, and when another close colleague, Dr. Ernest Jones, began to publish his intimate
biography, I seized eagerly the opportunity to know Freud
a little better. I wanted especially to continue our argument about the concept of the Unconscious.

So far as concerns Freud's charm and the "obdurate hard cranky streak" I felt underlying it, Dr. Jones bore me out, I thought, completely. Freud's confession, quoted by Dr. Jones on page 8 of the first volume, sounded "cranky" enough in all conscience: "An intimate friend and a hated enemy have always been indispensable to my emotional life; I have always been able to create them anew, and not infrequently . . . friend and enemy have coincided in the same person. . . ." As for Freud's passion against America, that proved only more obdurate on better acquaintance, and more morbidly bitter, than I had realized in our conversation. To the end of his days—according to Dr. Jones —or at least until it moved down and became recognized as mucous colitis—he used to describe his intestinal disorder as "my American indigestion." His nephew, Edward L. Bernays, who is also the nephew of Freud's wife, gave me an explanation of this anti-American fixation which differs somewhat from that of Dr Brill. He said that William James attended those pioneer lectures at Clark University in 1909, and being intrigued both by Freud and his ideas, invited him up to his summer camp in the Adirondacks. To entertain the distinguished guest, they all went out in the woods and cooked a beefsteak dinner, picnic fashion, over an open fire. That dinner was the awful beginning of Freud's indigestion, according to Bernays, and of his anti-Americanism.

"Why they're still savages over there," he grumbled, "they cook their food on heated stones out in the woods!"

As to Freud's equivocation about the concept of "the Unconscious," which I thought revealed so neatly the conflict in him between the scientist and the mythmaker:

that too received illumination as I got better acquainted with him. Dr. Jones himself is somewhat perturbed by criticisms like mine, and he answers them by saying that if the critics would read all of Freud's writings on the Unconscious, they would find their objections refuted. So I went out and bought Freud's *Collected Papers* and read all that he had to say on the Unconscious, as well as many fascinating things about related subjects. To my surprise I found, in his principal essay on the Unconscious, the very same unmediated leap from an *als ob* conception to an existent entity that had turned up in our conversation.

I also found out, in those *Collected Papers,* that while insisting that a mental element when absent from consciousness does exist as a psychic entity, Freud confessed that he had not the slightest idea what sort of an entity it was. To put it in his own language: "In what shape it may have existed, while present in the mind and latent in consciousness, we have no means of guessing." What does he gain then, as a scientist, by denying the quite obvious assumption that it exists "as a physical disposition for the recurrence of the same psychical phenomenon"? Freud himself asks the question, and his answer is that this denies to psychology "the right to account for its most common facts, such as memory, by its own means." But again, what does he gain, as a scientist, by erecting a barrier between psychology and the physiology of the brain? It is not important to psychology, or any other science, that its facts be explained "by its own means," but by the means which best explain them. Freud's insistence that there is causal determinism in the psychical as well as the physical world —by which he can only mean independently of the physical world—is adapted to make untrained minds think they are being very scientific, but it is a roadblock on the path of biological psychology.

These papers left me convinced that it is not the scientist in Freud but an artist—a demonological poet—who insists on peopling an underworld with masked demons who move about in the unlocal dark, controlling our thoughts and the action of our bodies; the id, the ego, the superego, the censor, the death-wish, the castration complex, the Oedipus complex, etc. We "have no means of guessing" what those creatures are, but they are endowed both with ideas and intentions, and behave at times almost exactly like little ghouls or demons. They resist, elude, deceive, suppress, kowtow to, or overcome one another in a region which has no existence anywhere on the real earth, and can have none, for the very name of it, "unconscious mental action," is a contradiction in terms. Brain action can be unconscious, and largely is, but to be mind and to be unconscious is, if words are to have genuine meaning, a contradiction in terms.

Although in that esoteric paper Freud says we cannot guess "in what shape" the psychic contents of the Unconscious exist, it can hardly be doubted that what most Freudians think of when they speak of "the Unconscious," is another conscious mind lurking beneath, or behind, or somewhere in the vicinity of, the one they are familiar with. Freud himself compared a wishful idea in the Unconscious to "a demon striving not to come to the light of day, because he knows that will be his end." And indeed it is hard to make real to oneself, except in such terms, the existence of a "wish" splurging around, bodiless, unlocalized, inside of something, but that something defined only by a negative attribute. Certain things may no doubt be accomplished with these demonological concepts, if they are regarded as merely handy ways of talking. How far Freud was from so regarding them is revealed in his article on psychoanalysis in the *Encyclopædia Britannica,* where he remarks that "the future will probably attribute far greater importance to psychoanalysis as the science of the Unconscious than as a therapeutic procedure."

I think the future will take exactly the opposite course, if it is not already doing so. Notwithstanding his vital and tremendous contributions to psychology, we shall go very wrong if we take Freud for the "true man of science" of Dr. Jones' adoring portrait. Science, to be sure, is no supernal enterprise; it is nothing but the skilled, persistent, and appropriate use of the mind, and the stores of human knowledge, about any problem. It does, however, require at least three qualifications in the scientist: the discipline of suspended judgment, a mastery of the knowledge relevant to his problem, a sustained passion for verification. Freud had none of these qualifications. He jumped to conclusions with the agility of a trained athlete. He was (to quote Dr. Jones) "ill-informed in the field of contemporary psychology and seems to have derived only from hearsay any knowledge he may have had of it"—he did not even sense, for instance, the elementary distinction between idea and perception. He had a temperamental distaste for experiment, and no impulse at all toward verification. The idea of submitting his "insights," his "intuitions," his "explorations of the unconscious," to confirmation *by someone else* seems to have been particularly alien to his

intensely emotional and recklessly inventive mind. His attitude toward other people's findings may be inferred from
the ferocious demand he made of his sweetheart that she
join him in hating her brother. He would break off his engagement, he threatened, if this happy consensus of opinion was not attained.

To me he was less like Newton, or Darwin, or any of the
great men of science, than like Paracelsus—a man who
made significant contributions to science, but was by nature given to infatuation with magical ideas and causes.
Freud's contributions were, to be sure, immeasurably
greater than those of Paracelsus, but there is a similar ad-
mixture of midnight fabrication in them. Way back in the
eighties when he was still working in brain anatomy, Freud
got seized with the notion that cocaine, then newly discovered, was a "magic substance"—the phrase is Dr. Jones'
—which would not only cure all sorts of ills, including
morphine addiction, but would increase a healthy man's
nervous and muscular strength without any bad effects,
and without habit formation. He reached this conclusion
"experientally"—again a word from Dr. Jones—that is,
on the basis of his own experience. While enamored of this
substance, and convinced it would make him world famous
and solve his dire financial troubles, he hit upon the idea
that, besides all these interior miracles, cocaine might possibly be useful in eye troubles as a local anesthetic. He
made this remark to a colleague, but did not himself bother
—being all wrapped up in the internal miracles he was going to accomplish—to make the tiny experiment indicated.
The colleague made the experiment and became world
famous, while Freud, clinging to his unverified belief in

the life-enhancing properties of his wonder-drug, damaged his reputation by killing a patient with an overdose of it.

This inclination to believe in occult hunches instead of trying out plausible hypotheses, is illustrated time and again in Dr. Jones' account of Freud's development. Throughout the ten years when he made his "Great Discoveries," Freud was in an almost pathological rapture of admiration for a quack philosopher in Berlin, a thoroughgoing phoney, who believed in numerology, and professed to have found the solution of all life's problems in the ratio between the numbers 28 and 23, which he derived in different ways from the periodicity in the sexual life of women. By manipulating these numbers, this Dr. Fliess professed to explain the inner nature of almost everything, not omitting the solar system and the interstellar spaces. From the age of thirty-nine until he was fifty years old, Freud accepted and believed in this man's shamanistic lucubrations, describing them as "your beautiful and sure biological discoveries," and Fliess himself as "the Keppler of biology."

Dr. Jones quite frankly describes Freud's condition during these years of the Great Discoveries as a psychoneurosis —which is all right, most of us have a touch of that—but that Freud's psychoneurosis expressed itself in an avid disposition to swallow grandiose and uninvestigated occult *beliefs,* is a point whose significance escapes him.

Dr. Jones is contemptuous of Joseph Breuer, Freud's collaborator in the early *Studies in Hysteria,* for having got off the Freudian bandwagon as soon thereafter as possible. I do not know whether Breuer ever said what he thought of Freud, but what Freud said about Breuer pretty well tells the story: ". . . he always knows of three candidates for one truth and abominates every generalization as a piece of arrogance."

The principal "one truth" that Freud was believing in at the time when Breuer got off was that all hysterias are caused by the sexual seduction of an innocent child by an adult. Freud even deduced the criminality of his own father from this obviously improbable generalization. After clinging to it for over four years, he did begin to feel some doubts, but one little piece of "experiental" evidence reassured him. I quote Dr. Jones:

> When, finally, he had a dream about his American niece, Hella, which he had to interpret as covering a sexual wish towards his eldest daughter, he felt he had personal firsthand evidence of the correctness of his theory.

If this is "science," where shall we turn for organized common sense!

Another generalization to which Freud leaped from a single experience was that he had been all wrong about hysterical disorders—they are *not* caused by sexual assaults in childhood; those are only imagined by the hysteric. The real, but still universal, cause is the "Oedipus Complex" in the child. The "experiental" evidence in this case was an item in Freud's psychoanalysis of himself. Again I quote Dr. Jones:

> He had discovered in himself the passion for his mother and jealousy of his father; he *felt sure* that this was a *general* human characteristic and that from it one could understand the powerful effect of the Oedipus legend. Evi-

dently his mind was now working at full speed, and we may even speak of swift intuitions.

We may indeed, and I inserted the italics because I think it is well to remember how much empirical basis there was for Freud's original *sureness* about the *universality* of the Oedipus Complex, one of his most fixed and cherished obsessions. "In closing this study I want to state that the beginnings of religion, ethics, society and art meet in the Oedipus Complex." Thus, in *Totem and Taboo,* he sweeps pretty nearly every human thing there is into the lap of this generalization about which he had so suddenly felt sure.

Another example of Freud's easy grace in jumping to conclusions is provided by Dr. Jones in these words:

> One day a patient suddenly threw her arms around his neck, an unexpected contretemps, fortunately remedied by the entrance of a servant. From then on he understood that the peculiar relationship so effective therapeutically [the "transference"] had an erotic basis.

When Freud first came out with his proclamation that sex traumas lie at the bottom of all neurotic disorders, it was generally inferred that his own sexual constitution must be a little abnormal, and I think this inference was correct. The abnormality, however, was not in the direction of lechery and loose living, but just the contrary. Freud was a prude and a puritan, a fanatical monogamist, not sexy by nature, and so "chaste" in speech and conduct that he "would have been out of place in the usual club room." He was, in short, the kind of man to be shocked into a new theory of therapeutics by a girl who jumps up unexpectedly and throws her arms around his neck. I surmise that it was this state of shock, the astonishment of a natural-born puritan at finding out how much frank and raw sexuality there is in the world, which led Freud to "proclaim"—again a word from Dr. Jones—that extreme and improbable "One Truth" about the sexual seduction of young children which brought him so much obloquy and pain.

> When he got hold of a simple but significant fact, he would feel and know [sic] that it was an example of something general and universal and the idea of collecting statistics on the matter was quite alien to him . . . that is the way the mind of a genius works.

So speaks his worshipful disciple, and we can only say: Yes, but a genius for what? Not scientific investigation certainly. And not literature, either, although Freud was a gifted writer. Freud himself in a humble moment invented a name for his genius which, had Dr. Jones accepted it, would have made his praise of Freud much wiser than it was:

"I am not really a man of science, not an observer, not an experimenter, and not a thinker. I am nothing but by temperament a *conquistador*—an adventurer, if you want to translate the word—with the curiosity, the boldness and the tenacity that belongs to that type of being."

It was a conquistador, truly, rather than a man of

science, who explored this darkest Africa of the Unconscious,* a conquistador and a poet. For the progress of scientific good sense, it seems to me as important to exorcise the faceless demons with which he peopled this unimaginable region, as to recognize his epoch-making contributions to science. But I hope it will not be imagined that a closer acquaintance has diminished my sense of the grandeur of those contributions. Freud played the major part in making psychology dynamic, bringing the wish into it, the instinctive drive, in place of the old unlifelike tale of stimulus and reaction, association and dissociation. And his discovery that these drives, when denied fulfillment and repressed out of consciousness, may take effect in hysterias, dreams, neurotic symptoms, etc., has given a new look to the whole study of mankind by man. His place among the giants of the history of knowledge is secure. It is not necessary to pretend that he explored a new world and a new order of being, neither mind nor matter.

---

* It should not be thought that Freud *invented* this dark continent. The idea of it was familiar to him, and to all German intellectuals, in the metaphysics of Eduard von Hartmann, whose remarkable book, *The Philosophy of the Unconscious*, published in 1859, went through eleven editions during Freud's life. Von Hartmann did not claim to have explored this region, but arrived by abstract reasoning at a knowledge of what was to be found there: will and intellect, namely, in a state of conflict.

Two Bertrand Russells

Bertrand Russell is the most readable of living high-brows; he also knows more than any of the rest of them. When Lenin died, his adoring disciples had his brain examined with a microscope to see if it differed in some occult way from the normal. Bertrand Russell's might be better worth examining, for it is a more variously prodigious specimen. George Santayana, in the final volume of his memoirs, described "Bertie" as the most gifted of all the men he had known.

"He had birth, genius, learning, indefatigable zeal and energy, brilliant intelligence, and absolute honesty and courage. His love of justice was as keen as his sense of humor. He was at home in mathematics, in natural science,

and in history. He knew well all the more important languages and was well informed about everything going on in
the world of politics and literature."

That is high praise indeed, but Santayana added that as
a great intellect Russell had somehow "petered out." In
discussing the subject with me he said, more harshly:
"Along with his genius he has a streak of foolishness."

I was reminded of this when reading a review by Maurice
Hindus of Russell's recent book, *Portraits From Memory
and Other Essays*. Hindus praises the book highly, as any
good critic must, but also remarks: "The goddess he wor-
ships is Sprightliness, and she can make him do and say
silly things at times . . ." I should say *irresponsible* or
light-minded, rather than foolish or silly things, but I have
long shared this two-fold opinion of Bertrand Russell: un-
bounded admiration for his mind, and a certain embarrassment about this trait of his character.

He is a funny-looking fellow, rather like some eager-
beaked bird, or birdlike gargoyle, and I sometimes wonder
what effect this had on him as he grew up. To discover the
finest brain of the generation in such a receptacle must
have been a surprise. He is not unpleasantly grotesque,
however, but pleasantly so when you see his eyes lighted
with interest in an idea.

It was thirty-two years ago (November 21, 1927) that he
and I entertained a crowded Cooper Union with a debate
on *The Road to Freedom,* and I came home and wrote
down the title of this essay: "Two Bertrand Russells." I had
then read some of Russell's philosophic writings, notably
*Our Knowledge of the External World as a Field for Scien-
tific Method in Philosophy.* The title is almost as long as

the book, and is not logically constructed, it seems to me. It should read: "The Problem of our Knowledge of the External World, etc. . . ." But the book itself is brief and is logical to a degree rarely to be found in books of philosophy, even the most famous. They are all, with but two or three exceptions, dedicated to proving, or building into a conception of the universe, some notion that is satisfactory to the emotional needs of the philosopher. This, at least was my firm opinion after emerging from a four-year course in philosophy. I cherished a feeling of admiring kinship with the few so-called skeptics—Hume, Montaigne, Sextus Empiricus, Protagoras perhaps—men who had attempted *without any other motive* to find out what could be known about the plight of man's mind in the universe. I believed, and believe still, that Bertrand Russell belongs among these cool and elevated spirits, and that in a wise history of philosophy his place would be secure. For that reason I approached the meeting in Cooper Union somewhat awed by the honor of being associated in conflict with so great a mind.

Proposed Roads to Freedom was the title of a book that Russell had published, and my opening speech, which as usual I wrote out and delivered from memory, was as thoughtful a criticism of it as I knew how to make. Indeed for those in the audience with a taste for proletarian revolution, it must have seemed quite conclusive. I took a backward glance at all the great advocates of a better social system, and pointed out that none of them, from Plato to Russell, had ever even looked for *the road* to freedom. They had merely told us what a free society might be like when we got there. Karl Marx, I declaimed—and I was then immature enough to regard this as very wise—did not bother his head about what it would be like when we got there. He concentrated on finding the road: the working-class struggle, namely, for the conquest of political power.

Russell replied, as I would now, that this was all very much more neat than convincing, that it was impossible to treat human history as though it were a process taking place in a laboratory—words, at least, to that effect. And he remarked how many years had passed since Marx predicted the revolutionary change I was still waiting for, and spoke of the folly of any man's imagining that he could predict the course of history over a long period of time.

"Not one of us can tell right now what is going to happen in the next seven years," he exclaimed.

Toward the end of his speech—which was not a speech, but just brilliant inconsecutive talking—he happened accidentally, as any impromptu speaker might, to get to telling us, rather explicitly, what might be expected of the rest of the twentieth century. It was a bad accident, and I made some good fun in my rebuttal out of the striking contrast between the prophetic genius of Karl Marx and of Bertrand Russell. His answer was magnanimous, and also clever. He acknowledged that with this lucky crack I had probably won the debate, but remarked that this did not prove the validity of the theory of progress through class struggle.

We walked across town together after the debate, and I tried to get him to say something illuminating about my teacher, John Dewey, toward whose instrumental philosophy I was still struggling to orient myself.

"I find him such a dull writah," was all I could get out of him.

I don't know why, but though I have often met Russell since, and ridden in taxis with him, and dined beside him, and made speeches from the same platform, I have never been able to get much farther into a conversation than that. Something rises up between us—whether my too humble admiration for his mind, or an opinion on his part that I haven't any mind, I can't pretend to say. Mathematics, of course, is an alarming thing to a man of my temper and experience. Although I passed examinations in both algebra and trigonometry, not to mention plane and solid geometry, I could not at this moment describe the binomial theorem, or state what a logarithm is, if the sword of Damocles were hanging over me. So perhaps it is just the phantom of Mathematics that rises up between us, putting me in my place with that mystic and impenetrable gesture that has the whole world of unciphering mortals buffaloed.

At any rate, this memoir will contain only one more phrase spoken to me by Bertrand Russell. That, too, was on the way home from our debate, and what he said was—and he said it disdainfully—"Anyone who takes these debates and lectures of ours seriously must be an idiot." I had taken my part of it seriously as my manuscript testifies, and whatever may have been my answer, I recoiled inwardly from this remark. As he was then making an enviable income out of these debates and lectures, playing up to the eagerness of a half-baked American intelligentsia to gaze upon, and gather pearls of wisdom from, a great British philosopher, this roused my democratic indignation. I thought he ought to give the best he had for the money and adulation he was getting. I also thought—at that time— that his political opinions were as trivial and superficial as his philosophic speculations were profound. That was the source of my title: "Two Bertrand Russells." I now see that his answer to my neat speech, in spite of that accidental lowering of his guard, was a good one. But I still resent his flippant attitude to that attentive audience. There is a point of view from which nothing that any of us "intellectuals" do or think seems very important. But from that point of view, I am not sure a book in the library on the Principles of Mathematics ranks so much higher than a speech in Cooper Union on the Road to Freedom. I would like to find the same Bertrand Russell in both places.

I will give another example of what I mean. Not so many years ago I attended a lecture by him in the Rand School for Social Science. It was a lecture on Aristotle, and was attended by a throng of young boys and girls, mostly working-class, all hungrily drinking up with burningly attentive eyes whatever gems of wisdom and guidance they could get from this famous and truly great man. And the great man delivered a very fine lecture—a chapter perhaps from his *History of Western Philosophy*. He was particularly illuminating on the subject of the virtue which Aristotle called *megalopsychia,* and which is often but incorrectly translated "magnanimity." It means something more like high-mindedness or dignity of spirit. You might say that it means "what *noblesse* obliges," for it is essentially an aristocratic virtue. Russell was engaging and wonderfully subtle in describing it. But afterward one of those burning-eyed youngsters, a girl in her teens, breathless with bashfulness and a zeal to understand, asked him a question—not a penetrating question perhaps, but not foolish. He brushed her off and out of the intellectual world with some frivolous jest about consulting Mrs. Aristotle. As I watched her sink back miserably into her chair, I thought: "Well, he has given a perfect discourse on *megalopsychia* and a perfect example of the lack of it."

It must have been after that lecture, for it was in an anteroom at the Rand School, that Bertrand Russell confided to me the genuinely desperate financial situation he was in. His radical opinions, particularly about military patriotism and marriage, had closed all the innumerable chairs of philosophy that would otherwise have been open to him. To climax this hardship, he had just been summarily ejected from a professorship at the rambunctious art foundation in Philadelphia established by the Argyrol king and ex-prize fighter and cranky connoisseur, Albert C. Barnes. He told me with genuine distress in his voice that he really did not know how he was going to earn his living.

This will surprise the reader now, but hardly more than it surprised me then. I was indeed so appalled that a great mind should be in such a plight—and my admiration for the delving mind was so much stronger than my distaste for the flippant tongue—that I went over the next morning to the New School for Social Research, and pleaded with its founder and director, Alvin Johnson, to give Bertrand Russell a job! Both Johnson and the New School, I thought, were bold enough to stand up to public opinion in such a cause. I realized how little Russell had exaggerated his plight when I received my answer. Johnson listened patiently, with the genial twinkle in his eyes and the genial pipe in his mouth that are both a part of him, and when my plea was finished, removed the pipe with friendly deliberation and said:

"Max, I agree with everything you said . . . But the question will have to come before the trustees. I will put it before them, but I can advise you in advance not to hope for a favorable answer."

The two-fold nature of Bertrand Russell has given rise to some other interesting reactions besides those I quoted. W. B. Yeats, in an imaginary letter to a schoolmaster about his son's education, made this amusing remark: "Teach him mathematics as thoroughly as his capacity permits. I know that Bertrand Russell must, seeing that he is such a featherhead, be wrong about everything but as I have no mathematics I cannot prove it. I do not want my son to be as helpless." Even the Encyclopædia Britannica shares this two-way attitude toward the great philosopher. It describes him in a biographical essay as "temperamentally desperate, loving extremes . . . almost querulously criticising the world's workings," and declares ironically that he "has been peculiarly successful in eliciting from contemporary physics those theorems that are most consonant with his own temper." But when it comes to getting an article on the most subtle and difficult subject in the whole encyclopedia, one requiring acuity and balance as well as learning of the most reliable kind, the article on Knowledge itself—what we can know and how we know it—the editors turn to Bertrand Russell! *

I have a feeling, which I cannot verify, that the trivial

* I owe this observation to C. K. Ogden, writing on "The New Britannica" in the *Saturday Review of Literature,* October 23, 1926.

and irresponsible member of this dual personality is apt to be uppermost when he is dealing with America. Many other distinguished Europeans have come overseas annually to tap the gold mine of our provincial adoration of Old World Culture—it was natural enough—but most of them tried hard, however unsuccessfully, to give a good lecture. Yeats, for instance, according to his biographer, "always gave of his best . . . and this consideration sprang no less from his inborn courtesy than from a sense of his own dignity and what was due to others." But Bertrand Russell was content merely to stand up and chatter about ideas. Perhaps, indeed, he was the only one who could stand up and chatter about ideas without fear of exhausting the reservoir, or losing control of the taps. I cannot help doubting, however, whether in lectures to a British audience he would have been quite so cavalier. "Love of England," he says in this recent book, "is very nearly the strongest emotion I possess"—a statement so surprising in one whose closest companion seems to have been the universe that it adds weight to my feeling that in order to understand him we have to divide him in two.

Russell himsef contributes a little to this feeling. "The serious part of my life ever since boyhood," he says, "has been devoted to two different objects. . . . I wanted, on the one hand, to find out whether anything can be known; and, on the other, to do whatever might be possible toward creating a happier world." He adds that he has found his work on social questions "much more difficult and much less successful" than his earlier work on mathematical logic. He thinks it is more difficult "because its utility depends upon persuasion." My feeling is that on social (and political) questions, he is inclined to spend more time in persuasion than in doing the work—the work, I mean, of establishing valid opinions. It is in this sphere, at least, that the light-minded Bertrand Russell seems so often to have sway.

Having said this, I must hasten to add that in 1920, when he paid his visit to Soviet Russia, Bertrand Russell arrived with speed at an opinion that time has verified. He was right when most of us who shared his bold views about World War One were making the mistake of our lives. He is entitled to all the boasting he so genteelly refrains from doing about that fact. At that early date, his adverse report on the "Great Experiment" said pretty nearly everything that the rest of us wasted so much time in summoning the mental force or humility to say. It was not as though he had gone over there with adverse prejudices, either. On the contrary, a month or so before boarding the train, he had issued a startling announcement of his conversion to Communism. He had to take that announcement back while it was still floating like a flag almost from the masthead of all pro-Bolshevik publications throughout the western world.

The memory touches me rather deeply because it was in my magazine, *The Liberator,* that he published the original confession of his faith. We printed it in extra-sized type on the first pages of the magazine, rejoicing that we had now a comrade-in-arms who would strike respect at least, if not fear, into the hearts of our enemy, the general public. He did not send his recantation to the *Liberator,* but to our rival the *Nation,* wishing perhaps to save me a rather painful embarrassment, for I believed in free discussion as

well as proletarian revolution and should have had to publish it. As it was, I felt compelled to answer the great philosopher, and I did so with all the scholarly heft I could
muster, entitling my essay, "Plato, Nietzsche and Bertrand
Russell." I am happy to recall that I did not dismiss his recantation as a class-conscious reaction, although that would
have been made easy by the fact that his traveling companion, Robert Williams, head of the British Transport
Workers' Union, came back with an exactly opposite reaction: "All my previous hopes and expectations were more
than borne out by my actual contact with Soviet affairs." I
brushed this easy argument aside, and answered according
to my own pretty thoroughly un-Marxian type of revolu-
tionism.

"It *is* possible," I said, "for persons of drastic and pure
intellect, or militantly sympathetic emotion, to abstract
from their own economic or social situation, conceive the
process of revolutionary struggle scientifically, and put
their personal force in on the side where lie the ultimate
hopes of human life." And I paid a special tribute to Russell's capacity for such disinterested logic, his championship of "scientific method in philosophy." "What is it," I
asked, "that prevents him from bringing over that austere
and celebrated method into his contemplation of the problems of society? It is the contagious Christian disease of idealizing the soft, and worshipping the ineffectual."

So I disposed of this most devastating intrusion on my
state of exalted belief. Bertrand Russell was in China when
my editorial essay came out. His wife, Dora Russell, wrote
a ponderous answer to it, and he sent her manuscript to me
saying that it expressed his views. I am not by any means a

touchy person; my inferiority complex takes other forms than that. But I must confess I was not flattered by this left-handed, or no-handed, way of answering my studious and deeply pondered criticism of his changed opinion. Twice since then, once in a letter, once in a personal encounter, Bertrand Russell has reproached me for betraying the principle of free discussion in not publishing his wife's letter. On neither occasion did I say in reply—what I thought should be obvious—that I did not care to advertise the position he put me in by replying to my dissertation through an unknown woman who happened to be his wife. I cannot help wondering, since I am still in the vicinity of that subject, whether he would have sent such a communication to a British editor.

I wish I might feel as happily confident as I did in those days about that "hard-headed idealism" which I regarded as the heart of the Marxian doctrine when purged of Hegelian metaphysics. My present feeling when Bertrand Russell expresses his "firm conviction" that "the only stable improvements in human affairs are those which increase kindly feeling and diminish ferocity," is one of nostalgia. I was brought up to think so, and I would like to go back to my childhood. But I do not believe we can increase kindly feeling and diminish ferocity on a large scale except by selective breeding. And I still think that the political Bertrand Russell fails to confront such facts with that unremitting, diligent and disciplined hardness of mind with which the philosophic Bertrand Russell confronts a proposition in logic or mathematics. One cannot be so sure, it is true, about political as about mathematical matters, but one can require of himself that he be as sure as possible before advising the world. And this, it seems to me, is what the political member of the Bertrand Russell combination fails to do. His recantation after the visit to Soviet Russia was an act of admirable devotion to an ascertained truth; it is beyond praise. But was not his startling proclamation of a conversion to Communism just before he went, by the same token, somewhat cursory and careless?

Bertrand Russell has made a good many such startling shifts of opinion in the course of his work on social questions, more, by a good deal, than the changing conditions have warranted. I remember—it cannot be so long ago—his announcing in the *New Leader* that love, after all, is the only force that can save the world. Yet in 1948, in an address at Westminster School which he took pains to publish, he said:

"There must be in the world only one armed force supranational and all-powerful . . . It is the only way to prevent Great Wars. There is singularly little hope of establishing such a force by international agreement. . . . The Western Alliance with the United States and the Commonwealth have the nucleus of such a force. It must impose itself on the whole world, and remain powerful, uniquely so, until the world has been educated into a unified sanity."

A very far call from love as the savior of the world.

Though sprightly enough, none of these rapid changes seems quite so featherweight as his shift of passion and opinion in the last seven years on the subject of the fight against Communism. In 1950, in the *New York Times Magazine,* he issued a battle cry that must have roused thousands who care about real values to join in that fight. He depicted with militant eloquence the horrors of life under the Communist dictatorship: "Soviet man, crawling on his knees to betray his family and friends to slow butchery"; "A world in which human dignity counts for nothing"; a world in which "it is thought right and proper that men should be groveling slaves, bowing down before the semi-divine beings who embody the greatness of the state.

"It is this conception that we have to fight," he cried, "a conception which . . . would, if it prevailed, take everything out of life that gives it value, leaving nothing but a regimented collection of groveling animals. I cannot imagine a greater or more profound cause for which to fight."

During the eight years since that battle call was issued, the "regimented collection of groveling animals," with no change in its nature, has steadily gained ground throughout the world. The fight to which we were so gloriously summoned, though more desperate, is still being fought. And what has become of our intellectual standard bearer now, our great philosopher who came down from the heights of pure reason to summon us into battle for "all human values?" He sits aloft once more and informs us that "anti-Communism" may be classified with Communism as a "dogmatic and fanatical belief in some doctrine for which there is no evidence." "Nationalism, Fascism, Communism, and now anti-Communism," he says, "have all produced their crop of bigoted zealots ready to work untold horror in the interests of some narrow creed." *

And to certify this surrender to the enemy of all human values, he contributes a preface to another book written by one of the most unabashed defenders of that "regimented collection of groveling animals" in the western world, Cor-

* *Portraits From Memory,* p. 38.

liss Lamont.* In this preface he reaches the climax of a series of slanders against America that would, in a man less famed for the achievements of his mind, seem very nearly insane. I will quote but one example of this wild talk, since it is no pleasure to dwell on these flights of the feather-like partner in the firm of Bertrand Russell.

"Members of the FBI join even mildly liberal organizations as spies and report any unguarded word. Anybody who goes so far as to support equal rights for colored people, or to say a good word for the UN, is liable to visit by officers of the FBI and threatened, if not with persecution, at least with blacklisting and consequent inability to earn a living. When a sufficient state of terror has been produced by these means, the victim is informed that there is a way out: if he will denounce a sufficient number of his friends, he may obtain absolution."

I imagine that Bertrand Russell regards it as an example of unprejudiced logic to liken the extremes of intolerance to which the passion of the fight against Communism has carried certain individuals in America to the systemized brutalities of the totalitarian police state. To my mind it suggests, rather, a deep-lying and irrational prejudice.

But that is not the point I wished to make in concluding this essay. The error underlying everything Russell now says about the "great fight" to which he summoned us so gloriously was present already in the summons. It is not a *"conception"* we have to fight, but a *conspiracy*—a conspiracy by seizing political power to force that conception upon an unwilling world. The problem is indeed complex and

* *Freedom Is as Freedom Does.* Preface in the English edition only.

subtle how a relatively free society can, without destroying its own freedom, defeat such a conspiracy. There is room here for a wide latitude of opinion. But no opinion deserves respect which ignores the fact that it is a conspiracy. Not only did Russell ignore this in his original battle cry; he ignores it now when the whole thinking world is alive to it. He might without loss of dignity argue against the congressional investigation of subversive activities, but when he calls them *"supposed* subversive activities" (my italics), it appears that he has not had enough conscience or intellectual pride to study the subject he is persuading us about. He has not examined the programmatic literature of international Communism, or given a glance to such critical texts on the subject as Sidney Hook's *Heresy Yes—Conspiracy No.* He is avoiding, as though deliberately, the factors in his problem which make it difficult to solve. That is not the way one employs his mind when delving to the logical *Principles of Mathematics,* or attempting to establish beyond a possibility of doubt the extent and limitations of human knowledge. For his own sake, as well as ours, we have to perceive that there are two Bertrand Russells, one disciplined and conscientious, the other glib and in a measure irresponsible.

Charlie Chaplin: Memories and Reflections

Motoring down from Paris to Florence not long ago, I paused at Vevey on the Lake of Geneva and drove up the hill to the villa where Charlie Chaplin is living his new life, surrounded with green sloping lawns, wide-spreading trees, and six—if you can believe it, six—beautiful children. It is so amazing a conclusion to the life he is supposed to have led, and so large a surprise even to me, his quite close friend in the life he did lead, that I felt I must have a look at it. We had a very beautiful Muriel, a Parisian girl, in the car with us, and this, I was sure, would mitigate an unannounced intrusion on Charlie's fastidiously private life. Nobody showed up for a long time after I announced to the butler an old friend from America.

Finally, as we stood waiting, Muriel espied a grey head peering from an upstairs sun-deck to see who we were. Whether it was her beauty or my identity that brought him down, I don't know, but in a few seconds Charlie appeared at the door with a beaming smile and a two-handed welcome. He was nervous though—at least that was Eliena's opinion and Muriel's. He led us all over the estate, pointing out all the trees and flowers, the stone walls, the tennis court, the garage, the vegetable garden, and talking a blue streak all the time. He seemed, in their opinion, to be trying to put off the moment when I would say what I came for. I too noticed that his stream of talk was continuous and there were no questions in it, but it did not occur to me that our political differences might be prominent in his mind, and he might think I had come on some sort of propaganda mission. Whether that was true or not, the tension did not relax and the talk become general, until we got back to the house and Oona came down to serve tea— gracious and warm and simple-mannered—and a child or two showed up for a biscuit. Then Charlie's apprehension, if he had one, disappeared, and he seemed to realize that I had dropped in for old friendship's sake and nothing else.

He was the most famous man in the world when I met him in 1919. Woodrow Wilson had just made a triumphal passage through the capitals of Europe, but vaster crowds would have followed Charlie Chaplin. In the History of Great Fame—when that book is written—no chapter will be more astounding than that in which this little modest actor of one role, his birth timed and his genius cut and trimmed to fit a new kind of entertainment, became in three short years known and loved by more men, and more races and classes of men, than anyone, even the great religious leaders, ever had been before.

The story will give pause to those who think that subtle and mature art is incompatible with mass popularity. For Chaplin's acting was mainly distinguished from that of his colleagues by what, to my mind at least, is the subtlest and most mature of all values, power in reserve. He loves to *not quite* do something, letting his audience feel the more exquisitely what it would be if he did it.

Our friendship began on the note of this mutual taste. I was rather notorious at the moment, being about the only Socialist agitator who had opposed the World War and supported the Russian revolution, and yet managed to stay out of jail. I traveled to the West Coast soon after the Armistice, while the famous "Palmer raids" were still suppressing what they called sedition. It was more like a sortie from a besieged city than a lecture tour. My meetings were the first opportunity the radicals had had for a long two years to make their voices heard, and they came out in mobs. The police came too. There were forty of them lined up like great blue smooth-feathered birds-of-prey around the inside of the Philharmonic Auditorium where I spoke in Los Angeles. My friend Bob Wagner came up afterwards, while I was shaking hands with people, and whispered:

"Charlie Chaplin is in the wings and would like to meet you!"

If he had said "Julius Caesar," I would not have been

more astonished or delighted. To crown my delight, Charlie's first words when we shook hands were in genuine admiration of what he termed my eloquence.

"You have what I consider the essence of all art," he said,
"even of mine, if I may call myself an artist—restraint."

"Well—did you see those policemen?" I said.

But we both knew that was not what he meant. For my
part, I was so surprised to hear just that remark coming out
of Hollywood that it has remained verbatim in my memory: "If I may call myself an artist!"

We had supper together that night, and the next day I
went out to the little row of English-village houses on La
Brea Avenue that formed the street front of his studio. It
was the only studio in Hollywood that did not look like a
freight yard. We swam together in his marble pool, and
talked again all afternoon, and had our "movie" taken
eating raw lemons like apples off a tree. I was, as almost
everyone is, quite as captivated by the real Chaplin as by
the Chaplin on the screen.

Humor is a playful thing: it isn't there if you take it
seriously. It is natural, therefore, that the world's favorite
humorist should have turned out to be the world's most
charming playmate. I would back Charlie Chaplin against
anyone I ever met to cast a spell—if he wanted to—over
the most hardboiled and leather-hided visitor of either sex
that you could bring around. Something, however, deeper
than his charm appealed to me in him that day. Perhaps
his prodigious fame had to do with it; any instinctive hero-
worshipper has a weakness in that direction. But that was
not all. Charlie Chaplin seemed to my mind and my immediate perceptions a great man, and I was moved, with that

in the back of my head, to study and try to understand him. Maybe my understanding of him will throw some light on his equivocal position in the world today.

Most entertaining people are egotistically aware of it, but Charlie has a deep modesty. Like all actors, of course —and actors in this are very much like human beings—he would rather be in the center of the stage than off in a corner. But he has the gift of admiring others, and the rarer gift of listening to them with vivid and prolonged interest. He is high-strung and aesthetic, with an instantaneous distaste for anything false-faced or cheap, and no hesitation about extruding it from his attention or abruptly leaving it. That got him lots of enemies, especially in Hollywood where plenty was false-faced and cheap. But among people he likes he is in the depth of his heart humble, a poor boy who had no opportunities and is eager to learn. Once long ago, but when already at the height of his prodigious fame, he showed me with the pride of a child who has won a prize, a letter of appreciation from H. G. Wells.

"He's quite a writer, isn't he? Isn't he pretty well thought of?" he said, putting the treasured letter carefully back in his breast pocket.

Next to this ability to receive as well as to give, without which all charm is brassy and hard-surfaced, I found the main elements of Charlie's magnetism to be a restless intellect and imagination, humor, good looks, grace, agility, and a gift of bringing, or if need be dancing, everything he mentions into being by the instinctive motions that accompany his speech. I say "intellect" with malice toward some, who, lacking the real thing themselves, liked to think that Charlie's endless, genuine, and fertile interest in thinking was a pose. People naturally at home in the world of ideas are always thus misjudged if they happen to be alive also in the world of things. Charlie is alive all the way around. He never had any schoolroom discipline to speak of, and he reads a big book like Spengler's *Decline of the West,* for instance, by a hop-skip-and-jump process that is remote indeed from scholarship. But he makes no bluff to the contrary—not with me, at least. And he offers what he has to say about such a book as a curious shell picked up in a stroll along the beach, not a compendium of the ocean. The shell *is* always curious, always relevant, always has some curve or color of its own. That is why I say he has intellect as well as imagination.

"In the matter of reading," he said to me once, "I am an Epicurean—a very little food for thought is enough!"

"I went and *bought* a lot of books," he said at another time, "and now I've got to read them! But I have to be choosy because I'm a very slow reader. It's hard for me to concentrate on a book. For that reason I hardly read modern literature at all. Only very recently I discovered Joyce's short stories. Some of those I've read three or four times. That one story *Clay* says more about human character in ten pages than ten volumes of Dickens."

Charlie's eyes are of the very darkest blue, the color that the camera likes best. They are "honest" and "unflinching" eyes, set deeply in a noble brow, and when he lies to people because he does not like them or their questions, they make him very persuasive. They have filled the world full of contradictory stories about him, all honestly believed—a state of affairs pleasing to him because of his reticence. The lower part of his face is not so noble as his brow and eyes, his mouth not quite so unflinching. But the trim grace and veritable perfection of his build and carriage, which is that of the prince of tumblers, tap dancers, tightrope walkers— the prince of agility and poise—harmonize with the classic perfection of his head to make a unitary impression of great beauty. He seems to possess, above all, complete and exquisite integration.

And this too is misleading—or was at the time of our friendship—for he impressed me then as having no unity of character, no principles or conviction, nothing in his head that, when he laid it on the pillow, you could sensibly expect would be there in the morning. He was an actor so deep down and completely that, if you let his charm bewitch you into resting any hope on what he said, you would certainly sooner or later find that hope floating in the air.

"Oh I know Charlie well—we're intimate friends. In fact, he's dining at my house tomorrow. Why don't you drop in and meet him?" Thousands of people have said that, almost everybody, in fact, with whom Charlie ever enjoyed a long evening's conversation. And they have said it, usually, to all their best or most important friends and relatives. The friends and relatives *have* dropped in, all of them, bringing their important friends and relatives along. The board has been made festive, the cocktails have been passed around, the conversation has grown unnaturally animated, the ringing of the doorbell has been awaited with eagerness—surprise—impatience—consternation—mortification—despair—and Charlie never heard from again from that day to this.

Nobody "knew Charlie well" who did not know how deep down he was an actor. Barring a few elementary trends like a fine distaste for shoddy, an intellectual sympathy for revolutionists, a collector's mania toward dollars, and a frank and reliable liking for his own ease and comfort, it was safest not to bank on his qualities at all—much less his opinions. The day after he so praised my radical speech in Los Angeles I heard him express a glowing belief in slavery as an immortal institution, backing it up with arguments and illustrating it with a pantomime that left his hearers breathless if not convinced. About the same time—1920-21—he made this remark: "Any perfectly free and profound intelligence would be Bolshevik today. H. L. Mencken, for instance, if he should really get down and study the problems of life. But I hope he won't, for he's more entertaining as an acrobat."

To the best of my belief he expressed both these opinions, or acted both these parts, without any mental reservations, and he has acted many others quite as contradictory and conclusive. His genius is essentially dramatic, and in the long run subtle understanding has to content you in the place of character. It did content me, and I think that is one reason why we were good friends for so many years. I sensed very early, through watching with keen attention these wholly unintegrated flights of his mind, that he could not be relied upon to be, or continue to be, anything in particular, and I never expected him to. If he was irresponsible toward me, instead of nursing the injury, I cured it by being irresponsible toward him. Chained down as I am by a puritan conscience in matters of social obligation, I enjoyed the moral holiday.

Another matter in which I got "wise" to Charlie very early was that collector's mania I spoke of. I was raising

money for our magazine, *The Liberator,* on the trip West
when I first met him, and when he so generously praised
my speech I hoped he might react similarly to an appeal
for funds by my traveling companion, Isaac McBride. He
did say he wanted to help, and said it with some warmth,
and then gave us twenty-five dollars. If he had said he
didn't want to help and given us twenty-five dollars, I
would have learned something else. As it was, I learned
right there never to try to drag Charlie in, as I did most of
my rich friends, on various schemes of social reform.
Charlie liked radical ideas; he liked to talk about trans-
forming the world; but he didn't like to pay for the talk,
much less the transformation.

Of course, when you've made an emphatic remark like
that about a born actor, you have to turn right around and
make another almost opposite. Once Charlie happened to
arrive in New York just as our bookkeeper ran away with
the last three thousand dollars in *The Liberator's* till. I received a lot of commiseration from all sides, but Charlie
said the only thing that seemed to me halfway logical. He
said:

"I can't make it all up to you, but I've got a thousand I
can spare."

He isn't stingy, you see. It is more subtle than that. He
is *anxious* about money. He might just as well have given
me the whole three thousand, or a million. But he
couldn't, because he lives in dread of poverty. He grew up
in dread of poverty. When he was nine, his mother took
him to an orphan asylum and left him there for two years
because she could not feed him. Experiences like that in
childhood leave channels of scar tissue in which the feelings

flow, no matter what the mind says. Charlie is afraid all the time that he will be taken to that orphan asylum again. I spent a luxurious month once in his house on Summit Avenue, and the coffee came up every morning not in cups, but in two-handled soupbowls from which one of the handles had been broken off. It seemed a sensible idea—they were just *like* cups—but somehow it didn't fit into the general atmosphere of life among the movie millionaires of Beverly Hills. It was the little waif Chaplin, the poor boy from London's East End, almost the same one you saw on the screen, being careful about expense.

The harvest days of our friendship were in 1920 and 1921, when I went out to Hollywood to be far from *The Liberator*—and near a beautiful actress I loved—while writing a book on *The Sense of Humor*. Charlie was devoted to my actress too, and our friendship became a three-cornered one in which a lot of unusual emotions were given a place in the sun. As I look back upon those winters, Charlie and I seem to have been together almost every evening, playing charades and the speechmaking game and the drama game. We had to give up charades finally, because we found our whole energy going into all-night sessions of it, and neither of us doing a stroke of work in the daytime.

I must explain that those charades of ours were not little impromptu guessing games; they were elaborately worked out dramas and scenic spectacles, in the preparation of which all human experience and the entire contents of Charlie's house would be levied on. His dining room opened through a wide archway into the library, and it had two exits at the opposite corners, one into the kitchen and one that went upstairs. There was a curtain in the archway that could be drawn, and thus the whole living part of the house would be converted into a theater. Without disturbing the guests, you could sneak up those back stairs and ransack their wardrobes, if any of them had had the hardihood to come for the night. Charlie and I would always choose the sides, and we would choose them the day before, inviting to dinner those whom we each wanted on our team. We got so expert at this game that we thought a charade was no good if it didn't have continuity—the first syllable being the first act of a play, the next the second act, etc.

It is not easy to get people into a mood at once energetic enough and relaxed enough to enter into such exploits, and that is where the speech-making game came in. It was a creation of mine, a revenge I took for my long years of suffering before audiences who wouldn't give me any help.

We played it this way: one end of the room would be cleared of people, and regarded as a platform. Everyone would write the subject of a speech on a slip of paper, fold it tight, and drop it into a hat. We always had to warn them to write a serious subject, not a funny one—the fun would come afterward. And we had to make everyone in the room honestly agree to play: if anyone hung back, they all would. Then the host or ringmaster—whoever was engineering the game—would take out his watch, and pass the hat to the first person on the left of the platform. He— or she—had to draw a folded paper from the hat, mount the platform, face the audience, unfold and read it aloud, and make a speech one minute long on the subject read. If he could not think of a word to say, he had to stand there facing the audience just the same, until the minute was up.

It is one way of finding out how long a minute is. And it is an unfailing means of limbering people up to the point of playing charades. After they have suffered through one of those lonely minutes, they are ready for anything that is done in company.

Charlie improved on my speech-making game by passing two hats, in one of which a subject was dropped, in the other the description of a character. Then we had to make a speech *on* the subject and *in* the character. This soon involved costumes and became almost as formidable as charades. I vividly remember Charlie as a "Toothless Old Veteran" discoursing on "The Benefits of Birth Control." He rises before my mind's eye, too, completely costumed and made up as Carrie Nation, delivering, hatchet in hand, a lecture on "Some Doubts as to the Origin of Species." It was in one of our games that he first preached the sermon on David and Goliath that forms a hilarious climax in *The Pilgrim*. When I saw it my mind traveled back to the evening I first introduced him to the speech-making game, and he stood up there valiantly for one minute—fussed and embarrassed as a schoolgirl, giggling and saying absolutely nothing. He was trying to be himself. As soon as he caught on to the trick of acting a part he adored it.

Charlie devised what we called the drama game, to take the place of those charades after they got so elaborate that neither his picture, *The Kid*, nor my book was getting any attention at all. For this game we would drop into the hat titles suitable for one-act plays. We would divide the company into couples, and each couple would draw a subject. After consultation, and a raid on the wardrobes upstairs, they would put on a one-act play corresponding to that title, making up the dialogue as they went along. Of all the "parlor games" I ever played, that is the best fun.

In Moscow, a little later, I saw this same kind of fun put on the stage. In the mood of creative adventure that followed the revolution, an impromptu theater called *Semper Ante* was set up by a group of witty actors, and played to full houses for almost ten years.

Besides these inimitable night's entertainments, the gayest events of that kind in my life,* I used to hang around Charlie's studio and watch him make pictures, learning much of what I put in my book on humor there. He was doing the cocktail-shaker gag in *The Idle Class* one afternoon. The hero, you may remember, is an alcoholic, and he receives a letter from his absent wife saying she will never come home again unless he stops drinking. He is standing in front of a table on which sits her portrait, and also some bottles and a cocktail shaker. He takes up the portrait and gazes at it, tears pouring from his eyes and great sobs shaking him. He turns around to set it down on a table, and the sobs continue to shake him, his shoulders rising more and more rapidly, until the audience can hardly bear it. Is Charlie going sentimental, after all? Then he turns gradually back, a look of sublime abstraction in

* To show that this was not a one-sided gaiety, I will quote from *Mes Voyages*, the French edition of Charlie's little book describing his trip to Europe in 1921:

"Lunch today with Max Eastman, one of my best friends. He tells me of a party at his house the same evening, and I gladly accept his invitation.

. . . What an evening! I really escaped from myself. My emotions ran the whole gamut from laughter to tears without an artificial moment. It was for this that I had left Los Angeles . . ."

his eyes and his shoulders in motion because he is gently agitating a cocktail shaker.

Charlie performed that little act nine times while I watched him, consulting me each time, of course—that too is a part of his charm—and later we went to the projection room together and chose the best of the nine. It did not satisfy him, and he went back on the set the next day and did it nine times more.

It was understood between us that I was going to write about him some day, and I would often take down remarks he made, or answers to my prying questions. I asked him about that cocktail-shaker gag:

"How did it come to you? Did you think it up when you were writing the scenario, or just happen to do it on the set?"

I liked his answer even better than the gag.

"Max, it isn't mine at all. It was suggested to me by a man on the set."

Charlie brought his mother over from England while I was in Hollywood, and gave her a comfortable house to pass her last days in. She was a little crazy, but was aware of it and able to manage it some of the time.

It had been difficult on account of her mental state to get her into the country, and she had been instructed to be very careful when talking to the immigration officials. Her mind got out of hand, however, and her first word when one of them approached was:

"You are Jesus Christ!"

Then she remembered what she had been told, and added with a sane and engaging smile:

"I mean by that, sir, that when I looked in your eyes I

realized, notwithstanding the blue cap, that you have a gentle and spiritual nature!"

She came through with flying colors—a perfectly bewitching woman. Almost nobody knew that she was in Hollywood, and it was a day in my life when Charlie took me to see her. She was rosy-faced, red-haired, very cockney English, a music-hall singer and dancer by profession. She put on the phonograph and did us a merry little song and dance. There was a canary on the piano. He chirped in the midst of her dance, and she stopped—her gay expression turned to utter pathos. "Poor thing, he's lonely here!" she said, or sang—for it was all in time to the music—and then she was dancing merrily again, and she twirled at the end, and with the last note sat down accurately and lightly in the chair she had risen from.

Charles Spencer Chaplin, Senior, was an entertainer too —a "topical vocalist" is the way he is billed on a yellowing poster in his son's possession. Maybe he was a good topical vocalist—nobody seems to know—but I thought I saw the source of Charlie's genius in his mother.

There was a large gap in our friendship after those Hollywood days. I went away to Russia and France and was a long time coming home. Charlie meantime seemed to have been entertaining the world more with his marital problems than his pictures. I hate marital problems, and was glad the Lita Grey episode evolved to its inevitable end without my personal attention. Fourteen years had elapsed since our gay evenings together, when I found myself again strolling over to the little studio on La Brea Avenue. I wondered if I would find Charlie as much changed as all the rest of Hollywood. The lazy little toy village I remembered, with its population of child millionaires, had turned into a "business center" now. There were three small memory-laden cottages I wanted to get sentimental over, but I couldn't find them—they were gone!

"Will Charlie also have turned into a business center?" I asked myself. And I asked it with trepidation, for that is one of the ways in which he could degenerate. At least so I thought, for I never could understand his passion for the national currency. Moreover, there was a general impression then that Charlie was about through making pictures. I found him in the projection room, discussing with his staff the first two reels of *Modern Times,* which had just been run off. Paulette Goddard was there, looking so intelligently and brightly beautiful that it seemed as though the heavens themselves had dropped a star into his lap. And he himself was at the top of his form, standing out in front of the little audience, entertaining them with an illustrated lecture on the picture's merits and defects—illustrated, I mean, with the old inimitable pantomime. I saw no change to speak of.

We went up to his new home, after he had run off those two reels for me, and played a game of tennis, and spent a long evening talking. Far from having degenerated, or being in the least unbalanced about his work, Charlie seemed to me to have gained both in poise and self-confidence. It did not bother him that most people thought he was on the shelf. He answered quite casually when I asked him why his tempo of production had slowed down from a picture every seven days on the old Keystone lot to a picture every seven years.

"I'm more finicky, I guess," he said. "I care more about

making it good. Besides, it was new—the whole industry was new in those days. Everything was exciting. We had no scenarios even, at first. We would finish a picture on Saturday, and say, 'Well, now we must get a story for Monday.' On Monday we wouldn't have a story, but one would develop out of the props and the people who happened to be standing around. You'd say, 'Well, can I have a couple of policemen this morning?' And if they said yes, you'd say, 'How about a coupla bricks?' And if you got those too, there was your story. Everybody has slowed up, as a matter of fact."

"Yes, but not the way you have," I said, "not so much that the public is worried for fear they've quit altogether."

"Well, why worry?" he said. "Why this terrible insistence on work? Work is a beastly thing, especially when it gets to be a kind of religion. 'If you don't work, you can't eat'—they've got to offer us something better than that in the communist society. It's too damn irksome and nasty. I'd like to see a state of society where everybody could get up in the morning and say, 'Well, it's all right, I don't have to work!'

"Look at the animals. They don't put the moral aspect on life all the time. So many gorgeously beautiful creatures —with poise and dignity! Think of a lion—unmolested by these bustling humans. He lives a magnificent life, works when he has to, and then sits, leisurely and sufficient, blinking at the sunset and playing with the cubs!"

I could not possibly help thinking of a lion while he spoke, for he became the lion. And I could not worry quite so much about his slower tempo. Within limits, it seemed reasonable. It seemed, in fact—this revolt against the high-pressure production mania that has corrupted so many American artists—another sign of promise in a remarkably promising young man.

"Besides," he added, "I find less satisfaction than I used to in merely entertaining people. As one grows older he wants to do something that will give him some spiritual satisfaction. I hate that word 'spiritual,' but you know what I mean."

In one way we had both changed in those fourteen years —our being together no longer compellingly suggested play. Jimmie Cagney was there, I remember—a natural for the drama game—and two other people limber enough to enter into one of the old hilarious evenings. But something else wasn't there—youth, I suppose, and the gay, intelligent laughter and vivacity of the girl we had both been so fond of. Instead of playing we talked, and what we talked about was work.

I asked him how he had come to make the picture *Modern Times*.

"It started from an abstract idea," he said, "an impulse to say something about the way life is being standardized and channelized, and men turned into machines—and the way I feel about it. I knew that was what I wanted to do before I thought of any of the details."

I reminded him that he had conceived of the picture years before, and had even photographed one of the gags. I described it to him: a beggar sits on the sidewalk at a busy intersection; the public hurries by, like automata or German soldiers on the quick-step; every so often one of them turns briskly aside to hand the beggar a nickel; he receives it in the same perfunctory manner and rings it up on a cash register!

"That's modern life," he said to me then, "everything mechanized and regimented—even charity!"

Charlie had completely forgotten this; he did not even remember the gag. But it is a fact—and one which acquired some significance later—that for several weeks in 1921 he was sowing this brilliant notion abroad in conversations, careless, as he always is, with such riches. One of our playmates in those days was the French director, Maurice Tourneur, and it is not unimaginable that through him Charlie's idea for a modern comedy traveled to France. When *Modern Times* came out, René Claire and the producers of *À Nous la Liberté* sued Charlie Chaplin for plagiarism. After a while they withdrew the suit—wisely, as my recollection proves. Whatever sins this genius may have on his conscience (or what takes the place of conscience in a complete actor), plagiarism is not among them.

I had another book on humor, *Enjoyment of Laughter,* in mind, and I fell back that evening into my old habit of studying my gifted friend with pencil in hand. I will recall here what he said about his creative moods and methods. I asked him if his pictures always start from an abstract idea, and he hesitated.

"That is the way I like to have them start," he said. "I like to wake up some morning with a desire to say something—a feeling, I suppose I mean, about something. To take a simpler example, I find the idea of a tramp and a gamin together attractive. They meet in a patrol wagon and start life again. That is attractive. I must find out what exactly is the thing that is attractive about it. That's where the intellect comes in. I must bring this idea or feeling to the fore. I must bring it to the noetic mind. I must work back from it to a total situation by reasoning. I enjoy that phase. I enjoy gnawing at an idea.

"Maybe I enjoy it too much, and that's why I don't produce as often as I used to. These days, if I don't feel jolly I just put it off. I've got used to these spells of dullness now, and they don't worry me. They used to worry me to death. 'You're through,' I'd say. 'You've lost your creative streak for good!' Now I just stay in bed and think. I start in thinking at seven and finish at four when I'm seeking a story. It's a pure matter of sticking to it. I've gone as much as a month without a creative thought, messing around with some notion that seemed to me as though it ought to contain one. 'Hell, you can't make a story out of that,' I'd say. 'Yes, but you can stick to it until a story comes!'

"There's no use just sitting down and waiting for an inspiration, though. You've got to play along. The main thing you've got to do is preserve your vitality. A couple of days of complete rest and solitude helps. Not seeing anybody. I even conserve my emotions. 'I'm not going to get excited about anybody or anything,' I say, 'until I get this gag worked out.' I go along that way, living a quiet and righteous life, and then I stay out late one night, and have a couple of drinks—perhaps all night—and the next morning the reserve pours out. But you've got to have the reserve. Dissipation is no use except as a release. You've been damming it up inside of you, and all of a sudden you say: 'Oh, here it is!' And then you go to work."

A couple of years after *Modern Times* came out, I received a telephone call from Paulette Goddard asking me if Eliena and I wouldn't come out to Hollywood and stay with them for a while. She said she thought I would do Charlie good. I surmised that "do Charlie good" meant get him to make another picture and put Paulette in it. But that was all right, and I said I would come if he also wanted me. I got a telegram the same night:

"Expecting you. Charlie."

For various reasons we put off going for almost two months, and were extremely casual about it, merely telegraphing toward the last the probable date of our arrival. I found Charlie surrounded with a pile of manuscripts almost half his size.

"I'm learning to write," he said. "All these papers you see around here are scenarios with dialogues in them."

"You're learning to talk!" I said.

"Well, I may not talk myself. I may just direct a picture for Paulette, but what I'm interested in now is writing. I don't see how you do it. It all seems wonderful to me when it pours out. I thought every one of these sheets was a masterpiece when I wrote it. But when I look at it the next day I think it's terrible."

The upshot of it was that he thought we might work together—we had played together so often.

"I really would like to collaborate with you on a talking picture," he said.

It seemed natural—indeed it was not a new idea—and with Paulette's ambition pushing in the same direction, it even seemed probable. But Eliena, who adored Charlie, was a good deal more excited about it than I was.

"Remember what I've told you," I said. "Enjoy any

Charlie Chaplin you have the good luck of a chance to. But don't try to link them up into anything you can grasp. There are too many of them. The one that wants to collaborate with me is, in my opinion, sensible, but I doubt if he lives through the night."

He did live through the night and all the next day. After tennis in the afternoon, Charlie said:

"If you'll come up to my room after breakfast tomorrow we'll start in by going through some of these mountains of stuff I've written, and see if any of it is any good."

The next morning before I got up, Charlie left for Monterey, thinking he could write better if he got away from Paulette—which, at the moment, was undoubtedly correct. He left word that I was to have his sunny bedroom to write in. When he came back to play host again, the idea of our collaboration had vanished from the agenda. He never mentioned it again, nor did I. Nor did it make any difference. I had no complaint. I had paid off his casualness in advance.

One day, after he had had time to get tired of the social maelstrom that followed the premiere of *The Great Dictator,* I sent Charlie a telegram at the Waldorf Astoria:

"Come on up Sunday and bring a companion. I've got a new game."

When Frank, his Japanese parent-valet, called up to say that he would come, I invited Edmund Wilson, the literary critic, and his gifted wife, Mary McCarthy, to come over from Stamford, and got my friend Charles Reitell, a doctor of sick industries by profession, to bring some of his intelligence and personality tests along. In inviting these guests, I explained that Charlie Chaplin might or might not be there.

Charlie arrived at noon with a gentle and warm-eyed companion from Brooklyn, and we played with those tests, and discussed them, and discussed everything under the sun, until one-thirty that night. It was like old times in Hollywood. Somewhat to our surprise Bunny Wilson, who is a distinctly literary person, made a phenomenal score in the test for operators of delicate machinery. Dr. Reitell guaranteed him a sixty-dollar-a-week job on application. On the same test, I was marked way down for "labored accuracy." "Don't hire this man" was written across my sheet.

Charlie pleaded the absence of his reading glasses and did only one eighth of the test—perfectly. The rest of the time he spent denouncing the whole idea of classifying human beings.

"These tests tell nothing," he said. "People are individuals; they aren't bunches of attributes. You have to know them with your intuitions before you know them."

The Wilsons left about midnight, and a few minutes after they went out, Bunny stuck his head back through the door:

"Max, I can't seem to start my car. I wonder if you know anything about engines!"

Charlie jumped right out of his chair with delight. "There you are!" he exclaimed. "That shows you what these tests are worth! Wilson the great machine operative—sixty dollars a week as a mechanic—and he has to come back and ask a poet to start his car!"

Just the same, Dr. Reitell knew a lot more about us when

he went home than he could have found out in months of ordinary conversation. In particular, I thought, he had the low-down on Charlie and me, and the reasons for our long mutual understanding. Our "personality inventory" showed a surprising number of traits in common. On "emotional instability" Charlie made a score of 84 per cent —50 percent being the average, and 98 per cent indicating a visit to the psychiatrist, at the very least.

"Your high score there," Dr. Reitell said in a kindly way, "assures you of the ability to dramatize your public. You overfeel for them their emotions. . . ."

He did not offer any such consoling reflections on my still closer approach to the loony bin. My score was 87 per cent.

The doctor's inventory attributed one trait to Charlie that indubitably belongs to him, and makes him stand out almost solitary among the weakly gregarious and garrulous brain wasters of the movie world. That is a high degree of "self-sufficiency."

"Your score of 77 per cent in this trait indicates," the doctor announced, "that you prefer to be alone, rarely ask for sympathy, and tend to ignore the advice of others."

The phrase is a picture of Charlie in Hollywood—or above it. It explains both the awe—if the word is not too strong—and the resentment with which many of its more convivial celebrities regarded him. It explains also the dreadful state of mercy-turned-into-rage that girls would get into when their almost universal impulse to become his mother—welcomed at a certain distance—found the inner citadel impregnable.

And not girls only. There is an impulse in all affection to

try to "get hold of" its object—to make sure that he depends enough upon its warmth, to be there whenever a returning warmth is needed. Charlie doesn't depend upon any warmth that much—not even when he is in love. He is sufficient unto himself.

This trait frightens some people and gets them mad. It gives me the pleasure of admiration. I do think, however, that in the later years it grew on him and gave rise to flaws in his work. Like most brooding artists, Charlie is hypersensitive, and gets very sad if you tell him something he has just done is no good. Nevertheless, he always used to have some robust critic around the studio, like Eddie Sutherland, a good director himself, who would say: "Aw, Charlie, cut that gag short—it's a bore!" Charlie would go into a gloom, and maybe quit work for a day or two. But when he emerged, he would emerge with a perfectly objective and correct appraisal of the criticism.

I remember feeling that in two of his later pictures he lacked that sort of corrective. He was indulging his touchiness. He was getting a taste for yes-men. It was a glaringly obvious flaw in *The Great Dictator* that there was no build-up toward the momentous speech made by the little barber at the end. The speech was crudely tacked on and, however pleasing to our passions during those war years, remains an addendum rather than a part of the picture. All he had to do to correct that was to give the little man a yen for speech-making—put in one or two ludicrously unsuccessful attempts to grab an audience before the grand chance comes. In matters of comedy or pathos Charlie is just the one who knows this best. He was thrown off his balance here, I think, by the weight of his feelings. A trifle less indulgence of that admirable "self-sufficiency" might have made both *Modern Times* and *The Great Dictator* better even than they are. There is no man so great that he cannot be helped.

In Charlie's inventory the score on "introversion" was 88 per cent—so high that the doctor exclaimed with surprise: "You are not so damn far from being a recluse! Seclusion from the world with solitude seems to be your idea of heaven!" This again increased my respect for the doctor's methods, for I had heard Charlie express that idea of heaven many times. Years ago, when we both thought—some of the time, at least—that a proletarian revolution was coming, he remarked:

"It's all right with me. I'm for the working class. But they needn't expect me on the barricades. I'm no hero—I've got too much imagination to be a hero. When the shooting starts, I'm going to take a loaf of bread and a can of sardines and beat it to the mountains."

He was climbing the mountains in a hurry while he said that—and then he climbed cautiously down again.

"I'll probably come back for a can opener, but that's all I'll ask of the revolution."

In those days, the general notion of living a hermit's life was never far from his thoughts. His home at that time was tucked away on a little walled-in hill with trees enclosing its private sky.

"If I had a moat and a drawbridge," he said when he showed it to me, "I could live here the year round all alone and be happy. I might let you in once in a while for a game of tennis, but only because I need exercise."

Another thing that vastly surprised our examiner was

Charlie's low score of 18 per cent on "dominance versus submission."

"You certainly fooled me on this one," he said, "I had always thought you would dominate others, but I find you a very submissive, peaceful, quiet type indeed."

On "self-confidence" Charlie's score was still lower— only 11 per cent.

"You are very hamperingly self-conscious," the doctor decreed, "and harbor definite feelings of inferiority. Any bold indications of aggressiveness, or strong assertions of power, are but a defense, a thin veneer, the cloaking of a timid, worried, and perturbed soul!"

Here I thought the doctor's system showed a serious defect. It failed to distinguish dominance as an ultimate fact from dominance as an immediate social attitude. It failed to realize that shy and diffident people often have a sovereign confidence in their own judgment, even if they have to go home and lock themselves into a soundproof chamber to find out which judgment is their own.

You could safely bet that, in any group engaged in making moving pictures, Chaplin, even though unknown, would soon turn out to be the boss. He would either become the boss or get kicked out as unmanageable. And yet you would see no clash of wills. He would never bristle or try to domineer. He hated that kind of thing so much that he evaded meeting one of our excessively red-blooded writers who, on a visit to Hollywood, was entertained by all the other stars.

"I like civilized people," he said.

It took this "submissive, quiet, peaceful type" only two months, after arriving in Mack Sennett's studio in Holly-

wood in 1914, a young kid and a total greenhorn, to become the director of every picture he appeared in. It took
him less than six months to change the whole character
and conception of cinema comedy prevailing there, if not
everywhere. But there is no record of any "indications of
aggressiveness" or "strong assertions of power." On the contrary, he bewildered everybody by behaving deferentially,
and even humbly, but just not doing what the director
told him to. Indeed, until the great news began to arrive
from the box offices, Charlie's independence on the set
was generally regarded as a special kind of stupidity. Mack
Sennett finally allowed him to direct a picture of his own
in sheer desperation.

"Let the damn fool find out for himself that it's not so
easy!"

But Charlie told me another story from those same days
which illustrates his self-distrust:

"Mack Sennett was paying me $175 a week, and when
the contract expired, Essenay offered me $3000 a week. I
went to Mack Sennett and told him I had had this offer. I
said that I would prefer to stay with him, if he would pay
me $1000 a week. He came back with an offer of a three-
year contract—$500 a week the first year, $1000 the second,
and $3000 the third.

"I knew I was popular. I had seen the crowds in the
street outside the theatres. But I also knew how transitory
such popularity is. I had grown up in the shadow of the
uncertainties of an entertainer's career. I wanted to cash in
on my popularity before it ran dry. I said to Mack Sennett:

" 'I'll accept your offer if you'll reverse it. Pay me $3000 a week the first year, $1000 a week the second, $500 a week the third, and I'll stay.'

"Sennett said it was an idiotic idea, and he wouldn't sign such a contract. But I meant it. I was ready to sign."

There is a shrewdness in such timidity, or near it, and Charlie is extremely shrewd. As a businessman he fell down only in matters demanding an adequate estimation of his own size. It did not seem funny to him to make out his income-tax reports on the theory that he and his half brother, Syd, who also "acts in the pictures," were partners. Even after paying up a million dollars in back taxes and penalties, he could not quite follow the government's logic!

Here is another example of his shrewdness—or inferiority complex, I don't know which:

I came into his room one morning at the Waldorf Astoria, and found him still in bed. His face wore, or assumed when he saw me, that expression of unutterable pathos that so often and so suddenly breaks your heart on the screen.

"What's the matter, Charlie?" I asked. "Why are you so sad?"

He reached over and picked up a slip of paper from the bed table.

"Look at this!" he said.

I took the paper and read—in the handwriting of his valet-secretary:

"The X——— Company offers you $877,000 for twenty-five fifteen-minute broadcasts."

I laughed. I thought his pathos was a joke. But it wasn't.

"I can't do it, you know," he said. And then, with in-

creased mournfulness: "I need the money too! The government just relieved me of a million dollars."

"Why can't you do it?" I said, "You can make a speech!"

"It isn't that," he said. "You know how I love speech-
making. I can't come that close to my public. I have to
remain a little remote and mysterious. They have to
romanticize me. I would lose more than that at the box
office if I made myself real and familiar over the radio."

To me, I must say, Charlie remained a mystery no
matter how real and familiar he grew—a baffling combination of cool and high judgment, with total submersion in
blind emotional drives. He loved advice; he loved a long
conversation in which the best minds in the world would
devote themselves to his problems and feel that they were
guiding an untutored and yet great creative genius. He
loved it the way a duck loves a shower bath. The advice was
always thoughtfully weighed and, in so far as it was really
good, "accepted." Everybody went home with a feeling
that important and rather intimate decisions had been
made. But if they were made on the other side of the moon,
they would have had as much effect on Charlie's course of
action.

There seemed to be some almost weird disconnection
between his earnest judgments and his acts of will. He is
not more neurotic, I think, than most creative artists. They
do have to be easy of access to all currents of emotion—the
doctor was perfectly right there. But Charlie makes less
effort to swim, less effort to keep his *head* above these
currents, than most thinking people. He not only never
acquired in childhood the habit of self-discipline, but
never apparently even caught on to the idea. It just doesn't

occur to him that he might stand up to a strong flow of feeling, or even move against it for a time, because his mind reminds him of something else. It doesn't occur to him to feel sorry when he hasn't. I have never heard him express regret. . . . But all of this applied only to his relations with people. Toward his art he had—in those days at least—conscience, integrity, discipline, patience, persistence, every good and great quality. Here again he had to be understood as an untrained waif, a dream-endowed gamin, a delicate-minded guttersnipe—a leaf of paper with sacred writings on it blown through the streets of a London slum.

You would understand him in that way if you knew him long enough. And very respectfully also—for he has great dignity—you would pity him a little, as you would his namesake on the screen. His life, when I knew him, was filled to the brim with what most lives consist of yearning after—wealth and fame and creative play and beautiful women—but he never knew how to enjoy any one of the four.

His failure to revel in fame is, I suppose, a credit to him. He is not only impatient of it, because he really loves to wander in the streets alone, but he is distrustful of its meaning. A person of his aristocratic tastes, if noble-born, might adore the masses and drink their adulation with credulity. But Charlie knows them too well. He is, so far as I can judge, sincerely and stubbornly unimpressed by numbers. If he had a choice between world-wide popularity and the praise of a few people whose judgment he respects, I believe he would veer toward the latter with the simplicity of a compass.

One day when he had been up to Croton to see me, I

drove him to town in my open Ford car, a Model-T that had seen better, and also more hushed and integrated days. I pulled it up alongside a Childs restaurant near Broadway, and we went in to have some griddle cakes and milk. Although we sat way back in the room, I became aware before long that the big window was filling up with peering faces. I watched Charlie with a curious interest, for to my more omnivorous egotism this trait of his was hard to believe in. He was at first smilingly annoyed. He got up and turned his back to the window.

"In my business you have to erect fortifications before you can enjoy a griddle cake," he said.

We finished quickly, and walked over to the car. . . . I neglected to mention that that old Ford was responsive to my every mood—if I happened to feel slightly embarrassed and in a hurry to get away, she never failed to burn out a spark plug or kick loose a connection. We sat there, painfully high up from the pavement, with the crowd steadily augmenting, and the car spitting and jerking in response to "Hello Charlie!" "Attaboy, Charlie!" "Go to it, Charlie!" "Give her the gas, Charlie!" Charlie bore up under it with apparent good nature. But when we got away, he cursed that crowd with a venom that astonished me.

"I can't understand that," I said, "I should think you would like their affection."

"It isn't affection, it's egotism," he said. "None of those people cared a damn about me. If they did, they wouldn't embarrass me. They were thinking about themselves, feeling bigger because they had seen me and could go and brag about it."

After he cooled down, he told me how differently the London crowds behaved.

"When I went down to the East End to visit my old haunts," he said, "word got round, and a regular mob collected. But they always stayed as much as a hundred feet away, kind of hushed and whispering to each other. They never addressed me. They made me feel that I was loved—but not these New Yorkers. I know them!"

As usual, he had sensed an underlying truth and delved it up, but it is a truth that most people would be willing to leave buried for the sake of their own complacence. Mark Twain had a similarly undeluded perception of men, but it never marred his childlike joy in his own popularity.

Charlie's failure to get any fun out of his money was not so healthy. It was more purely due to his deprived childhood. He was so much more keenly aware of the enormous expense of running a studio than of the infinitely more enormous income from his pictures and securities that he felt poor all the time. The whole fable of his sudden fortune was beyond the grasp of this unhappy infant, and his imagination got hold of the size of it only on the debit side. Hence he took no pleasure in giving, no pleasure in having, no pleasure in spending, money—a misfortune that kept him in touch, at least, with the common man!

Another thing that I thought Charlie did not know how properly to enjoy was girls. Girls occupied almost as important a place in his life as dollars, and they caused him even more anxiety. It was not because there were more of them. There honestly weren't so many. But girls unfortunately are not, like dollars, all just alike. They differ fantastically. A susceptibility to their charms, therefore, is not a steady and firm propulsion like the trade winds, in relation to which a certain trend of character can be established and the hope cherished of really getting somewhere. They are a permanent source of contrary breezes, fluctuating and sudden gusts, gales, billows, storms, typhoons and hurricanes, which tear the character all to pieces.

Anybody in a public position who tries with some force and resolution to solve the problem of happiness in love gets surrounded with a lot of scandal which has no relation to any reality but the famished lusts of the scandalmongers. Charlie, as I knew him, would not have been easy to live with, not any easier than Lord Byron or a kaleidoscope. It required, as I have shown, a large initial act of understanding to be, or continue to be, his friend. Some of his girl friends had this understanding, and some hadn't. Some hadn't any understanding at all. But they all went in with their eyes open, and the opinion that there was something abnormal or monstrously heartless in his behavior toward women was an invention of the public, not a private fact. The private fact that explains Charlie's early matrimonial disasters is a very simple and very old one—namely, that love in people of poetic imagination is often blind, but if these people also possess intellect, love opens its eyes after a while, often quite suddenly, and *sees* the object of its attachment.

I once asked Charlie about one of his celebrated loves whom I had never met, and he answered:

"I thought she was divinely natural and real—I found she was only gawky and crude."

It was said in the manner of a person who has bought a fountain pen at the five-and-ten-cent store, and thrown it away when he looked it over. But that is the ruthlessness of a mind with a taste for knowing, however late, the essential truth. He did not need to tell me that the experience had been, in its lifetime, tinged with Eternity, as they incurably and always are.

There are few mismated wives who could not make a monkey out of a man by dragging out in the divorce court all the worst incidents they could remember—and then some. There are few mismated husbands who could not reciprocate, if they chose to. We are discussing the ways in which Charlie differed from others.

He was, to express it very simply, incurably romantic. He was as susceptible to feminine charms as Tom Moore or Robert Burns, and as given to lavish idealizations of the vessel in which they dwelt. He had a veritable genius for lyrical raptures about girls. At the same time, and deeper, he had the need for a woman friend and companion—a companion not of his senses only, but his mind. The classical approach, the approach of George to Martha Washington, to take a remote example, itemizing her qualities and status, and choosing her for a life companion on the grounds of her fitness for the job, could never occur to Charlie. He belongs to a different age and cult of living. He could not mold his personal life as he molds a picture, bringing its central problem to "the noetic mind" for analysis. In real life he skipped that delectable phase altogether. It just wasn't in him—at least when I knew him— to use his brains about women.

And the situation was complicated, if I am not mistaken, by the fact that he knew this. He sensed the total process before it began and watched it unfold with a sad, helpless, abstract understanding that must have been very trying to the victims of his adoration.

Charlie was in love, when very young and for a long time after, with a beautiful girl named Hetty who played in the theater where he first went on the stage. He came to America—he will admit in some moods—because Hetty was already booked to come. But he did not look her up when she came. He just thought about her. He could not believe she loved him—he was not egotistical enough. He let her slip out of his ken because of his diffidence—so the story goes. And when he went to London years after, still conscious of Hetty, still cherishing a dim yet tender "perhaps" in his breast, he learned that she had died. He brought home her photograph.

"It was nothing," he said when shyly showing me the photograph. "She was a fetish. I knew nothing about girls then." From which I inferred that Hetty was one of the momentous things in his life.

Still, I have a hunch that excess of self-protection, as well as lack of self-confidence, played its part in this sad story. He knew that he loved Hetty too much. He knew even then that she was a "fetish." He was afraid of her actual self. He was afraid if he won the girl, he would lose the romance.

And that hyperprudence, a kind of timorous canny clinging to what he's got, is the reason Charlie has not enjoyed his creative art to the full, or exploited to the full his unparalleled chance to enjoy it. His studio used to be as still as a cemetery a good deal of the time. This was not because he lacked energy or invention, or the funds, to fill it with a riot of experimental miracles. He lacked freehearted abandon. A good shot of generosity and recklessness—right into the blood stream—would have made a big difference.

If it is true, as Alexander Woollcott hazarded, that with his one little mute creation on the screen, Charlie Chaplin was "the foremost artist in the world," it is not extravagant to say that, if he had gathered a great gang around him, and *let himself go,* intellectually as well as poetically and financially, forgetting the box office, casting loose from the motion-picture industry altogether, he might have been one of the foremost artists of history. He might have rivaled Molière and Aristophanes—and had a good time besides.

How much this is Charlie's fault, and how much Hollywood's or America's, or the twentieth century's I do not not know. I only know that I have seen him do things when discoursing about what *might be done* in the modern cinema, if it were not for the "cost of production," the "ignorance of the public," the "risks of experimentation," the "censorship," or some other "if" that ought not permanently to paralyze the foremost artist in the world, which, if presented on the screen, would startle men's eyes, and their minds too, as much as his first appearance did. He has an audacity of invention and a versatility, or rather universatility, in the pure art of acting, of which his screen comedies conveyed no more than a hint.

I am afraid we are all implicated in this, Charlie, and Hollywood, and the twentieth century, and America—above all, America. For Charlie Chaplin is essentially an American humorist. Notwithstanding those early years in London, where he struggled up out of poverty by learning to tap dance and do an act, it was in the rough, democratic,

money-mad and sentimentally friendly atmosphere of an
American studio that he developed the art and imagined
the character that made him famous.

His not becoming an American citizen, about which so
much fuss has been made of late, was due to an indifference
to political institutions, not a preference for one or the
other. Had he been born in America and made his career
in England, he would not have bothered to become a
British subject. That is a fact which perhaps only artists
and anarchists can understand.

"Of course I am essentially American," he said to me one
day (and I wrote this down). "I feel American and I don't
feel British—that's the chief thing."

How he may feel now, I would not venture to guess. And
in our brief visit at Lausanne I was careful not to inquire.
The world is politically in such high tension these days that
old friends can hardly meet after a lapse of time without
rubber gloves on. I must say too, that I don't extend an un-
gloved hand to the servants of the totalitarian powers,
whether fascist or communist. But I have known Charlie
too long and too well to place him in that category. He
is not a joiner, and he has neither the strength of character
nor the firmness of conviction to serve a conspiracy. He is,
or is apt to be, in a general way, "for the underdog." And
he has gulped down as gospel—for what reason I do not
know—a major portion of the lies manufactured in Moscow to prove that the ruthless new exploiting class of
opulent bureaucrats in the Kremlin are, or represent, that
underdog. He used to be more astute than that. Indeed, in
the old Hollywood days, it was I who was the dupe—not,
to be sure of Stalinism, but of Lenin-and-Trotskyism—and

he was the wary skeptic. But in 1947, meeting accidentally in the streets of New York, we dined together, and I found him as innocent of the facts of recent political life, as though he had just been born. I tried for a time to stem the stream of cold-war clichés that Charlie poured out, but gave up when he declared that his persecution* in the notorious paternity suit had been due to the fact that America was going fascist and he had attacked Hitler in his film, *The Great Dictator!*

"If that's really your opinion," I said, "let's not try to talk politics because to my mind it's crazy."

He agreed and we spent the evening in reminiscence and philosophic discussion. So this accommodation had already been reached when I came to Lausanne, and I did not feel obliged to take Charlie's flirtations with the Chou En Lais too seriously. My feeling about that—and the feeling, I think, of essential America—was delicately expressed in a New York *Times* editorial of June 5, 1954, when he accepted the "peace prize" of the Communist-sponsored World Peace Council.

If he knew more about Russia, or if he were perhaps less bitter, Charlie Chaplin would be well aware that the "peace prize" is not a peace prize at all, but a prize offered to those who serve the purposes of a brutal and tyrannical imperialism. Charlie Chaplin once stated that his ideology was a sympathy for "the little man—his right to have a

---

* That it *was* persecution was well known to me because a friend of mine spent with the girl involved the night on which she is supposed to have slept with Charlie and become the mother of his baby. At the first hint of a trial, my friend left town in a hurry to avoid having to state the fact in court.

roof over his head and to work and raise a family." He should know, but we hope he does not, that the little man who moves so touchingly, so humorously, with such pure genius, through most of the Chaplin films could not survive and prosper in today's Russia. . . .

He has allowed himself to be used by a sinister conspiracy of which the little man he so touchingly represented is the victim. The little man he once portrayed and with whom he has now parted company will some day be at home in the world and untroubled. Perhaps the memory or revival of the early Chaplin films will help the little man in his struggle for freedom. But Charlie Chaplin, whether he knows it or not, has gone in the other direction. He shuffles off leftward, toward Moscow, perhaps not even realizing where he is going, most probably not calling himself a Communist or a fellow traveler—but there he goes and the sag of his back, the flap of his coattails, the set of the little derby over his ears and the sadly reminiscent twirling of his cane move us almost to tears.*

Almost as distressing as Charlie's break with the "little man" he created, was the unseemly behavior toward him of the United States government when he went abroad in 1953. The Department of Justice, finding no ground for legal investigation or action against him while he was resident here, turned over to the Department of Immigration the job of holding him up when he should apply for re-entry. I had the pleasure of telling an Immigration agent who came to me seeking data for the case, some of my feelings about this sly manuever. To wait until a man leaves

* It is worth mentioning that Charlie gave the Stalin Peace Prize money to Abbé Pierre, "the rag-picker of Paris," to distribute among the poor.

home on a visit—any man, least of all a great and beloved artist—and then slam the door and say, "Now see if you can get back in!" struck me as beneath the dignity of the American government. It was flagrantly unrepresentative of the American people.

Inexcusable as it was, however—and the moralistic clamor against Charlie among certain scandal-addicts, really hysterical—this did not justify him in stepping down from the heights he occupied and composing vengeful propaganda. In France last year I saw his film, *A King in New York,* and found it, but for one or two spontaneous laughs at traits of American life that we all ridicule while participating in them, so dull and contrived as to suggest that his whole heart was not in it. I think the last twenty minutes of *Limelight,* the union there of utterly hilarious comedy—not with pathos, for that has been done before— but with the ultimate tragedy of death itself, stands high among the greatest achievements of dramatic art. I would like to hold him to those heights. I don't want him to be American or anti-American. I want him to belong, as he once did, to truth and the human race.

John Dewey:
My Teacher and Friend

Since this memoir takes the form of a story of Dewey's life rather than of my meetings with him, it may be well to describe our association in general terms. I studied under him at Columbia for three years, teaching logic under his supervision and occupying an office next to his with the door usually open between us. For the first of those years I dined at his home every Sunday, and we spent the afternoon and often the evening conversing together. For another year I served by his appointment as his assistant in philosophy. I helped him revise the English and improve the expression of his thoughts in his chapters of the book on ethics which he wrote in collaboration with Professor Tufts. I attended his course of lectures on Logical

Theory and another on modern Philosophy. I submitted
to him my Ph.D. thesis, "The Quality of Plato," and we
discussed it more than once—the last time in 1940! And
then finally, I interviewed him three or four times, a
notebook in my hand, with a view to writing this portrait
of him and of the development of his ideas. His daughter
and collaborator, Evelyn, read the manuscript and helped
me with comments and suggestions, but Dewey himself
never examined it. Nothing could be farther from an "offi-
cial" biography, but any remarks I attribute to him were
put down immediately in my notebook and are quoted
verbatim.

Dewey had passed his eighty-second year when I undertook this engaging task, but there was not a quaver in his
voice or a quiver in his handwriting. Up in Nova Scotia,
where he went in summer, he still kept the local people in
a dither by swimming in all weathers in the deeps of Solar
Lake. Besides surviving this himself, he surprised them one
morning by going out an extra two hundred feet and
rescuing, in a deferential way, a drowning woman. At his
occasional cocktail parties on Central Park West, which
were attended by a motley aggregation of all ages, faiths,
colors, and social positions, from grandmothers of Ethical
Culture to prophets of the ultimate wrinkle in modern
painting, he always seemed the most agile person present—
agile in pretending to remember who they all were, agile
in sliding around among them with the drinks.

John Dewey may best be described as the man who saved
our children from dying of boredom, as we almost did in
school. The Encyclopædia Britannica in its article on
Education puts it less succinctly: "By 1900 the center of

gravity had shifted from the subject-matter of instruction to the child to be taught. The school, in consequence, had begun to change from a place where children prepare for life. . . . to a place where children live. . . . These changes, largely due to the teachings of John Dewey, have become dominant purposes of the American elementary school of the twentieth century." That is half of who John Dewey was, and the other half was a philosopher in the technical sense—a man who made his living arguing about such questions as "How We Think" and "What Does Thought Do to Being?"

The University of Paris, in conferring a degree upon him in 1930, described him as "the most profound and complete expression of American genius." And not so long ago, Waldo Frank called him "the most influential American."

Two things made this grade-A brand of fame surprising. One was Dewey's perverse and obdurate neglect of it. He never blew his own horn and never listened when kind friends undertook to blow it for him. He did not attend the banquet given in his honor on his eightieth birthday, although some of the world's most distinguished citizens were there. He found he had a previous engagement at his daughter Evelyn's cattle ranch in the northwest corner of Missouri. The whole thing had been done once before when he was seventy.

"I just can't stand it again," he told Evelyn.

The other thing that made Dewey's fame surprising was the total lack of fireworks in his nature. He published 40 books and 815 articles and pamphlets—a pile 12 feet 7 inches high—but if he ever wrote one "quotable" sentence it got permanently lost in the pile. Not only was his own style dull, but this dullness infected everybody who had anything to say about his theories of education. A reform which might be described as a grown-up formulation of the necessity, long known to lively-minded children, of raising hell in school, was put over in the language of the prosiest of disciplinary pedagogues. No flash of wit or poetry illumines it.

Perhaps Dewey's origin had something to do with this. He was born, like Calvin Coolidge, in Vermont, and he was born with the same trick of concealing whatever was, or was not, going on in his head under a noncommittal exterior. Vermonters have a dry humor of understatement—an understatement so remote that you can't quite guess whether they are joking or just failing to warm up. So it is just possible that Dewey concealed the dynamite of his educational theories in a pile of dry hay merely to amuse himself.

His father was famous in a small way as a joker. He "kept store" in Burlington, a town of ten or twelve thousand, and sold more goods than anybody else in town because of the whimsical way he went at it. A sign outside reading "Hams and Cigars—Smoked and Unsmoked" apprised his customers that they would not be taken too seriously. On a frequently borrowed wheelbarrow he painted in big red letters: "Stolen from A. S. Dewey." Notwithstanding his popularity, A. S. Dewey never got along very well because it hurt his feelings to ask people to pay their bills. He stuttered, too, and that made it seem an especially good joke when he asked for money.

Mrs. A. S. Dewey—Archibald Sprague is the name—was

the daughter of "Squire Rich" of Richville, and her grandfather had been in Congress. But the Riches hadn't gotten along very well in a property sense, either, and John's boyhood home was run on lines of watchful thrift. If he wanted any spending money he had to earn it—which he did, as befitted a complete expression of American genius, by delivering papers after school. That netted him a dollar a week, and in the summer when he reached fourteen, he got a real job "tallying" in a lumber yard, which netted him six dollars. He had to do chores around the house besides, and got punished when he chiseled with an appeal to conscience, which he found more painful than a licking.

His parents belonged to the White Street Congregational Church, the father being religious mostly for the reason that it wouldn't have occurred to him not to be, the mother putting a little more feeling into it. She had been brought up a Universalist, which means one of fifty to sixty thousand Christians kindhearted enough to believe we shall all be saved—a far cry from Calvin's doctrine of the Elect of God which did so much to keep New England mean and snobbish. She had attended revivals in her youth, and was, to quote her son's exact language, "not emotionally repressed and not austere, but pretty moralistic." Reading dime novels and playing marbles for keeps were immoral, but dancing and card playing were not. John was an excellent whist player—and he would, in my opinion, have shone still more brilliantly at poker—but not so bright a light, it seems, on the dance floor.

There was something painfully, or if you will, divinely average in John Dewey's early life and circumstances. He swam and skated on Lake Champlain, but not any too well.

He liked to play, but was no good at "set games"—not competitive enough, I think. He was a great reader, but did not care for "set lessons," either. He worked fairly hard during school hours, but only because he didn't want to carry his textbooks home. There were books in the village library that he liked better. He went through grammar and high school fast, but without getting high marks. People were more impressed with his sweet temper and selflessness than his brains.

Dewey thought he probably would not have gone to college if there hadn't been a college right there in Burlington to slide into. As it was, he slid into Vermont University at the early age of fifteen—an unusual accomplishment, but one which caused no particular comment, least of all from him. He slid through his first three college years also without throwing off any sparks, or giving grounds to predict anything about his future except that he was not going to be a mechanic—to convince yourself of which you only had to watch him try to drive a nail. He joined the church during his sophomore year, and did so with sincere religious feeling, but with no profound experience of conversion. He was a good boy, and wanted to be better, and thought God would help him—and that was all.

He wanted to be better, however, with the inward glow of a boy whose sexual life is almost entirely sublimated. He was shy too far inside of himself even to think of making love to a girl.

"I tried to work up a little affair with my cousin when I was nineteen," he told me. "I thought something ought to be done. But I couldn't do it. I was too bashful. I was abnormally bashful."

This fact, combined with the moralistic inculcations of his mother, enabled John Dewey to make his start in life as an impeccable Sunday-school teacher. He mildly questioned some of the dogmas of the White Street religion; he was pained one Sunday when in the midst of prayer the question rose up in his mind: "Isn't this, after all, just a routine performance?" That question bothered him a good deal and a long time. But he never had any doubt about the supreme importance of "being good," and helped along by bashfulness, he managed not only to teach it but achieve it.

It was toward the end of his junior year that this placid process of development was crashed into by an event that unsettled the whole scheme, and may be described as the chief crisis or turning point of John Dewey's life. It would not have been a crisis in your life or mine, but we also did not get a degree from the University of Paris as the most profound expression of American genius. The crisis was a short course in physiology with a textbook written by Thomas Henry Huxley. That accidental contact with Darwin's brilliant disciple, then waging his fierce war for evolution against the "impregnable rock" of Holy Scripture, woke John Dewey up to the spectacular excitement of the effort to understand the world. It woke him with a shock, for in reading Huxley's objective explanation of the working of man's body and brain, Dewey felt himself to be in a different world altogether from that in which as a White Street Sunday-school teacher he was telling boys' souls to be good. He found Huxley's world exciting; he was swept off his feet by the rapture of scientific knowledge. And yet the old moralistic attitude had too much momentum to give way. He could not abandon thinking about human life as a thing to be shaped by moral will and meditation; and yet he could not deny the validity of Huxley's account of how material forces shaped it. There seemed to be some separation, some gap, some intimately ominous chasm here, over which this lanky, mild, shy, black-eyed boy yearned in the intense way that most boys do over the yawning gulf that separates them from the body of their best girl.

As a result, his senior year at college was an ardent effort and adventure. He plunged heart and soul into his studies. He read and labored far into the night. He led his class and got the highest marks on record in philosophy. At times he seemed to his classmates, when answering a question, to be somewhat diffidently explaining the lesson to the professor. By the time that year was over, there was very little hope left in the Dewey family that John would turn out to be anything more useful than a philosopher. The question was: what are you going to do with a nineteen-year-old philosopher? And to this, nobody in that small farming community, John perhaps least of all, had any practical answer.

As a temporary solution John went down to Oil City, Pennsylvania, and taught in a high school run by a female cousin. He earned forty dollars a month. Two brokers living in the same boarding house urged him to borrow some more money and invest it in the town's newest excitement, Standard Oil. Instead, he borrowed books and used the oil in a lamp.

One evening while he sat reading he had what he called a "mystic experience." It was an answer to that question which still worried him: whether he really meant business when he prayed. It was not a very dramatic mystic experience. There was no vision, not even a definable emotion—just a supremely blissful feeling that his worries were over. Mystic experiences in general, Dewey explained, are purely emotional and cannot be conveyed in words. But when he tried to convey his in words, it came out like this:

"What the hell are you worrying about, anyway? Everything that's here is here, and you can just lie back on it."

"I've never had any doubts since then," he added, "—nor any beliefs. To me faith means not worrying."

Although his religion had so little affirmative content—and had nothing to do, he was sure, with his philosophy—Dewey likened it to the poetic pantheism of Wordsworth, whom he was reading at that time, and to Walt Whitman's sense of oneness with the universe. To forestall your own remark, he would remind you that it was very likely a sublimation of sex, and point out that this didn't make it any less normal or important.

"I claim I've got religion," he said, "and that I got it that night in Oil City."

At the end of the year Dewey's cousin resigned her job, and his went with it. He found himself back in Burlington with a new tranquillity in his heart, but still the old tension in his head about that chasm that he saw yawning between the material and moral sciences. To close that chasm always seemed the big problem to John Dewey; he said once that he had devoted his entire intellectual life to its solution. It was not, however, a problem that anybody in Burlington was just then offering money to have solved. To keep going while he worked on it, he took another job, this time teaching in the little district schoolhouse in Charlotte, Vermont. Charlotte is not far from Burlington, and while teaching everything from the alphabet to plane geometry, Dewey devoted his spare hours, under the direction of his old philosophy professor, H. A. P. Torry, who made a free gift of his time and knowledge, to reading the philosophical classics. He also started writing a little philosophy on his own.

In 1879, when John Dewey set out on his life task of reconciling ethics with physiology, there was hardly such a thing as a career in philosophy in America. The whole country was little better in that respect than Burlington, Vermont. Professors of philosophy were ministers of the gospel who for some reason, located as often in their vocal organs as their brains, had found it easier to teach than preach. They were a sort of plain-clothes chaplain employed by the colleges to see that science did not run away with the pupils' minds. One of the few exceptions was W. T. Harris, who published a *Journal of Speculative Philosophy* in St. Louis, Missouri. Harris was what they called a "lay philosopher," and Dewey, although still a churchgoer, was "lay" enough to send his first original work to Harris. It was a little piece he tossed off after school hours in Charlotte on "The Metaphysical Assumptions of Materialism." He hardly offered it as a contribution to the journal; he merely inquired of Harris whether it showed signs of promise. When it was accepted for publication, he decided that he would become a lay philosopher too. There would be a career for one, he guessed, by the time he got ready to have it. He also guessed that it was not necessary for an American who wanted a philosophical education to study in Germany. That sounds obvious now, but in those days it was a revolution.

An imaginative merchant named Johns Hopkins had just founded a new kind of research university in Baltimore, and Dewey's annunciation angel, Professor Huxley, had delivered the inaugural address. The new university was offering twenty-five-hundred-dollar fellowships to be competed for by college graduates. Dewey tried for one and failed. (Thorstein Veblen also tried for one and failed.) But Dewey had an aunt with five hundred dollars, and he borrowed that and went to Johns Hopkins, anyway. After studying a year, he tried for the fellowship again and got it. He also got a job teaching the history of philosophy to undergraduates. So who said there wasn't a career in philosophy in America? To be sure, there was no pay attached to this job, but then, on the other hand, he did not have to pay for the privilege of doing it. He was happy. He had found a wonderful teacher, a Hegelian named George Sylvester Morris. His brainy big brother, Davis R. —an economist, who had a longer section in *Who's Who* than John had—came down to live and study with him. He had no sex problems. And he was falling in love with Hegel.

Unless you understood how exciting it is to fall in love with Hegel—and what hard work—there was very little Dewey could tell you about those three years at Johns Hopkins. They were entirely filled up, from morning to midnight, with philosophy. And philosophy is a large thing, not easy to define. It is generally assumed to be an effort to go behind the returns made by science. Science tells us how things are like each other, and how they follow each other in certain sequences; but why there should be any things at all, or any telling about them, science can not decide. Neither can philosophy really, and the philosophers who say so, the skeptics, are the ones who give us a feeling of profound truthfulness. What the others do, for the most part, is to think up ways of mitigating the rather desolate conception of things arrived at by science. A very large part of Western European philosophy is, in fact, an effort to read God back into the universe as fast as science crowds him out. Even when you get it out of the hands of the clergymen, metaphysics is still largely, as Feuerbach remarked, a "disguised theology."

And Hegel invented a most ingenious disguise, a truly wondrous scheme for keeping deity in the world, no matter how harsh, fickle, bloody and reckless of ideal interests the world turns out to be when honestly examined. His scheme was, in brief, to say that all reality, good and bad together, *is* the Divine Spirit in a process of inward, and also onward and upward, struggle toward the realization of its own free and complete being. Many years before natural scientists began to see the world as in process of evolution, Hegel was ready for them with his theory that God himself *is* a world in process of evolution. Nothing more prodigiously ingenious was ever invented by the mind of man than this Hegelian scheme for defending soulfulness against science. Only it takes a very hard-working soul to get the hang of it. . . .

That much of a technical nature is necessary if you want to know John Dewey's life story. He belonged to the White Street Congregational Church in Burlington; he was brought up by an evangelical and "pretty moralistic" mother; and he was aroused to philosophic speculation by Thomas Henry Huxley, the "prophet of science," the man who in order to describe his skeptical attitude toward deity, invented one day, in consultation with his wife, the word "agnostic."

It was not deity, however, that Dewey was worried about after he read Huxley; it was not religion that he felt concerned as a young philosopher to defend. His discovery that the real world is arranged somewhat differently from the plans presented in the White Street Sunday School had upset him pretty badly; he described it to me as a "trying personal crisis." But that crisis, so far as concerns religion, seems to have been passed through and a working adjustment arrived at before he came to Huxley. I do not mean that he had rejected religion, or denied all meaning, as Huxley did, to the word God. But he had rejected the more incredible parts of religion as expounded on White Street, and had ceased to regard what was left as a thing to reason about. He had decided, to put it in his own words, that "any genuinely sound religious experience could and should adapt itself to whatever beliefs one found oneself intellectually entitled to hold."

That poised and unexcitable attitude toward God— keeping him, so to speak, waiting in the anteroom while you interview the world—was characteristic of John Dewey. As an example of social behavior, I don't know but it is characteristic of Vermont. It has not appeared elsewhere in history, so far as I know, and is basic to an understanding of this very American philosopher. It was not God but man that Dewey was worried about. He saw that by comparison with the hard implacable body of fact presented by Huxley, there was something soft and unconvincing about Christian ethics—about the whole "spiritual" way of discussing human problems. It contained too many pious wishes, too much that could not be verified. He wanted to make it hard and sure and solid. To put it in his own words to me: "I was reacting against the too *moralistic* morals in which I had been brought up, and trying to find something that would be more objective, more like physical science. In more technical terms, the problem I was at work on, and have been all my life, is whether there is any common method applicable both to the material and the human sciences."

That was the problem that Dewey thought he had solved by believing in Hegel's idealistic metaphysics. And the solution was, roughly speaking, to subordinate the material sciences, or bring them in under the "human," by asserting that materialness is an illusion. Properly understood the whole world behaves like a mind. That Professor Morris, who led him into this philosophy, was a man of rare moral character, a man as good if not as "moralistic" as his mother, was not accidental. "I have never known," Dewey says, "a more single-hearted and whole-souled man."

Here then is this "most complete expression of American genius" caught fast at the age of twenty-two in a completely German system of metaphysics. It sounds like a misfortune, and perhaps on a long-time estimate of John Dewey it will prove to have been one. But to him, for the time being at least, it was a tranquilizing experience—as blissfully tranquilizing to his mind as the Oil City "conversion" had been to his heart. Sixty years later, when the whole thing seemed to him a sentimental German self-deception, he still felt a pious love toward Hegel, and groped for words that might express the emotion of release that this mystical conception of the cosmos gave him. Some "sense of separation," some "dividedness," or "loneliness," as though the world were cut off from his soul, or he himself were cut off from the world, had troubled him. He had been in painful tension. Hegel's metaphysics gave him back the sense "of unity, of things flowing together."

If Dewey had not been such a hopeless extrovert, we might have a little more light on this philosophical romance—or if he had been sick and gone to a psychoanalyst. But he remained perfectly healthy, and couldn't quite remember what it was all about.

"I was unduly bashful and self-conscious," he said, "always putting myself over against other people. Perhaps that was it. Or perhaps an overemphasis on evangelical morals had given me a feeling of alienation from the world. I can't recover it. If I could, I could write something about adolescence that really would be interesting."

Whatever the cause, the effect was long-lasting. It was in 1881, his first year at Johns Hopkins, that Dewey was rapt away by Hegel, and he remained pretty Hegelian for ten or twelve years, coming back to earth, appropriately enough, in the vicinity of Chicago in the early nineties. It is unusual for a Hegelian to recover at thirty-five. If they stay up that long, they generally get lost in the stratosphere. And it is safe to say that one of the main factors in bringing Dewey down was a flesh-and-blood romance—a romance with a girl who had her feet very firmly planted on the earth.

When Dewey took his Ph.D. at Johns Hopkins, President Gilman offered him a loan to continue his studies in Germany. Dewey was deeply gratified, but said that he would rather not borrow money, and felt perfectly at home in America. President Gilman also offered him some advice: "Don't be so bookish; don't live such a secluded life; get out and see people." That offer Dewey was more inclined to accept, although he did not know exactly how to act upon it. What he needed first was a job, and he spent another rather wistful summer in Burlington before he got one. It was a nine-hundred-dollar job as instructor in philosophy at the University of Michigan, where his friend Morris was teaching.

In Michigan Dewey began to "see people," and among the first he saw was a coed named Alice Chipman, who lived in the same boarding house with him. She was a strong-minded girl, descended from a family of radicals and freethinkers, an ardent woman suffragist, deeply religious but of no church, and brilliantly intolerant of "bunk." She was shorter than Dewey and thicker, not beautiful and not well dressed. By a purely physiological accident her eyelids hung so low over her eyes that to a timid judgment she looked forbidding. But her features were handsome in a strong way, and her mouth was gentle. Her pioneer grandfather had joined the Chippewa tribe of Indians and fought for their rights; he had also opposed Lincoln and the Civil War. She inherited his crusading spirit and his moral courage. And she had a passionate interest in the life of ideas. It was good luck—or was it good sense?—that John Dewey fell in love with such a woman. An adoring sissy might have left him half of what he did become. That does not say, however, that their relation was uneven. Dewey also was strong-minded. In his mild and limp way, with neither inward conflict nor outward fuss, he would stick to his own course of action, barring rational arguments to the contrary, with the momentum of a mule. Besides that, he had the advantage of superior knowledge; Alice was a pupil in his classes. There was, in short, a full-sized moral and intellectual admiration between them. "No two people," Dewey remarked to me, "were ever more in love."

They were married at the home of the Chippewa Copperhead in 1886. In the same year Dewey was made assistant professor, and his salary was raised to sixteen hundred dollars. The next year their first child, Fred, was born, and Dewey published his first book—significantly not a philosophy book at all, but a textbook in psychology. Dewey was willing to see psychology break loose from philosophy and become a natural science, and this book places him among the pioneers of that process. But still it winds up with a piously Hegelian reminder, quaint in a scientific textbook now, that the ultimate reality is God.

The next year, without any wangling on his part, Dewey was given a professorship at the University of Minnesota and a salary of twenty-five hundred dollars. The year after that, his friend Professor Morris having died, he returned to Michigan to succeed him as professor and head of the department of philosophy, with a salary of three thousand dollars. Dewey had guessed right about careers for "lay philosophers." They were growing on the bushes—especially for those who could still weave God into a textbook of psychology.

By the time he came back to Michigan in 1889, however, Dewey was losing interest in Hegel's world made out
of Spirit. The social atmosphere of the Midwest in those
years, when population was spreading like wildfire, was
hardly one to sustain a faith in mystic systems that made
real estate unreal. Moreover, John and Alice were both
fascinated by concrete human problems connected with
the novelty of a democratic state university. Under James
B. Angell, whom all who taught for him regarded as the
ideal college president, the university was the active head
of the public-school system of Michigan.

One of Dewey's tasks as a member of its faculty was to
visit high schools throughout the state, and investigate
their qualifications to send up students to the university.
This first set his mind to work on that general problem of
Democracy and Education—which was to be the title of his
major work in this field. It also took his mind off the
Hegelian cosmos. He still formally believed that Hegel had
correctly described the logical structure of Reality with a
large R. But he was getting more interested in what he
called the "instrumental logic" by which people who are
real with a little r think out ways of getting what they
want. This tendency was vastly reinforced by the appearance in 1890 of William James' famous *Psychology,* which
foreshadowed the philosophy of pragmatism, formulated
by its author seventeen years later. In 1891 Dewey announced a book called "Instrumental Logic," but he then
still meant by the phrase: what logic is like when it is used
as an instrument. He never wrote the book, and before
the end of the century he was teaching that logic is an in-

strument, and that is all there is to it. The Hegelian cosmos, as he put it, "just dropped away."

Before that happened, however, Dewey's own personal place in the cosmos had taken a large upward leap. The University of Chicago had been founded with a plentiful endowment by John D. Rockefeller, and its president, William Rainey Harper, had conceived the novel idea of combining the departments of philosophy, psychology, and education into one. In 1894 Dewey was invited to come to Chicago at a salary of five thousand dollars and be the head of the whole thing. It was a piece of rare good luck, for Dewey's philosophy was taking more and more the aspect of a psychology of the thought process, and his interest in education was running neck and neck with his interest in philosophy. Moreover, the Dewey family was growing and was destined to grow far beyond the limits set by the income of any ordinary lay philosopher. Mrs. Dewey, notwithstanding her free-thinking grandparents, held some streak of puritanism that made her think it wicked to decide when and under what conditions you are going to bear children. The second child, Evelyn, had been born in 1890, and the third, Morris—named after Dewey's revered teacher—early in 1893. The difference between three and five thousand dollars was beginning to look important, and the letter from Chicago was in all ways a joyful piece of news.

Mrs. Dewey, they decided, would spend the summer in Europe with the children, and Dewey would go ahead to Chicago and earn some extra money teaching in the summer school. Dewey hated to say good-bye to his two-year-old baby, Morris, for he had already made up his mind, by what signs it would be hard to say, that the child was a kind of saintly genius. This was not all a parent's fondness, either. A stranger on the boat going over made the peculiar remark: "If that child lives long enough there will be a new religion." Morris died of diphtheria in Milan, and fifty years later Dewey could not mention the event without a catch in his throat.

Three other children were born in Chicago—Lucy, Gordon, and Jane—and thus there were still five of them rioting around the house during the best years of this philosopher's life. They did not disturb his meditations in the least. As a logician Dewey was at his best with one child climbing up his pants leg and another fishing in his inkwell. He had not only mental concentration but a way of doing two things at once that was at times almost alarming. Friends were known to follow him several blocks down the street to make sure he would negotiate the crossings, he seemed so unaware of where his body was going.

I don't know whether this belongs in the same category of facts, but one sunny afternoon John Dewey and four of his colleagues on Morningside Heights walked a half mile down Broadway to attend an open-air movie—"none of us realizing until we got there," as Thomas Reed Powell recalled, "that movies require darkness, which in this part of the world is not rampant in the daytime."

In his New York apartment Dewey used to do his meditating with a telephone beside his ear. He found that it only took a minute to dispose of an inquiry from the landlord about washing the windows, a request for a consultation from the Chinese ambassador, a question from Sidney

Hook about the policies of the Committee for Cultural Freedom, a summons to a meeting in honor of the old rebel, Angelica Balabanoff, a plea for a "moral affidavit" for some obscure refugee, an invitation to address a World Congress of Sciences in Cambridge. In one second after he hung up the receiver, the old typewriter would be jumping along finishing his interrupted thought.

Dewey never bothered about physical exercise; brain work, he thought, was just as good, if there was enough of it. So for recreation he would go on long automobile rides, and sit in the front seat solving crossword puzzles and conversing with his companions—a slightly irritating habit that was not made any more agreeable when, at the end of the journey, he turned out to have a more accurate memory of the landscape than they had.

To such a mind a half-dozen or so children would obviously be a help philosophically. But Dewey's children, besides clambering on his philosophy in a helpful way while he was writing it, made another contribution more important to the course of history. They kept the problems of philosophy thoroughly mixed up in his mind with the problems of education.

It is customary to regard Dewey's educational theories as an inference from his instrumental philosophy, but more accurately they are an inference from his children. Dewey was interested in reforming education and wrote a book about it long before he became an instrumental philosopher. The book was called *Applied Psychology,* and that indicates what his doctrine about education is. Education is life itself, so long as the living thing continues to grow; education is growth under favorable conditions; the school is a place where those conditions should be regulated scientifically. That is about all there is to it.

The household also needed a little renovation along this line, and Dewey's influence on the relations between parents and their children has been as great as his influence on the schools. It was a reform that in the nature of the case began at home.

Once Sabino, the boy he adopted in later years, ran away from a boarding school in the country. The principal reported it to Dewey by long-distance telephone, and concluded:

"As soon you find him send him right back and we'll see that it doesn't happen again."

Dewey said: "Well, I rather think on the whole that if Sabino decided to leave the school, he probably used his judgment about it, and he may very likely be right."

In his house at Ann Arbor, Dewey's study was directly under the bathroom, and he was sitting there one day, absorbed in a new theory of arithmetic, when suddenly he felt a stream of water trickling down his back. He jumped out of his chair and rushed upstairs to find the bathtub occupied by a fleet of sailboats, the water brimming over, and his small boy Fred busy with both hands shutting it off. The child turned as he opened the door, and said severely:

"Don't argue, John—get the mop!"

You might think that a family of five children, brought up along these lines, would be something of a riot, and they did have a rare good time. But they were, as children go, a remarkably well mannered bunch of rioters. They were at times, indeed, a little too well mannered. Jane used at the age of twelve to discuss the causes of prostitution

in a disturbingly judicious manner. And Evelyn developed
so early the poised and sagely humorous good sense which
surrounds her now with loving friends that you wished
sometimes she would be a little foolish for a minute.

Both as philosopher and educator, John Dewey reached
his high point in Chicago. In a book called *Studies in
Logical Theory,* published in 1903, he formulated that
very American philosophy which was left in his head
after Hegel's German cosmos "dropped away." All thinking, it declares—even Hegel's about his cosmos—is instrumental, and basically concerned with bringing human
beings to their ends. Dewey finds rest in this idea because
it closes, in a way that does less violence to common-sense
reality than Hegel did, that chasm which he had felt yawning between the physical and moral sciences. The material
world is real, but our very knowledge of it is moral in the
largest sense. It is practical. It is a solving of problems in
the very proposing of which, and thus inevitably in their
solution, human needs and aspirations play a vital part.

When William James came to Chicago a short time after
Dewey's *Studies* were published, he spoke of the book—
with a little too much modesty—as "the foundation of the
philosophy of pragmatism." Dewey, equally modest, did
not know that he had been founding pragmatism, and was
greatly surprised when James greeted him in this way. A
case of "After you, Gaston!" not at all common among
philosophers—or other human beings.

The other half of John Dewey reached its high point in
the founding of an elementary school, two years after he
came to Chicago. This school was regarded by him literally as the laboratory of the department of philosophy, and

was called the Experimental or Laboratory School. But it lives in history as the Dewey School, a name which might well be written "Do-y School," for "to learn by doing" was one of its chief slogans. Its founder had the rather naive notion that in its operation he was putting his instrumental philosophy to an experimental test.

The revolt against Dewey's teachings these days is nothing to the clamor that was raised in 1896 by the idea of a laboratory school. "A school where they experiment with the children—imagine!" He could hardly have shocked the parents of the nineties more if he had proposed vivisection in a kindergarten. Even when closely examined, his idea seemed to be to let children do just what they wanted to, which was then generally regarded as equivalent to letting them go to hell. Dewey was, indeed, somewhat utopian in his rebellion against the old puritanical pumping-in system of education, summed up by his contemporary, Mr. Dooley, in the remark that "it don't make much difference what you study, so long as you don't like it." But he never did believe in consecrating children's whims, much less in forcing them to have more whims than is natural to them. He had more horse sense than many of those who now run "progressive schools" in his name. His idea was that life in school ought to be enough like life outside so that an interest in knowledge would arise in the child's mind as it did in the mind of the race—spontaneously. If you provide a sufficient variety of activities, and there's enough knowledge lying around, and the teacher understands the natural relation between knowledge and interested action, children can have fun getting educated and will love to go to school. That is the kind of thing Dewey was saying. And the little book, *School and Society,* in which he first said it, was translated into dozens of languages, including those as far away from home as Chinese and Japanese.

Dewey would never have started a Dewey School, however, if it hadn't been for Alice Chipman. Dewey never did anything, except think—at least, it often looked that way to Alice—unless he got kicked into it. Nothing seemed important to him but thinking. He was as complete an extrovert as ever lived, but the extroversion all took place inside his head. Ideas were real objects to him, and they were the only objects that engaged his passionate interest. If he got hold of a new idea, he would sneak around the house with it like a dog with a bone, glancing up with half an eye at the unavoidable human beings and their chatter, hoping they wouldn't bother him, and that's all. Only a man of this temperament who nevertheless took human lives and problems for his subject matter could have made the contribution Dewey did.

Mrs. Dewey would grab Dewey's ideas—and grab him—and insist that something be done. She had herself a brilliant mind and a far better gift of expression than his. And she was a zealot. She was on fire to reform people as well as ideas. She had an adoring admiration of his genius, but she had also a female impatience of the cumbersome load of ideological considerations he had to carry along when arriving at a decision. Her own decisions were swift, direct, and harshly realistic—not always aware of their grounds. "You always come at things backhanded," she would say. Dewey's view of his wife's influence is that she put "guts and stuffing" into what had been with him mere intellectual conclusions. He also recalled that she taught him not to be such an easy mark. He did not use that phrase. "She liberated me," he said, "from certain sentimental moralisms of the 'judge not' variety, and taught me to respect my adverse as well as my favorable intuitions." In short, she kept pulling him down into the real world. And as his own philosophy insisted that that is where a man ought to be, he was, theoretically at least, always willing to be pulled.

Mrs. Dewey, then, as might be guessed, was the principal of the Dewey School. To her, and to Ella Flagg Young, Chicago's famous superintendent of schools, belonged most of the credit for its concrete operation. Dewey called Ella Flagg Young "the wisest person about actual schools I ever saw." "I would come over to her with these abstract ideas of mine," he said, "and she would tell me what they meant." Another woman memorable in this connection was Mrs. Charles R. Crane, wife of the bathroom-fixture millionaire, who put up a large part of the money for the school, and helped the Deweys raise the rest. Still another was Mrs. Emmons Blaine, who, besides sharing the enthusiasms of this little group of glowing reformers, shared in the McCormick dollars. Those dollars aided very considerably in the birth of the Dewey School, and it was from being forced to swallow a million of them at one gulp that the school rather suddenly died.

That sad story, which altered the direction and to some extent the tone of Dewey's whole life, was a long time getting told. Mrs. Dewey wanted him to make a public statement at the time, but Dewey decided to swallow his chagrin, and so everybody else, for some thirty-five years, remained sitting decorously on the lid. The story in brief, as it stood in Dewey's memory when we discussed it, is this:

Mrs. Blaine gave that million-dollar endowment originally to another educational reformer, an educational genius too, named Colonel Parker, who founded a school with it called the Chicago Institute. Parker had more genius for handling children than for handling dollars by the million, and moreover, he soon began to lose his health. With his consent, Mrs. Blaine finally proposed to President Harper that Parker's school and Dewey's school unite, and the endowment be turned over to the University of Chicago. At that time the Dewey School was a flourishing institution with twenty-three teachers and one hundred and forty children; it had none of the troubles of the Chicago Institute; its theoretical principles, while significantly similar, were not the same—and it had no need of a million dollars. The change was therefore vigorously resisted, and for one year staved off, by the parents of the children in the Dewey School.

But Harper wanted that million dollars for the University, and the following year, while Dewey was conveniently absent in the East, he reopened the negotiations with Mrs. Blaine. When Dewey returned, the merger was all but accomplished. The president called him to his office and spoke with unction about "their dream at last realized." As Dewey had never dreamed this dream, but quite the opposite, and as Harper had never put up any money for the Laboratory School, he felt that he might have been consulted before the realizing got quite so far along. The interview was a tense one, and when President Harper asked him to come in on the final negotiations, Dewey abruptly refused.

"Since you've chosen to start this in my absence, I suggest that you finish it," he said. "After you get the terms arranged, I will decide whether I can cooperate or not."

"I should hate to go to the trustees," Harper said, "and tell them that your obstinacy had cost the University a million dollars."

Dewey explained that he was interested in an experiment in education, not in providing an endowment for the University of Chicago. He also told President Harper—although not in these terms, I am sure—that if he did find it possible to come in, he would expect a raise in salary from five to seven thousand dollars. President Harper expressed a fear that a salary of that size might embarrass him with his colleagues, but Dewey thought he could survive the pain. "That demand for more pay," Dewey remarked, "did more to make a man of me than any other act of my life."

Another stipulation Dewey made was that his teaching staff, including Mrs. Dewey as principal, should continue to serve in the new set up. Harper agreed to this when talking to Dewey, but when talking to Mrs. Blaine, whose main interest was in Colonel Parker's staff, he explained that the arrangement was only for the first year. Mrs. Dewey, in particular, he said, intended to resign as soon as the school got going. This put him in rather a tight place, but left him a year in which to wiggle out of it. His way out was to wait until Dewey was again absent in the East, and then send for Mrs. Dewey and inform her that Professor Dewey had told him she was going to resign.

As Dewey had never told her that, and, moreover, was not in the habit of telling her what she was going to do, she received this communication with a silence that President Harper found vastly impressive.

"Mrs. Dewey," he told her husband when he returned, "is a woman of extraordinary dignity!"

But Dewey had his back up now. He was aware that Mrs. Dewey had, as an administrator, the faults of her virtues. She was not a good mixer. She had an uncanny gift of seeing through people who were faking, and made such witty game of them that she alarmed even those who were not faking—or, at least, not faking very much. And she had a kind of inside-out timidity, a fear of being presumptuous, that because of her obvious superiority looked sometimes like snooty coldness. She was, however, the sole channel through which Dewey's ideas could naturally get down into action. She was too deeply bound up with bringing them down to be eased out as incidental to a "Dewey School." Dewey surmised, besides, that his other trained teachers would be eased out in the same sly fashion. Nominally he would be head of the school, but he would not be in a position of control. He ended that interview with President Harper, which was a hot one, by presenting his resignation as professor of education. As soon as he got outside the door he realized that Harper's expression on hearing this had been one of relief. He went home and wrote out his resignation as professor of philosophy, psychology, and education.

That was the end of the Dewey School, as the long hushed-up story lived vividly in John Dewey's mind. When I asked him to let me tell it, he said at first:

"I don't like to do that now that Harper is dead."

"If he's dead, it can't hurt him very much," I said.

"Well, if he were alive, he could answer."

"Somebody's going to tell it," I argued, "and if you don't hurry up, you won't be able to answer either."

"Well, all right, go ahead," he said at last. "Mrs. Dewey always said I made a mistake not to publish the whole thing when it happened. She had more nerve and courage than I have."

With the end of the Dewey School, there ended a joyful and very affluent epoch in Dewey's life. Mrs. Dewey's salary, together with the extras that he earned from books and lectures, had raised the income of this "lay philosopher" to heights never dreamed of in Charlotte, Vermont. The family lived in two adjoining apartments and employed two servants, a nurse, and a laundress on part time. They had built a comfortable summer home in the Adirondacks. Mrs. Dewey was not a neat or very thoughtful housekeeper—not a brooding, maternal, or even a loving person. She was, however, too intelligent to neglect the physical essentials—good food, good rugs and furniture, good company. And she had been, on the whole, gay and easy to live with, notwithstanding her underlying determination to reform you if she got the chance. But this shabby and yet tragic injustice to her husband's great ideas and her own intense work for them—a work that she felt was destined to change the foundations of social life forever— awoke an anger in her breast that never quite died down.

Dewey, of course, was not many days out of a job. Aside from his rising fame in philosophy and education, he had recently filled a term as president of the American Psychological Association. He could have had a chair in philosophy, psychology, or education in almost any university in the country. It was, in fact, a psychologist, J. McKeen Cattell, who took the initiative in getting him invited to Columbia as Professor of Philosophy, and it was stipulated in his contract that he continue to expound his views on education at Teachers College.

Both he and Mrs. Dewey might have recovered with more buoyance from the blow to their life work had not Fate chosen this moment to repeat, so exactly as to suggest deliberate malice, the tragedy of their previous personal loss. On a trip to Europe in the interval between jobs, their very gifted son, Gordon, died—in Ireland, of typhoid fever. We have only Dewey's words for the rich endowments of his baby, Morris, but Gordon had so impressed those around him that a service in his memory was held at Hull House, in Chicago, and Jane Addams gave a talk that is preserved in one of her books. Reading what she said about this "tiny protagonist of his time," an "indefatigable reader of the newspapers," a "fine and gallant spirit," possessed of "wide and tolerant wisdom" and "a sense of the humor of life," it is hard to believe that the child was only eight years old. It makes plausible, notwithstanding the unscientific moisture in his eyes when Dewey speaks about them, his own judgment of the phenomenal gifts of these two children whom he lost.

In Italy the Deweys adopted the orphan boy, Sabino, attempting in this common-sense way to fill the void in their hearts. But Dewey never quite escaped the pain of that double loss of his chosen life work and his best-loved child. President Harper's action rankled in him so deeply that, thirty-five years afterward, he expressed surprise on finding that he could laugh at the man's crude way of being astute.

In this, I suspect he was influenced by Mrs. Dewey, in whom the wound was even deeper. Stricken thus as a mother at the same time that she was deprived of any outlet for her violent zeal and genuine gift of leadership, she fell gradually into a habit of resentment. She grew caustic where she had been keen, captious where she had been critical. Her health began to decline. She had already done more work and borne more children than her physique, unless sustained by joy, was equal to. The less she could do herself, the more her perfectionism, her insistence upon everybody's doing his best and doing it just exactly right, turned into a vice of ironical nagging. Her husband's bland way of going around with nothing on his mind but thoughts, when she herself so longed for action, got on her nerves. Increasingly until her death from arteriosclerosis in 1927, these habits of perpetual objection became fixed in her, giving a bitter flavor to her witty charm.

Notwithstanding the mood in which the change was made, Dewey's eastward migration at forty was a good thing for him intellectually. He found a new group of stimulating minds at Columbia. His philosophic friendship with George H. Mead, a teammate in developing the philosophic implications of biology, was replaced by a more argumentative friendship with Frederick J. E. Woodbridge, a philosopher of the classic mold. Dewey says that he "learned a lot from Professor Woodbridge, but not what he was teaching." He learned a lot also from James Harvey Robinson, who used to begin his course in The Intellectual

History of Western Europe by remarking: "Now when I mention God, I want the class to relax"; from Charles Beard who was teaching American History with a similar irreverence toward the founding fathers; and from Wesley Mitchell, who was leading a like revolt against the "economic man."

In general, ideas were sprouting up through the bricks at Columbia in those days, and Dewey's mind was happy there. Also, he found it easier, while living in New York, to play a part in civic movements of national scope, to be a factor in the nation's political life, as is appropriate to a philosopher who believes that the truth of an idea lies in its practical effectiveness. By taking an apartment at the corner of Broadway and 56th Street, a fourth-floor apartment fronting on both streets, he managed to surround himself with enough noise so that he could get some thinking done. He wanted to avoid academic abstraction, I suppose. He wanted to think about real things, and Broadway street cars seemed as real as anything else. To one with sensitive eardrums, the place was hell itself.

Later, he moved out on Long Island, and preserved his contact with reality by raising eggs and vegetables and selling them to the neighbors. With characteristic vigor he learned all about farming and actually earned money enough during one year to "pay for his keep." His farm was but a short walk from Walt Whitman's birthplace—where still the lilacs in the dooryard bloomed—and like Walt Whitman he loved the companionship of the humble earth. He loved to identify himself with lowly people. He was pleased when one day a hurry call came from a wealthy neighbor for a dozen eggs, and the children being in school, he himself took the eggs over in a basket. Going by force of habit to the front door, he was told brusquely that deliveries were made at the rear. He trotted obediently around to the back door, feeling both amused and happy. Some time later, he was giving a talk to the women's club of the neighborhood, and his wealthy customer, when he got up to speak, exclaimed in a loud whisper:

"Why, that looks exactly like our egg man!"

Dewey looked like a young man then, a man just starting his career. He looked like the portraits of Robert Louis Stevenson, having the same flat hair and dark mustache and the same luminous eyes. Dewey's eyes were wells of dark, almost black, tenderly intelligent light such as would shine more appropriately out of a Saint Francis than a professor of logic. The rest of him was pleasant, but not quite so impressive.

He used frequently to come into the class in Logical Theory with his necktie out of contact with his collar, a sock down around his ankle, or a pants leg caught up into his garter. Once he came for a whole week with a large rent in his coat sleeve which caused a flap of cloth to stick out near the shoulder like a little cherub's wing. His hair always looked as though he had combed it with a towel, and being parted, if at all, in the middle, gave his face a rather ewelike contour which emphasized the gentleness more than the penetration in those wondrous eyes. He would come in through a side door—very promptly and with a brisk step. The briskness would last until he reached his chair, and then he would sag. With an elbow on the desk he would rub his hand over his face, push back some strands of his hair, and begin to purse his mouth and look vaguely over the heads of the class and above the windows, as though he thought he might find an idea up there along the crack between the wall and the ceiling. He always would find one. And then he would begin to talk, very slowly and with little emphasis and long pauses, and frequent glances up there to see if he was getting it right.

He was thinking rather than lecturing, evolving a system of philosophy *ex tempore,* and taking his time about it. The process was impersonal and rather unrelated to his pupils—until one of them would ask a question. Then those glowing eyes would come down from the ceiling and shine into that pupil, and drew out of him and his innocent question intellectual wonders such as the student never imagined had their seeds in his brain or bosom.

Education does not, according to the Dewey system, mean "drawing out." But drawing out was never better done than it was in his classrooms. John Dewey's instinctive and active deference, and unqualified giving of attention to whatever anybody, no matter how dumb and humble, might have had to say, was one of the rarest gifts or accomplishments of genius. He embodied in his social attitude, as Walt Whitman did in a book, the essence of democracy.

Another trait of John Dewey's, very impressive in the classroom—and very little conveyed, I fear, in the above paragraph—was his personal dignity. Careless as his dress used to be, he never seemed, as so many eccentric professors do, inwardly sloppy. You felt his moral force. You felt the rigorous self-discipline beneath his sagging manner. You felt also, or soon found out, that with all his taste for heresies John Dewey knew his trade. He was an expert philosopher. He wrote a great many things that drove his colleagues of the academic tradition wild, but he never wrote anything that was amateurish, as did both James and Schiller, his co-leaders in pragmatism. He had a prodigious memory, and was a learned scholar as well as an unforgetful friend.

There was one act of learning, however, which Dewey never performed and whose neglect was deeply regrettable. He never studied, at least until his very last years, the philosophy of Karl Marx. While occupying for two generations of young people the position of a leader in radical democracy, and that in a period when Marxism was sweeping the militant majority of them into the anti-democratic, or supposedly super-democratic, camp, he was content always to say when the subject came up: "I have never read Marx . . . I cannot speak with authority on the subject." He ought to have read Marx, and he ought to have spoken on the subject not only with authority, but with vim. Marx was his chief enemy, the only other man on the left who backed a political program with a system of philosophy.

Once when Sidney Hook and I, two of his egotistical pupils, were waging an unseemly war over the question whether Marx was a "scientific pragmatist," I wrote Dewey to know if he would preside at a debate between us on the subject. His reply shows that he himself was not unaware of a neglected duty:

> Your idea is an ingenious and intriguing one. But the trouble is I don't know enough Marx to go into the scheme and I don't see the least probability of my getting the time to acquire the needed knowledge. When I talk with you I

incline to think you must be right, and the same—in reverse—when I talk to Sidney. This is doubtless a deplorable confession but there it is.

Sincerely, if delinquently,

John Dewey

This delinquency made all the more harsh the parting between John Dewey and his more intransigent pupils on the subject of America's entrance into the First World War. It was mainly Marx who backed them in their opposition to the war, and Dewey supported the war without refuting Marx. Those issues seem pale today when history has refuted Marx, and when Dewey's central theme, "Democracy and Education," may be almost the slogan of a third world war. But in those days there was bitter derision of John Dewey in the heart of some of his most devoted disciples—eminent among them the gifted cripple, Randolph Bourne. The crisis was momentous in Dewey's history as well as theirs. He was not only alienated from them, but somewhat from himself, I think, by his support of the war against Germany. It was not that he felt, either then or afterward, that he made a flatly wrong choice. But his philosophy had not contemplated such a choice. Facts, in forcing it upon him, proved more "brute" than he had anticipated. He wrote a book on *German Philosophy and Politics* which seemed—to us then, at least—a contribution to the war propaganda rather than to the history of thought. And he got into a state of tension that in most people would have been an illness.

In this emergency he had recourse to a very unconventional physician named Matthias Alexander, who opened a new chapter in his life. Dr. Alexander was an Australian of original but uncultivated mind, attacked by the medical profession, but possessed in Dewey's opinion of a valid theory about posture and muscular control, and a technique of "re-education" by which human beings were supposed to recover that integration of the organism which is natural to animals. Dr. Alexander was endorsed by men as brainy as Bernard Shaw and Aldous Huxley, and his system undoubtedly worked in Dewey's case. "I used to shuffle and sag," he said. "Now, I hold myself up." Every one of his friends endorsed that assertion. And when he added that "a person gets old because he bends over," it was difficult to argue with him, for he was obviously an expert on not getting old. It was simply impossible to believe when you saw him in 1940 that he had been around since 1859. Dewey gave 90 percent of the credit for this to Dr. Alexander, 10 percent to a regular physician who taught him to keep things moving through the alimentary canal.

The post-war period gave Dewey a chance to prove to his radical critics that he had not turned into a "bourgeois reactionary," and he proved it. When the smoke cleared, he was found, unlike most of the pro-war liberals, to the left of where he had been before. More accurately he was found adhering to the most radical of his previously expressed opinions. For as long ago as 1887—when on the lips of a college professor it was a prodigy, if not a crime—John Dewey had said: "Democracy is not in reality what it is in name until it is industrial as well as civil and political."

Accordingly, Dewey was among the first of the American liberals who made the pilgrimage to Soviet Russia—not

then quite throttled by the totalitarian tyranny of Stalin
—and he came back speaking bold words of praise for the
accomplishments, especially in education, of the regime of
Lenin and Trotsky. This act placed him, if not among the
"radicals," at least at the extreme left of the liberals in
America, and again in a position of international leadership. He was invited by the new revolutionary government
of Turkey to go to Ankara and draw up a plan for the re-
organization of the schools, which he did. And he was invited by the Chinese followers of Sun Yat-sen to give a
course of lectures at Peking University, which he also did
—and further distinguished himself by declining, for democratic reasons, the decoration of the Order of the Rising
Sun offered him by the Imperial Government of Japan.

In those post-war years, Dewey also turned his thoughts
toward the understanding of art. He had no ear for music,
but he had a connoisseur's appreciation of painting. His
dwellings were decorated with taste, and you would always
find a rare picture or two on the walls. While in Paris in
1926, he attended an art class in the Louvre conducted by
Albert C. Barnes, famous as the first systematic collector of
"modern" French paintings. Ten years before that, Barnes
had attended one of Dewey's seminars at Columbia, attracted by a reading of *Democracy and Education,* which
he was heard to speak of as his bible. Dewey on his side regarded Barnes as one of the finest minds he had known,
and the author of the wisest theory of aesthetics. Their
friendship was fruitful to them both, and Dewey was for a
time, at first formally and then informally, educational ad-
viser to the Barnes Foundation. The two men differed so
much in temperament that the friends of each sometimes

inquired what pleasure they could find in being together. Dewey delighted to report that Barnes once replied to such an inquiry: "Why, Dewey just comes along like my chauffeur—I can talk to him the way I can to a barkeep."

For a person who devoted his life largely to educating other people, Dewey had a surprising lenience toward their follies. Ascetic enough in his own personal conduct, his attitude toward others was one of philosophic tolerance. His favorite story was about a man who bought a secondhand suit for two dollars and, finding moths in it, took it back to the dealer with indignation. The dealer said: "What do you expect for two dollars—humming birds?" But this tolerance could become, at times, a militant passion for the rights of man.

Soon after Dewey came to Columbia as professor of philosophy, New York City was turned upside down by a scandal attending the visit of the great Russian writer, Maxim Gorky. Gorky had come to solicit help for the Russian revolution, and had brought with him his life companion, or common-law wife, the actress, Madame Andreeva. It required but a hint from the Tsar's officials to rouse the town against him. He was denounced in screaming headlines as a free-lover; hotels and private homes were closed in his face; he was virtually thrown into the streets. Even Mark Twain, although appealed to in the name of the republic of letters, refused to stand against the public hysteria. He turned his back with the rest. John Dewey offered his home, and the shelter of his prestige, to the bewildered Russian. He in turn was violently attacked for this act of magnanimity, so violently that he seemed for a time in danger of losing his job. Mrs. Dewey stood behind him like a rock. "I would rather starve and see my children starve," she said between clenched teeth, "than have John sacrifice his principles."

In his subsequent championship of a fair trial for Leon Trotsky on the treason charges made against him in Moscow, Dewey found no such support at home. The son and daughter-in-law who made their home with him after the marriage of his daughter Evelyn did all they could to dissuade him from taking the chairmanship of the Commission of Inquiry. He was too old for the journey to Mexico —he could not stand the discomfort and the change of food —he would probably be shot—he would contract some fatal disease. Dewey smiled at these anxious warnings. "I'll enjoy the trip," he said.

When Trotsky was asked afterward for his impressions of John Dewey, he said:

"Wonderful! He was the only man on the commission who didn't get sick!"

Dewey was no figurehead on that commission. He was, apart from the secretary, Suzanne La Follette, the one who did the major part of the work. And his work included an intense study of the Russian political situation in its historic development. He even went into its theoretical background to the extent of being able to deliver—at last—an authoritative judgment on the philosophy of Marxism, a judgment more important than his verdict of "Not guilty" in the case of Leon Trotsky: "Orthodox Marxism shares with orthodox religionism, and with orthodox idealism, the belief that human ends are interwoven with the very texture and structure of existence—a conception inherited presumably from its Hegelian origin."

The *Daily Worker,* of course, described his behavior as

senile. The *New Masses* regretted that a great philosopher
had made a fool of himself in the sunset of his life—a remark on which Dewey's comment was: "Twilight is the
usual expression." In the opinion of his colleagues on the
commission Dewey conducted himself with the dignity of a
judge and the shrewdness of a Vermont horse trader. He
had answered his adverse critics in an essay written forty
years before: "Better it is for philosophy to err in active
participation in the living struggles and issues of its own
age and times than to maintain an immune monastic im-
peccability." He did not answer them again.

The charge of senility looked a little foolish when he
published, almost simultaneously with the 800 page report
of the Dewey Commission, what may perhaps appear in history as his major work, *Logic, The Theory of Inquiry,* a
book of 546 pages. He wrote most of it in hot sunshine in
the backyard of his winter home in Key West, Florida,
stripped to the waist, and brown as an acorn. If you went
out there and asked him how his eyes could stand the white
glare on the paper, he would say: "Well, my eyes have always been weak—it's just a matter of getting them accustomed to it."

Besides good health, this lay philosopher had rare good
luck in his declining years. He continued to buy his socks
at the five-and-ten, but not because he had to. His salary at
Columbia was raised to $7000 soon after he came there,
and in the booming twenties it was raised to $12,000.
When he retired in the early thirties, President Butler
called him "professor emeritus in residence" and kept on
paying him that $12,000. In 1940, however, Columbia de-
cided to retrench, and Dewey had to fall back on his Car-

negie pension. He was accommodating himself to this with his usual composure, when he received a letter from the Barnes Foundation in Philadelphia stating that, if he didn't mind, they would pay him a pension of $5000 a year for the rest of his life. The news stunned him so that he "acted funny" for two days, and wouldn't tell the family why. But after a while he got adjusted to it.

Key West was a kind of winter-season Provincetown, a mingling place of staid citizens of a sea-faring complexion with transitory artists painting their pictures—enlivened too by a nightly rain of sailors from the naval station and a springing up of painted tarts on the highways and byways. John Dewey, dressed in brown sandals, white socks, a pair of blue shorts and a blue shirt open at the neck, fitted into this picture as though he had always been there. The artists called him "John"; the staid citizens wanted to. They both invited him to their cocktail parties, and he would drift in, usually a little late, still in those blue shorts no matter how dressed up the function was, and looking like a lad from school. If there were any affectation in this it would have been embarrassing, but Dewey always did exactly as he damn pleased—that is why he kept so young—and he continued to do it with a master's unconcern. A sailor coming out of Sloppy Joe's one early morning stopped him on the street and said:

"Say, Buddy, where's the brown-roofed house?"

"What do you mean by the brown-roofed house?" Dewey asked.

"I mean it's late and I gotta get back to the ship, and I want a whorehouse in a hurry."

"Oh!" Dewey said. "Well, I really don't know. I suppose

perhaps I'm a little too old to be interested in such things."

The sailor gave him a large pat on the back.

"Hell, you're just a kid!" he said.

Dewey consisted so essentially, so much more than most men, of unexcited thoughts, and his thoughts had still so long to live, that the remark seemed true. Even after the wondrously vigorous heart of the man stopped beating, it still seemed true.

There has arisen of late an extreme and intemperate re-action against John Dewey. It is due largely, I think, to the follies committed by some of his wooden-minded yet flighty followers in the name of "progressive education." They forget how persistently Dewey returned to the thought that his theories were experimental. Not only his educational theories, however, but his instrumental philosophy is under attack by the zealots of this angry reaction. One eminent editor, wishing to sweep the whole thing out in a pile, invented the term *Deweyism,* a word that of itself contradicts the whole meat and meaning of Dewey's teaching. Even some more discerning minds of the "libertarian conservative" persuasion seem to regard this mild philosopher as the fountain-source not only of teen-age delinquency, and a soul-destroying materialism, but of the creeping socialism of the welfare state.

In my life, Dewey functioned as a stubborn and somewhat fatherly *opposition* to my youthful impulse to take up with socialist ideas.

"Society is not divided into two distinct classes, as the socialists assert," he would say.

"Yes, but by acting on the hypothesis that it is, we can *split* society in two," I would answer. "What we need is a working hypothesis, something to act on, instead of a lot of vague ideas about how things might get better."

He was never in a hurry to answer such bright but incautious ideas. He would smile indulgently and rub his chin and not say anything, but I could guess what he was thinking. I was teaching logic out of Stanley Jevons' famous book on *The Principles of Science,* and I was recklessly glib in transferring the conceptual apparatus of the physical sciences to social and psychological problems where the subject-matter is so much more mixed-up and undelimited. Dewey had, it seems to me, an opposite fault: he clung to the flux of fact with so much prudence that his ideas lacked keen edges and his prose was apt to be vague and hard to remember.

At any rate, he exercised as a teacher a cooling-down influence on my revolutionary ardor. It was not until years later, in the thirties, the Red Decade, when I was traveling toward an opposite conclusion, that he came out for a "socialized economy," and for "organized social control" as a means of supporting "the liberty of individuals."* He was then seventy-eight years old, and I think his life-influence, taken as a whole, was in a contrary direction. He cared primarily about the liberty of individuals, and about democracy as conceived by idealistic Americans untouched by the Marxian mystique.

Another mistake made by many of Dewey's conservative critics is to imagine that his pragmatism, or instrumental

* *Liberalism and Social Action,* 1955.

philosophy as he preferred to call it, is a glorification of
America's tough-minded practicality as against the more
subtle values called "spiritual" with which other philoso-
phies have concerned themselves. Pragmatism does, to be
sure, regard scientific method as a model of the method of
all valid knowledge, and if one's conservatism involves a rejection of the authority of science, Dewey's instrumental
interpretation goes by the board with it. But the feat accomplished by his interpretation is not to glorify, but to
mitigate, the tough or narrow practicality—above all the
materialism—of certain fanatic extroverts of what is called
scientism. Pragmatism builds the needs and aspirations of
man into the very process of acquiring knowledge, no matter how objective, no matter how "scientific" it may be.
The meaning of an idea, according to pragmatism, is its result in action, and the true idea is the idea that, acted
upon, leads to the result indicated in its meaning. William
James, in his famous lectures on *Pragmatism* (which, by the
way, I had the good fortune to attend), was naïve enough to
infer that this justified a belief in God. If the truth is what
works, he said in effect, and it works to believe that God
exists, then it is true that God exists. Dewey was miles
away from this facile notion. He was, moreover, primarily
concerned with morals rather than with religion. His original motive, as we have seen, was not to glorify the authority
of material science, but to give moral judgments a similar
authority. It was, to employ once more the illuminating
terms invented by James, a "tender-minded" rather than a
"tough-minded" motive. Broadly enough interpreted, it remained an underlying motive in all his philosophizing,
finding its concentrated expression, if anything Dewey

wrote can be called concentrated, in a paper on "The Logical Conditions of a Scientific Treatment of Morality," to be found in the Publications of the University of Chicago for 1903.

I do not myself believe in the pragmatist definition of truth, either in the mature and cogent form in which Dewey elaborated it, or in the more naïve manner in which William James abandoned himself to it. But I think many of its detractors on the so-called Right are making a total mistake when they dismiss pragmatism as a philosophic attack on the values called "spiritual." It would be truer to say, although the terms are far from technical, that pragmatism in all its forms is an effort to build spirituality into science.

On the subject of education as well as philosophy, I think the reaction against John Dewey's theories has gone beyond reasonable bounds. Undoubtedly there has grown up under the aegis of "progressive education" a generation of rude and ill-behaved youngsters, to whom a strict training in the amenities of life, a course of implacable instruction in reading, writing and arithmetic, and, when indicated, an occasional sound spanking, would be, or would have been, an unmixed blessing. I think that an error, or a tacit assumption that is erroneous, underlies Dewey's educational theories which is to some extent responsible for this. But his insistence that children can and should be interested in what they do in school, and that discipline should be a demand that they carry through faithfully what they have set out spontaneously to do, rather than that they should do what some irrelevant ogre called "teacher" tells them to do, was of immense benefit to civilization.

"A person who is trained to consider his actions, to undertake them deliberately, is in so far forth disciplined," Dewey wrote in *Democracy and Education*. "Add to this ability a power to endure in an intelligently chosen course in face of distraction, confusion, and difficulty, and you have the essence of discipline."

As a revolt against the previously prevailing notion that certain "subjects," in themselves "disciplinary," should be rammed into the brains of children at all cost to their own enterprise and adventure of living, this was a grand event. Dewey was really a liberator of children throughout the world, and as the quotation shows, liberating them did not mean letting them run wild. He was profoundly concerned, here as elsewhere, with morals. Just as in his philosophy he wanted to combine moral authority with the authority of science, so here he wanted to combine moral character and conduct with freedom of choice for the individual.

The erroneous assumption underlying his theories, as it seems to me, is that the spontaneous interests of the human cub are to be regarded, by and large, as acceptable. They are to be taken as the starting point of education. The idea of training or disciplining the *interests,* although it is one of the first things that has to be done with a baby, does not seem to find a place when the baby goes to a Dewey school. One of the things modern biology has taught us, is that none of our distinctively civilized attributes, either voluntary or intellectual, are transmitted in heredity to our children. A certain selective breeding no doubt takes place when men become civilized, but since no one has been able to plot the direction of it, it can be assumed that the babies born today do not differ on a large scale from those born thousands of years ago. Nature is not interested in modern improvements. A civilized human being is an artifact. To make one out of the little savages we are at birth requires a molding of the impulses, not just of the efforts we make to fulfill them. Probably Dewey has discussed this point somewhere and it has escaped my attention, but he failed, I feel sure, to give it the emphasis I think it needs. He was carried away by the role his philosophy gave to human purposes, not only in the development of knowledge, but in the very constitution of truth. I have recalled his saying to me, speaking of the Dewey school in Chicago: "I was naïve enough in those days to think of the school as an experimental test of my philosophy." Remembering that surprising remark, I have fallen to wondering whether, without being any more naïve, I might not regard the excesses to which the school has led as an experimental demonstration of the error in his philosophy. They both give too high and guiding a function to the offhand volitions of this, alas, too animal human.

I trust this remark does not place me among the reactionary martinets, who want to abandon the definition of education as growth under favorable conditions, who resent the world-rejoicing discovery that children can have fun going to school—it has rejuvenated the whole family from grandpa down—or begrudge John Dewey his place among the immortal benefactors of the human race. Like most daring innovators, he went to extremes; a period of reaction, a dimming of his world-wide fame, was inevitable; but he will ride clear of that. And meanwhile those who imagine they are dancing at the funeral of another wild radical, will be surprised, if they open a book and read a few lines actually written by him, to see how moderate he was, how cautious, how bent on conserving as well as multiplying the finest values of life in a free society.

My First Great Companion

She was a Christian minister—the first woman ordained in the Congregational Church of New York State, and she became the pastor of one of its large and famous churches. She was of medium height, with light-brown hair and green-blue eyes, a gently curving beauty both of face and figure. She wore in the pulpit a simple black robe of her own design which she called a surplice. It was pleated in front and made feminine by a little black lace in the opening at her throat. Her manner in the pulpit was as simple as her gown. She made few gestures, and never a motion that was not native to her. She had the two indispensable gifts of the orator, self-possession and a thrilling voice. When she rose to speak, you knew at once that she was in complete command of the situation, and you felt at ease. As there was nothing in the least degree mannish about her, you stopped bothering about whether she was a man or a woman. And when she began to speak, you were taken possession of, first by the tones of her voice, and then by the surprisingly candid and wise and joyous, and often humorous, things that she would say.

She believed in joy. As a freshman at Oberlin she had written a theme in which she advanced the theory that God himself *is* joy—a vast stream of joy surrounding all of us. And she believed in growing. She believed that the essential secret of a joyous life, no matter where you start from, is to be forever in a state of growth. These two beliefs, or instincts, comprise the essence of her teaching. They are at least what most distinguished it from the usual messages of those who put on black cloth as a mark of their profession. What also made her unforgettable was the undying gallant courage with which she carried into life whatever she believed.

Her father, George Ford—grandson of a Henry Ford— had been a gunsmith in Peoria, Illinois, and a big boss around the house. He believed that woman's place is the home, and proved it by getting drunk frequently and making the home hell. She grew up, perhaps in consequence, with a quiet but firm belief that women ought to learn a trade. She decided while still in high school—and that was in 1870 when such decisions were rare—that she was going to be economically independent. When Susan B. Anthony came to lecture in Peoria, this ambitious high school girl introduced the famous suffragette, and did it with so much eloquence that, according to a clipping in my possession, her speech was "the talk of the town." What George Ford contributed to the talk on that occasion is not recorded.

At Oberlin, where she went to learn to teach, she fell in love with a theological student just graduating. And like many a feminist, she loved so hard that after one year of college she gave up her own career and married him. They settled in a parish in Canandaigua, near Rochester, New York. There she kept house for him, bore him four children, and helped him with his sermons—helped him almost like magic, for she could write so fluently and fast.

He needed help, for he had been a soldier in the Civil War and had come back with only one lung. When the youngest child was still a baby, that lung seemed to be giving out. He would come home after preaching, or even after prayer meeting, pale with exhaustion, hardly able to lift one knee after the other. When he gave up at last, he was so weak that she had to write his resignation for him. She found herself with five dependents and no means of support.

Well—she had always believed that women ought to do something. They ought to *be* something besides wives and mothers. Now Fate was saying: "Let's see you make good!"

There was a deserted church with a proud steeple but a leaking roof in the village of Brookton, not far from Ithaca. She persuaded the trustees to let her open the doors one Sunday, and invite the people to worship. The whole village came, of course, as they would to a side show to see a freak. But they came again the next Sunday, and the Sunday after that, for warmer reasons. Inside of a month the roof was mended, and the parish was paying her twelve dollars a week for her Saturdays and Sundays. In a little while she was called to a larger church in West Bloomfield, which provided her a commodious parsonage and a salary of eight hundred dollars a year. By that time, however, the fame of her eloquence was beginning to spread throughout all western New York, and she added to her income by giving lectures and by marrying and burying people in the surrounding towns. Although her knowledge of theology was only what she had picked up by helping her husband with his sermons, she had risen high enough in her profession by 1893 to be invited, from her little country parish, to address the World's Congress of Religions in Chicago.

All this was accomplished without the slightest affectation of importance. Her sermons were so simply and directly spoken from her heart to yours that she seemed to have no art at all, but merely self-possession.

In one of them that she preached on "Children's Sunday," she began by telling the congregation of the hard time she had had finding a sermon. There seemed to be nothing around the house or out in the garden, or in fact anywhere in town. She finally went anxiously into the country and started down an old road through the woods looking for a sermon.

"I was walking very fast, and I know that the straight lines between my eyes were very deep, when all of a sudden I heard a voice. It was a slow, rather drawling voice, and it said: 'Why—don't—you—saunter?'

"It was the old road itself speaking.

" 'I am a worker; I have no time for dallying,' I replied. And I quoted to the road a sentiment that had been printed on a little plate I used to eat from when I was a child: 'Dost thou love life? Then do not squander time. There will be rest enough in the grave.'

"The road laughed rudely, and said:

" 'I suppose you think there's nothing worth while in a road but its end! That's where you and a lot of people get fooled! Believe me, no road has any end; what you call its end is only another beginning. . . .

" 'A lot of people in your church,' the road remarked, 'are so intent on getting to heaven that they haven't time to be good on the way. I'm afraid they will be turned back when they get there because they have no wedding garments on. You have to get your wedding garment, your immortality, as you go along, you know. If you do not find love and joy and peace on the road, they will not be waiting for you at the end. . . .' "

That is the way she would preach.

"I could not help seeing that the old road was talking sense," she added, "and of course you can't help feeling respect for anybody who can quote Scripture correctly."

While still at Brookton she had been ordained by a ministerial council headed by Thomas K. Beecher, a more radical member of Henry Ward's family, who had established an undenominational church at Elmira, New York. Mr. Beecher was heretic enough to be proud rather than critical of her rapid flight over theological education. He said many times that she had preached the greatest sermons he ever heard. He loved her and watched her career with a father's pride. When his own strength began to fail he invited her, with the eager consent of his congregation, to join him in the pastorate of the Park Church at Elmira. She came with the understanding that her sick husband should help with the parish work. He helped increasingly and even soon began to do a share of the preaching. When

Mr. Beecher died in 1899, she and her husband were unanimously elected joint pastors of the Park Church.

Such was her public career. It was distinguished enough so that her name appeared in *Who's Who in America.*

My relation to her was a peculiar one: I was her youngest son. From the age of six to nine, I was the child of a woman who disappeared every Saturday and, after being a preacher and pastor for two days, returned on Monday to be my particular mother. To me at that time the arrangement seemed perfectly natural and all right. When some young lad in the neighborhood announced that he was going to be a minister, I piped up:

"You can't, you're a boy!"

I think many families would be happier if they didn't stick so tight together. Half the fun of loving people is having them come home after an absence.

Of course, my mother's energy was unusual, and I am not laying down any rules, but life for us children was richer and not poorer because of her public career. I never felt any lack either of mother love, or good housekeeping, or even of mending. I never saw a home that made me envious. She was, as my sister said, "the kind of mother that tucks you in and tells you a story, the kind that drags you to the dentist to have your teeth straightened." Perhaps her going away weekends put us on our mettle in a wholesome way not unlike that adopted in the modern schools. She would gather us on Saturday before she left, and tell us just how to meet any contingencies that might arise. I faced the situation, she used to tell me, with the imagination of an engineer.

"What shall we do," I said, "if a baby should be born?"

Later on, I found it a little painful to be marked out in this peculiar way among boys. It's bad enough to be one minister's son, let alone two! But what I suffered during the smart phase, the phase of trying to be *like* everybody else, was more than made up to me by her wise counsel in the hours of real ambition.

"Be an individual," she wrote when I was away at school. "Nothing you can gain will make up for the loss of your self. Conformity with the crowd is beautiful until it involves a sacrifice of principle—then it is disfiguring."

"Become interested in everything that is going on in the world, and train yourself to think about it. It's better to have your own thought, even if it's a mistaken one, than to be always repeating other people's."

"Life isn't really so hard when it is faced as when it is evaded. Keep yourself in good physical condition, and mind and soul will take care of themselves. Or is it just the other way round? I am puzzled sometimes about it!"

"Hold your head high—even if your heart is low—and look straight into everyone's face. It is much more important for you to stand up straight than to understand Latin."

A letter she wrote to my sister Crystal, will suggest what her life was like, and her character too.

> Saturday evening
> alone by the fire.
>
> . . . I came home at half-past four, baked some sour-milk graham bread, and Daddy and I fairly revelled in it, it was so good hot with lots of butter on it. We had nothing else but oatmeal.

I also baked apples so that our dinner tomorrow is all ready.

I have mended a little and Daddy has gone to make a call.

Oh yes, and I bought you the flannel for a kimona— Scotch flannel, soft, and it washes, they say. Maybe Julie and I will make it. . . .

Sunday, nearly 2 p.m.

I've preached and helped with the communion service and I've lain down a long time. Now the soup and salad and baked apples are ready when Dad comes in.

The musical numbers were awfully long and many. I'm sure there was an extra one. I asked if the Offertory couldn't be omitted because I knew I'd feel hurried, but no, it couldn't, so just before I began, Mr. MacNaughton, our fat tenor, got up and yelled to some angels ever bright and fair to take him into their care. He yelled it over and over again, but they never took a bit of notice so far as I could see. The idea of an angel taking care of Mr. Mac-Naughton got on my mind so that I felt naughty when it came time to preach. But I got thro' and the people seemed happy.

My mother was wiser than the modern schools, for she knew how to insert into a general diet of freedom an adequate dosage of discipline. One of her inventions was to have "children's meals" when the grown-ups at table were not allowed to talk. But these were offset by "grown-ups' meals," and both regimes were vigorously enforced. The child must have a chance to grow—yes, but so also must the parent, and neither one in self-importance. Moreover, our household was run on feminist principles. In West Bloom-field my sister took her turn at hoeing the garden and cleaning out the stable for Merrilegs, a superannuated racing mare that took my mother on her pastoral calls. And my brother and I took turns at making beds and washing dishes. In short, while my "individuality" was held ade-quately sacred, I was allowed from earliest years to know that life consists largely of doing what you don't want to, and for that privilege I am profoundly grateful.

My father—you will have to believe this, too!—was something of a saint. Within the demands life made upon him as a citizen, husband, parent, minister of the gospel, he was unfailing in his goodness. But the Christian ideal, if you really mean it, demands more of you than "life" does. It demands that life itself, as we live it, shall be transcended and superseded and changed. It is a utopian ideal—ethi-cally, at least, revolutionary. That is what zealots like Saint Francis and George Fox and Tolstoy, and others so sin-cerely Christian that they had to renounce the existing forms of Christianity, realized. And that my mother real-ized. In her simple and unself-conscious way, without zeal-otry—for she had too much humor for that—but with perpetual inward struggle, she tried to live a life the core of which was doing, and not just being, good. She adopted one waif after another into our overcrowded and far from prospering family—took them in and brought them up and educated them on a shoestring. I cannot remember a time when there was not some boy or girl living in our house because he had nowhere else to live.

And these were only the large chunks of her benevo-lence. She was always secretly putting herself through some discipline of sacrifice and generosity. I remember once, during a period when, besides running the church, she was cooking three meals a day and helping us children with the dishes, a lonely old lady, who had been accustomed to ride in from five miles in the country to hear her preach, was stricken with paralysis and went blind. My mother got on a street car and traveled out to see her. When she came back she said:

"Max, Mrs. L—— tells me that my sermons were the only thing that gave her courage to live. She has absolutely nothing left, you know. I told her I would come out every week and read my sermon to her. I'll read her a novel too —that will do her more good."

I was old enough to be appalled. "Can't you send the sermon and let someone else read it to her?" I urged.

"You know that isn't what she wants," my mother said.

As long as the woman lived, my mother would get on a street car every Thursday afternoon and take that tiring trip out into the country to read to her. No worry and no weariness could deter her from this almost wanton regimen of kindness, as to which no murmur either of complaint or of complacence ever crossed her lips. It was to her a pitifully tiny crystal drop contributed to the ocean of black and cruel human relations that she felt called upon, as a believing and yet clear-seeing Christian, to purify with good deeds.

In a person shrouded in solemnity this goodness might not seem so beautiful, but she carried a gay, unmasking humor with her everywhere. One of her parishioners who believed in spiritism once persuaded her to visit a medium. It required a long walk, and when they arrived in the seance chamber my mother sank rather eagerly into a comfortable chair. The medium started forward in agitation:

"Oh, you mustn't take that chair—George is sitting there!"

"Well, I wish you'd ask him to move," she said. "I'm tired!"

She had an amused sensitivity to those distinctions of pecuniary caste which prevail in a democratic society, and the minister's peculiar relation to them. She took five dollars out of a lecture fee once, and firmly announced to the family that, come what may, she was going to buy a silk umbrella.

"There's nothing in this world," she said, "that sustains a woman when she walks along the street like knowing she's carrying a silk umbrella."

I borrowed that umbrella one morning about a week after it was purchased, and came back home at night without it. After retracing my steps and making every effort to discover its hiding place, I had finally to bring her the sad news that it was lost.

"Max, you have destroyed my sole claim to respectability!" she said. "However, I knew all along it was a false claim—that silk umbrella never really belonged to me!"

People concerned with extending the boundaries of kindness are rarely courageous about advancing the frontiers of knowledege. But my mother had that merit, too. In stating publicly what her study and meditation led her to accept privately as true, stating it without compromise or qualification, she seemed to me heroic. Her rather pagan belief in joy, and the right of everybody to have it, was disturbing to many a somber churchgoer, but she never pre-

tended to be any more churchly than she was. To someone
who complained about the poor attendance at prayer meeting she said:

"I wouldn't go to prayer meeting, if I weren't the minister."

Her everlasting interest in growth, too—her feeling that
the very will and bidding of Almighty God is that we keep
on growing—led her to positions that sometimes alarmed
the aging pillars even of the very liberal church in which
she preached. Besides being undenominational, this Park
Church had been one of the first "institutional" churches
in the country—certainly the first Temple of God with bil-
liard tables and a theater in it. But still it clung to the old
creed handed down from the days of Jonathan Edwards.
My mother, keeping abreast of the most advanced Christian opinion of her day, ceased to believe in this creed. She
felt that its elaborate details prevented that union of all in
the worship of God and the good life outlined by Jesus,
which to her was the real function of the church. She could
not keep this change hidden in her breast. At any risk, she
had to tell her true thoughts to her congregations. It is a
tribute to her diplomacy as well as her strength—a diplomacy that consisted largely of letting them think it was her
husband's idea—that she changed this old-established and
very large church, the largest in Elmira, substantially from
Trinitarian to Unitarian without losing a member.

Although my mother had presided at so many funerals,
or perhaps for that reason, she did not believe in funerals,
and did not want one for herself. On the Sunday of the
week after she died we held a memorial meeting in the
church, and it was addressed among others, by Z. R. Brock-

way, for years the head of the Elmira Reformatory and one of the pioneers of modern criminology. As a son's praise of his mother is in the nature of things a little suspect, I want to quote a few of his words. Testifying that of all his religious teachers she had been the closest to his own thoughts, he said:

"Annis Ford Eastman was brave—possessed in full measure the courage of her convictions—but her bravery was so mingled with gentleness, delicate considerateness, and was so unpretentious that this characteristic did not always appear upon the surface. She was hotly intolerant of sham and consoling sophistries. At the same time, she was most tolerant of honest difference. . . . Withal she was extraordinarily tactful, far beyond mere adroitness and finesse."

And I will add these words, spoken by the Baptist minister from across the Park:

"I may say here what I said in my own pulpit last Sunday morning, that she was the only woman I ever knew who took up public speaking that did not, by so doing, lose something of that fine flavor of womanliness which is so attractive to us all. . . . I do not mean simply that in everything that she said and did she was natural, sincere, and unaffected. I mean something more than that. I mean that in herself she was natural according to God and according to the harmonies of the universe. As I understand her theological views I do not agree with them, but I do believe that Mrs. Eastman was one of the choicest saints of God. . . ."

As I sat there, bereft and yet proud of my heart's possession of her, it seemed to me that her rarest trait was that one which she preached with the most eloquence—unceasing growth. It seemed to me as though almost every morning of my youth I had been lifted and launched anew by some vividly conceived scheme she would propose for making life a great thing. In this she never surrendered, not one inch, to the advancing years.

Looking back over our correspondence, I realize that in the very last twelve months of her life she did four things having in them the boldness and the suppleness of youth. She learned to preach without a manuscript; she learned to swim; she consulted a psychoanalyst; and she decided to leave the ministry, encouraging a movement set on foot to make her dean of Barnard College. The psychoanalyst, Dr. A. A. Brill, was the first in this country, and she was one of his first patients. To him as to me—to all who ever touched her poised and humorous and dauntless spirit- -she was unforgettable.

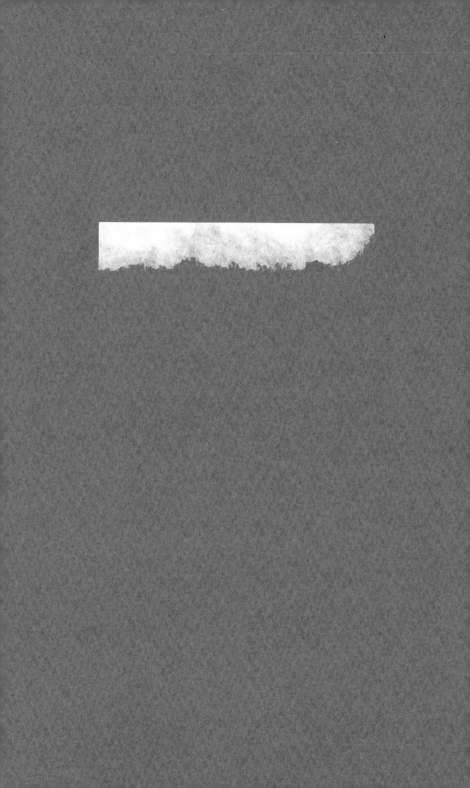